**THERE'S NOTHING MICRO ABOUT
A BILLION WOMEN**

THERE'S NOTHING MICRO ABOUT A BILLION WOMEN

Making Finance Work for Women

MARY ELLEN ISKENDERIAN

The MIT Press
Cambridge, Massachusetts
London, England

The MIT Press would like to thank the anonymous peer reviewers who provided comments on drafts of this book. The generous work of academic experts is essential for establishing the authority and quality of our publications. We acknowledge with gratitude the contributions of these otherwise uncredited readers.

This book was set in Adobe Garamond Pro by New Best-set Typesetters Ltd. Printed and bound in the United States of America.

Library of Congress Cataloging-in-Publication Data

Names: Iskenderian, Mary Ellen, author.
Title: There's nothing micro about a billion women : making finance work for women / Mary Ellen Iskenderian.
Description: Cambridge, Massachusetts : The MIT Press, [2022] | Includes bibliographical references and index.
Identifiers: LCCN 2021030806 | ISBN 9780262046442 (hardcover)
Subjects: LCSH: Women—Finance, Personal. | Women—Economic conditions.
Classification: LCC HG179 .I84 2022 | DDC 332.0240082—dc23
LC record available at https://lccn.loc.gov/2021030806

10   9   8   7   6   5   4   3   2   1

Contents

Preface

I have been a banker, of one kind or another, for my entire professional career. After college, I went through Bank of America's credit training program and did a short stint in the bank's international trade finance group before jumping to the fast-paced, foul-mouthed foreign currency trading desk. After earning my MBA, I went into investment banking at Lehman Brothers, pulling all-nighters, primarily in the Mergers & Acquisitions Department. I had taken these jobs quite deliberately, having decided early on that I wanted a career where I could use my finance skills to work with investors, banks, and governments to drive positive change in the developing world. I had gone off to college with visions of a career in the Foreign Service, but after a yearlong internship at the State Department I sensed that I could accomplish more if I understood how the financial system worked from the inside. I believed I could be a more effective agent of change by starting my career in the private sector rather than in government. Through these jobs, I gained a superb education in the immense power of the financial system that has stayed with me ever since. And I took these lessons with me when I joined the International Finance Corporation, the private sector arm of the World Bank, where I would specialize in investments in financial institutions in the developing world.

During the eighteen years I worked for the World Bank, I was conscious of being one of relatively few women in a large international bureaucracy, and I made it a priority to act as a mentor to several younger women along the way, as some women had helped me. But not once in all those years did I or anyone I worked with ever ask how many women clients were served by the financial institutions we were lending to. It never crossed my mind to question whether the benefits of the investments I made as part of the premier development organization in the world were equally distributed between men and women. And I certainly never questioned whether the impact of those investments might have been even greater if the money had gotten into the hands of women. Equality of access to finance was simply assumed.

By the time I was recruited to run Women's World Banking, a global nonprofit organization, in 2006, I had seen the difference that gaining access to finance had made in the lives of millions of people in countries throughout the world. But what I still hadn't grasped was how much more effective all of my World Bank investments might have been had they considered the different needs of women. In joining Women's World Banking, I stepped into an organization that worked to strengthen women-focused microfinance institutions. Founded at the first UN Conference on Women in 1975, Women's World Banking is dedicated to ensuring access to financial products and services to low-income women in the developing world. My first trip in this new role demonstrated to me what was possible when women were intentionally included in the design and delivery of financial services. On that trip, I went to a few countries in both East and West Africa, where I met some of the women clients who were being served through Women's World Banking's microfinance partners. I listened as women one after another expressed enormous pride in their businesses and observed how their success had helped their children. They described how hard it had been to get the money together to start a business, and the difference a loan made. Often it represented the first opportunity for these women to gain some financial independence.

I learned about the impact that financial services can have on the lives of low-income women from the women themselves and from the visionary leaders who had built the microfinance institutions that served them. But it also became clear that to reach the more than one billion financially underserved women throughout the world, these lessons would have to extend beyond the borders of microfinance. They needed to be brought home to those financial service providers that can operate at scale but don't know how (or why) to extend their services to that clientele.

This book is the culmination of all that I have learned from women clients and the leaders of the financial institutions that serve them. I draw on academic research to support these firsthand insights and to highlight the broader systemic impacts of women's financial inclusion. Ensuring that women are full partners in the financial system has benefits that go beyond any individual woman's circumstances. Women's financial inclusion improves the lives of women and the lives of all of those around them while strengthening communities, financial institutions, and national economies.

INTRODUCTION

Seeing Joyce Wafuko sitting in her small office at the back of the hardware store she owns, papers stacked on a large table that takes up most of the space in the room, invoices and other notices tacked up on the bulletin boards that line the walls, it would be difficult to imagine the road she has traveled in the last seven years. Joyce lives in a small village outside Mombasa, Kenya's second largest city, where she and her husband had settled a decade earlier to raise their three children, near both their families. After a few years, her husband had been unable to find steady work in the village and reluctantly had gone to the city to become a policeman. But the money he sent home wasn't enough to support their family, so Joyce decided to start a business to supplement his earnings. She noticed that her neighbors lacked the supplies to make even the most basic repairs to their homes, so she thought a hardware store would be a good addition to the village.

She was a member of an informal savings and loan group with other women from her village, but the amount she was able to borrow according to the rules of the group was relatively small and not enough to launch her business. When she asked about a larger loan at the local bank branch, the manager told her they didn't finance "startups" and that she should come back after the business was up and running. When it was her turn to take home the monthly "pot" from her savings group, she put most of the money into starting her business, although in a smaller way than she had originally hoped. Joyce has kept a photograph of her first shop pinned to the corkboard in her office. It depicts a small corrugated metal shack on the side of the road with a smiling Joyce standing beside her inventory: some two-by-fours, loose nails, eggs, and tomatoes.

After operating this stand for a few months, she heard about a microfinance institution called Kenya Women's Microfinance Bank a few miles from her home and applied for a loan at the branch. The bank gave her a $70 loan and some training in bookkeeping and budgeting, which she parlayed into a booming hardware business that, seven years on, sells a full range of home improvement tools and housewares. Joyce is still a client of Kenya Women's and maintains a $3,000 unsecured revolving line of credit with the bank. A few years ago, she went back to see the bank manager who had previously turned her down for a startup loan. They discussed her growth plans for the business at length, and he expressed enthusiasm about supporting her with a loan. But when he broached the subject of collateral—he estimated that the bank would need her to pledge property equivalent to about 130 percent of the value of the loan—she thanked him and left the branch as quickly as possible. The interest rate on her loan from Kenya Women's was high at 35 percent, but neither she nor anyone in her family had the kind of collateral a bank loan would require as security.

Even though Joyce has a banking relationship with Kenya Women's Microfinance Bank, she continues to participate in her community savings group because she enjoys the social interaction with her neighbors and the discipline of having to save a certain amount every month as a requirement of group membership. However, she also derives a sense of security from keeping most of her savings in an account at Kenya Women's (she had previously thought that interest was only something you paid on a loan, not something you could earn on deposits). But the real game-changer in her financial life took place a few years after she began banking with a microfinance institution. M-Pesa, Africa's first mobile money transfer service, burst onto the scene, upending all her ideas about convenience, security, and the cost of doing business. M-Pesa made it possible to pay vendors or utility bills, deposit funds in her bank account, or receive money from her husband or her customers through the cell phone in her pocket. This was a far cry from having to take a bus to a bank in another town during her peak business hours, nervously carrying cash if she was making a deposit, and then waiting in line to transact her business.

As Joyce's business has grown, she has employed twenty-five people, mostly women. She is especially proud of her newly hired twenty-sixth employee, her husband. He returned home to work with Joyce on expanding into a new side business, a lumberyard and construction company. Almost in the same breath that Joyce describes these outward, commercial signs of growth and prosperity, she begins to talk about the investments she has made in her family's well-being. It's clear that both represent measures of success. Most notably, she points with pride to the fact that all three of her children have completed secondary school and are weighing different options for continuing their education. In addition, she put her younger sister through graduate school.

Reading Joyce's story here, neatly printed on the page, risks missing how extraordinary her success is. Joyce just wanted to be able to care for her family and, in the absence of gainful employment for herself or her husband, started a business; she became an entrepreneur out of necessity. She then sought the most basic financial services to support that effort, and while she was eventually able to cobble together different products that suited her needs, they were expensive and often inconvenient. Joyce effectively had two sets of objectives. The first was to provide for her family's security with food, clothing, and housing. Her second set of goals was more aspirational: to provide a better life for the next generation by educating her children and to build a thriving business in her community. The right financial tools can make both sets of goals attainable, but at present, they are out of reach for nearly a billion other women around the world. Ensuring that women have access to the financial resources they need to achieve both security and prosperity is the motivating force behind women's financial inclusion.

Every man and woman, no matter how poor, needs the means to make and receive payments, as well as a safe place to store funds. The need to accumulate money remains a constant throughout life: in the short term to conduct daily transactions; in the intermediate term to provide a safety net in the case of emergencies or to save up for a large purchase, and in the long term to build a nest egg for old age. Not having a lot of money doesn't eliminate the need to be able to save for these essentials. For centuries, communities of low-income people have come together to help each other secure the tools to do so. As the universality of this need for financial tools became better understood, people and organizations from outside the community emerged to provide them—motivated sometimes by greed, sometimes by good intentions, and sometimes by a combination of the two. The broader economic impact of expanding access to financial services also became apparent as poor people increasingly gained the means to improve their own lives. But human nature being what it is, any system with the power to change lives runs the risk of favoring some more than others. And when it comes to financial services, women are seldom among the favored.

Closing the gender gap in financial services would be the right thing to do as a matter of equity alone. While 72 percent of men have a financial account, only 65 percent of women do, and that difference has not budged in the decade that financial inclusion data have been collected. But ensuring women's independent access to finance is important for other, perhaps even more profound reasons of human development. If a woman has her own bank account and access to other financial services in her own name, there is a greater likelihood that she will have a say in how money in her household is spent. What's more, there is ample evidence that she will spend that money in ways that contribute directly to the well-being of her family. Numerous academic studies ranging across geographies repeat the same finding: when money in the household is controlled by women, more of the family members are healthier and eat more nutritious diets and children are better educated than when financial resources are controlled by men. This finding is at the crux of the argument in favor of women's financial inclusion: improving women's access to financial services not only improves individual outcomes, it improves outcomes for families and wider communities as well.

The aim of this book is to make unequivocally clear why women's financial inclusion is good for women, good for business, and good for the resilience of the global economy. Part I of the book provides the necessary context for understanding the challenges and opportunities associated with women's financial inclusion. Chapter 1 lays out the current state of women's financial inclusion and briefly surveys the ways in which low-income people have addressed their financial needs through history and how these strategies have or have not worked for the benefit of women. Chapter 2 explores the principal barriers to women's full participation in the financial system, ranging from the systemic level, such as lack of identification documents, to the personal, such as the effect of gender norms on women's access to technology. Women's financial inclusion consistently shows up on any list of enablers of women's economic empowerment, but what does it really mean for a woman to be empowered, and how is empowerment measured? Chapter 3 reviews the academic literature on empowerment and how empowerment has been defined to determine whether (and how) gaining access to financial services and the skills to use them might result in a woman's empowerment.

Part II of the book presents the business case for financial service providers to embrace low-income women as a rewarding client base, and what policymakers can do to facilitate the growth of this market. By any standard, the untapped commercial opportunity afforded by extending financial services to unbanked and underserved women in the developing world is compelling: more than $2 trillion in new deposits flowing into the financial system; $1.7 trillion in loans to capital-starved, women-led micro, small, and medium-sized businesses; up to $50 billion in insurance premium income annually. Chapters 4, 5, and 6 present examples of financial service providers that have successfully offered profitable savings, credit, and insurance products to low-income women. The nearly one billion unbanked women, and the millions more who are underserved, lacking full access to all the financial services they need (and deserve) to build wealth, manage risks, and grow their businesses, represent a formidable untapped market opportunity.

Digital technology has smashed many of the barriers that financial service providers previously encountered in serving low-income clients. Digital financial services offered through mobile phones rather than expensive brick-and-mortar banks can serve individuals and small businesses at dramatically lower cost, eliminating the burden and expense of transacting in cash. Biometric screening and other technologies have also changed the landscape of identification and documentation, just as many regulators have relaxed "know-your-customer" requirements and their associated costs to encourage banks to extend their reach to the unbanked and underbanked. Today, various providers have developed financial products—particularly those with built-in savings features—that are well suited to many women's preferences for frequent, low-volume transactions. Other factors, though, are equally important to winning women's business. Gaining their trust is at the top of the list.

In the last decade, developing countries have adopted a range of policy measures to encourage growth, including important financial sector reforms designed to reduce the cost of capital and spur investment. But if those reforms are not accompanied by policies to expand financial access, only wealthier individuals and firms will be able to take advantage of them. Without embracing financial inclusion, the reform may indeed boost growth, but it will also increase inequality. In fact, recent IMF research goes even further to say that beyond the level of financial inclusion in a country, it is the distribution of that access, specifically as reflected in the gap between men's and women's financial inclusion, that makes the real difference in addressing income inequality. The fundamental findings of this research bear repeating: a nation's highest possible level of growth and the most equal distribution of the benefits of that growth are not attainable without addressing the disparity between men's and women's access to finance.

The COVID-19 pandemic has made the linkage between financial inclusion and macroeconomic growth more relevant and more urgent than ever before. As a result of the pandemic, an estimated 96 million people are expected to be pushed into extreme poverty, and it's not just low-income countries that are facing greater economic fragility. Middle-income countries, where some of the greatest growth gains have been achieved in the last decade, are seeing their progress against poverty erased. In many countries, the contraction in the economy is directly tied to declines in women's labor force participation. Around the world, women are shouldering additional unpaid care burdens during the pandemic and have lost jobs at a disproportionate rate: while women represent only 39 percent of global employment, they have suffered 54 percent of global job losses. The

World Bank projects that the pandemic will leave lasting scars on the world economy and urges developing countries, in particular, to foster "growth-friendly" economic environments. As governments shift from providing relief from the pandemic to supporting economic growth, it is essential that they include investments in economic gender equality on any list of growth-oriented policy options.

Closing the gender gap in women's financial inclusion would be an essential pillar in realizing the potential for women to assist in rebuilding the global economy. McKinsey notes that digital and financial inclusion, particularly access to credit and mobile banking services, are closely related to women's labor force participation.

There has always been a range of persuasive arguments in favor of providing low-income women with the full suite of financial services. Perhaps the longest-standing claim is the simplest and the hardest to refute: when a woman controls the money in a household, more of the family benefits from the choices she makes. The second argument—that women are loyal, profitable customers for financial service providers—has been immeasurably strengthened in recent years with the advent of digital financial services. Financial service providers can no longer hide behind the defense that serving low-income women is too expensive and does not represent a viable business proposition. Banks and other legacy players are leaving money on the table for fintech companies and mobile money providers to scoop up.

The COVID-19 pandemic showed us that we can react fast and implement changes that would otherwise have taken decades. Millions of bank accounts were established for previously unbanked people so that they could receive government social protection payments. To do this, innovative remote account opening processes were used on a large scale for the first time. While lawmakers remained prudent, they nevertheless allowed previously sacrosanct regulatory barriers to fall. The crisis refocused policymakers' priorities and showed that broad-based inclusion is possible. If the world builds on this momentum, the promise of women's financial inclusion—the outsized commercial opportunity, the resilient economic growth, and the empowerment of women—is within our grasp.

1 WOMEN'S FINANCIAL INCLUSION: CLEARING THE ROADBLOCKS TO EMPOWERMENT

Fully one-third of the world's adults do not own a bank account or mobile money account and, as a result, are shut out from all formal financial services. Without an account they are effectively denied the ease and efficiency of making and receiving payments, having a safe place to accumulate savings, and, perhaps most impactful, borrowing through the formal financial system. But there has been a sea change in the effort to bring this excluded population into the formal financial system as the concept known as financial inclusion has emerged in recent years as a fundamental, evidence-based underpinning for a broad range of economic, social, and development goals. Financial inclusion is now widely perceived not so much as an end in itself but as a means for people to own the skills and the tools they need to bring about change in their own lives. The idea of financial inclusion as an essential enabler of broad-based change is best captured in the context of the UN's Sustainable Development Goals. In 2015 the United Nations General Assembly established a blueprint to achieve a better and more sustainable future for all by 2030, dubbed the 17 Global Goals, although the term "universal financial inclusion" was notably absent. And yet eight of the goals—including Goal 1, "End poverty in all its forms everywhere," and Goal 5, "Achieve gender equality and empower all women and girls"—expressly require the achievement of financial inclusion as a necessary condition for success.

While the term "financial inclusion" is relatively new, the importance of delivering financial services to people who do not otherwise have access is not. To understand the current landscape, it's critical to review how the field has evolved. Although this is not a comprehensive history of informal financial services or an exhaustive critique of microfinance, there are invaluable lessons to be drawn from these efforts. It's also essential to appreciate the ingenuity local communities have applied to meet their own financial service needs long before commercial financial services were available to them. From this point of view, there are important insights to be gained when designing successful financial solutions and considering how best to engage this population. This is especially true when taking into account the enduring value of group-based solutions, particularly regarding the needs of women, coupled with tightly held beliefs that inhibit trust building with formal financial service providers such as banks. Microfinance, for its part, provides equally constructive lessons about serving the needs of low-income women customers as well as a cautionary tale about transforming a development model into a sustainable, mission-focused business.

These lessons couldn't be more relevant now as digital financial services are accessible through cell phones, at a dramatically accelerated pace of change that represents only the latest stage in the evolution of financial inclusion. This drive to provide safe, affordable, and convenient financial services to underserved people has made exponential progress in the last half century. While the impact of digital technology on financial inclusion has been profound, the benefits have not been evenly shared, with women representing well more than half of those who remain financially excluded. Financial inclusion cannot and will not fulfill its potential as a driver of economic change unless the inclusion of women is made an explicit priority. It is therefore crucial to lay out the current state of play for women's financial inclusion, both in terms of the persistent lag in women's access to cell phones (particularly internet-enabled smartphones) and in terms of the outsize benefits that accrue to women and their families once they are able to take advantage of digital financial services.

The barriers and challenges women face in gaining access to financial services are different from—or sometimes just higher than—those encountered by men, so it is important to keep those challenges in mind when designing solutions to address the differences. While low-income men face many barriers to inclusion, such as a lack of access to identification documents and the need for greater financial and digital literacy, those same barriers are often more difficult for women to surmount because of prevailing gender and societal norms. That particular obstacle course is magnified by the persistent lack of gender-disaggregated financial data: regulators fail to require financial institutions to report information on product usage and behavior by female clients, while even the financial service providers that do collect these data often ignore them when making business decisions. This uniquely female barrier of data invisibility, combined with a dogged belief on the part of both policymakers and financial service providers that policies and products are gender neutral, leads to defaulting to solutions that meet men's needs, preferences, and lived experience. There really is no such thing as a gender-neutral solution.

Once a woman makes it past these barriers to inclusion, the way she spends, saves, and invests has a direct and measurable benefit on her entire family, and on children in particular. But what about the women themselves? What happens to a woman when she has full and unfettered access to a bank or mobile money account and other financial tools such as loans or insurance? Part I closes with a look at how women's agency is affected through their interactions with formal financial services and whether—and in what way—they are empowered by them. A framework is introduced that tracks how various changes affect the ways a woman might experience empowerment through financial inclusion, from changes in her material well-being and knowledge base to changes in her relationships with others around her, and even in her own self-esteem.

There is now wide-ranging confirmation that financial inclusion enables, accompanies, and accelerates the achievement of many economic, commercial, and personal goals. Making deliberate efforts to ensure that women are included will result in achieving those goals faster, more equitably, and probably less expensively than clinging to the false idea that gender-blind finance exists. An oft-quoted proverb advises, "If you want to go fast, go alone. If you want to go far, go together." Women's financial inclusion would suggest that if you want to go faster *and* go farther, go with the women.

1 THE ROAD TO FINANCIAL INCLUSION

Easy access to financial services is taken for granted by many people in developed countries. And yet 1.7 billion people—fully one-third of the world's adults—don't have a bank account in their own name. Of those, well over half are women living in the developing world, typically from the poorest households. They have no way to access even the most elementary services that are readily available to a majority of people elsewhere: a bank account to deposit a paycheck, pay bills, or save toward a child's education or their own retirement. It is notable that even in a country as wealthy as the United States, this most basic vision of financial inclusion is not available to everyone because of a history of discrimination in access to finance due, for example, to race, gender, or ethnic origin. In the United States and other developed countries, it may be difficult to imagine having to give up a day's work to walk for miles to deposit money into a personal account because there are no branches or even ATMs conveniently nearby and because the bus fare alone would be more than the amount of the deposit. This is why, in many parts of the world, payment of everyday expenses, from food to school fees to utilities, must be done in person and in cash. The time and effort involved in getting to a bank can be so prohibitive that the time-worn strategy of saving cash at home under the mattress may seem like the best option, even with the obvious risk of it being stolen or used for more immediate needs. While the focus here is on expanding opportunities in the developing world, in many cases the situations and solutions described may be equally applicable to developed countries where people lack access to convenient and affordable financial services.

Though definitions of financial inclusion vary, to be financially included means essentially to have a safe place to save, the ability to borrow, and the means to make timely payments. The plethora of actors engaged in providing and advocating for financial inclusion have reached a consensus around the idea that all individuals and businesses should have access to the full range of financial products and services that meet their needs, including means of saving and making payments and ways to obtain credit and insurance. To be truly inclusive, these products and services must be delivered affordably, responsibly, and sustainably. After this point, though, the terminology gets a little tricky. The basic measure of whether a person is financially included is ownership of a bank account in their own name, which is both simplistic and misleading. (One need only look at the disparity in some countries between a traditional bank account and mobile money account ownership. In Uganda, for example, only 11 percent of the population own a bank account, while 43 percent have a mobile money account on their cell phone. However, mobile money accounts generally do not count in many measures of financial inclusion.) Nevertheless, at both the global and individual country levels, the organizations tracking financial inclusion data, such as financial service providers and the agencies that regulate them, classify people without a traditional bank account as unbanked.

Both this terminology and the underlying measurement are incomplete, and even inaccurate, for a variety of reasons. For example, owning an account but not using it—as is the case with roughly 20 percent of account holders globally—would seem to indicate that the service is not adequately addressing these customers' needs. While these account holders technically may no longer be unbanked, they have instead voted with their feet, and clearly remain unserved. In fact, the World Bank adds an important addendum to its definition of financial inclusion, noting that access to a transaction account is only "a first step toward broader financial inclusion." Ownership of a bank account in a formal, regulated financial institution, while an imperfect measure, stands as a proxy for and a portal to all the opportunities and protections offered by financial services: a safe place to save, a line of credit to smooth over a shortfall at the end of the month, insurance to manage an unexpected illness.

By the time world leaders gathered at the UN General Assembly in 2015 to commit to the achievement of the Sustainable Development Goals by 2030, there was an explicit recognition that financial inclusion was an essential means to meet those lofty ends. Global policy fora such as the G-20 and national-level policymaking and regulatory agencies had begun to support enabling environments that would allow a wide range of retail financial service providers to serve previously excluded customers and to address the policy, legal, and regulatory constraints that prevent a financial sector from being inclusive. There was a particularly strong policy response across the developing world: according to the Alliance for Financial Inclusion, at least fifty countries have adopted national financial inclusion strategies and twenty more are in the course of doing so. This heightened awareness has yielded impressive results, with millions of adults gaining account ownership since 2011, when the World Bank and the Bill & Melinda Gates Foundation first started collecting data through the Global Findex database.

THE GENDER GAP IN FINANCIAL INCLUSION

Despite the recognition of the importance of financial inclusion and the progress made toward bringing more people into the formal financial system, women throughout the developing world remain significantly more excluded than men. There is persistent gender inequality in financial access, in fact, and the gap in account ownership between men and women in the developing world has not budged since 2011; only 50 percent of women hold accounts, compared to 59 percent of men. The stubborn truth bears repeating: of the 1.7 billion people still left unbanked around the world, nearly a billion of them are women. In every region in the world, in every age group, and at every income level, women are more financially excluded than men.

Nearly but not quite all unbanked adults live in the developing world, and they share certain demographic characteristics. That said, women are represented—indeed, often overrepresented—across all these groups. For example, the unbanked population in developing countries are likely to be poorer, and in developing countries more women than men in every age group live below the poverty line. Likewise, the unbanked typically achieve lower levels of education, and women account for two-thirds of the world's illiterate adults (most damningly, women's share of the world's illiterate population hasn't changed in more than twenty years). Also, employment in the formal labor force is a strong predictor of having a bank account, while the majority of women in developing countries who are economically active work in the informal sector, typically as home-based workers or street vendors.

Closing this gap so that women are assured equal access to financial services is a necessary condition if the promise of financial inclusion is to be achieved. Women spend, save, and invest money in profoundly different ways than men, but the most important difference is that when women have access to—and control over—financial resources, they invest them in their families to a far greater extent than men do. Improving a woman's financial access brings with it an intergenerational multiplier effect that leads to consistently better outcomes in the health, education, and lifelong earning potential of every member of her entire family, including both boys and girls. Women with greater control over financial resources overwhelmingly invest them in the most fundamental human needs that pay the greatest long-term dividends, such as food security, health, and education.

To provide just one example of the impact women have on the household when they have control over the financial resources, a study in China showed that every 10 percent increase in a woman's income led to a 1 percent increase in the survival rate of girls in her household, as well as improved educational outcomes for both boys and girls. By contrast, when a man's income increased by 10 percent, the daughters' survival and education rates declined, and though the sons' welfare may not have suffered, neither did the boys experience any benefits from their fathers' improved financial circumstances.

As low-income women and men juggle their financial lives, we see them express clear preferences about what they want in their financial tools.

Products and services that are reliable, convenient, and keep money safer than if it were kept at home under the mattress are the most frequently requested product attributes; receiving a return on money invested is less explicitly demanded as long as the other qualities exist. In addition, women prize confidentiality in their financial transactions more highly than men do. All these qualities are present with digital financial services; indeed, in the decade since digital financial services were launched, owning a mobile phone, ideally a smartphone with internet access, is nothing short of an indispensable first step toward a financially inclusive future. But the gap between men's and women's smartphone ownership in low- and middle-income countries serves to exacerbate women's exclusion from the financial system. Even in countries where the overall mobile phone ownership gap between men and women is fairly small, that difference widens to an average disparity of 20 percent for smartphone ownership. In low- and middle-income countries, the connection between women's smartphone ownership and their degree of access to finance is quite stark. While mobile money has made huge inroads in providing access to many basic financial services, women have yet to reap the full benefits; there is a 33 percent disparity between men's and women's use of mobile money accounts.

Digital financial services appear to be closing the gender gap in financial inclusion in some regions; in Africa and the Middle East, for example, the gender gap in digital financial inclusion is lower than for traditional financial services. However, the opposite is true in parts of Latin America and Asia where a lack of digital and financial literacy or restrictive social and cultural norms represent greater obstacles for women than for men. In a survey by the GSM Association (GSMA), the mobile industry association, men and women largely report the same barriers to phone ownership. Affordability, together with literacy and digital skills, tops the list for men and women alike. Lack of knowledge on how to access the internet and discomfort with the technology present barriers for both men and women, often coupled with gaps in their basic literacy skills. In Senegal, more than one-third of the women surveyed by the GSMA indicated that their inability to read and write was the principal impediment to mobile phone usage. Both men and women identified affordability as a significant obstacle to cell-phone ownership; however, research suggests that if a low-income household does manage to acquire a smartphone, it will most likely be controlled by the male head. If a woman has a phone at all, it is often a "hand-me-down" feature phone (which does not provide internet access) that she receives when her husband upgrades to a smartphone. Women also report sharing phones with their husband or another family member more frequently than men to make and receive calls and to gather information, but their desire for confidentiality precludes them from conducting financial transactions on a shared phone. There is also evidence that women have far less agency than men over the purchase of a smartphone, with substantially more men purchasing their own devices than women.

However, in the GSMA survey, only women listed a cultural barrier, such as the disapproval of their families, as a significant impediment to phone ownership. As digital technology reduces social barriers between men and women, cultural norms may also be challenged. As a result, women may be denied access to smartphones—and by extension, financial services—in some particularly conservative societies, with phone ownership gaps notably wide throughout South Asia. In Pakistan, 29 percent of the women participating in the GSMA survey listed "family disapproval" as the principal obstacle to smartphone ownership. Only 38 percent of Indian women own a mobile phone, compared to 71 percent of Indian men; women's phone ownership correlates with education and income in many countries, but the gender gap in India is significantly wider than in countries with similar education and income levels. Research by the Harvard Kennedy School's Evidence for Policy Design (EPoD) confirms that women's mobile phone usage poses a challenge to traditional Indian gender norms. For girls and unmarried women, phone usage raises fears of promiscuous behavior and the breakdown of long-established "purity" and courtship norms.

THE RISE OF DIGITAL FINANCIAL SERVICES

By dramatically lowering the cost of conducting low-value transactions even for people living in remote rural areas, digital financial services have effectively removed some of the most intractable impediments to expanding financial inclusion. Mobile banking transactions, whether to pay for utilities, school fees, or groceries, offer low-income people a safe and affordable alternative to cash. With bank branches (which don't want to accept small deposits) few and far between and even ATMs miles apart, low-income people previously had no option but to make cash payments delivered by hand. The mobile phone, and specifically a smartphone, has unequivocally emerged as the passport to financial inclusion.

Roughly two-thirds of the 1.7 billion unbanked adults own a mobile phone and the ease, proximity, and growing affordability of cell phones are helping to overcome the most frequently cited reasons unbanked people give for not having a bank account. At the top of that list is the concern that they don't have enough money to maintain an account. Distance to a financial institution runs a close second to cost as a reason for remaining unbanked. Without the expense of meeting banking regulations or of maintaining a brick-and-mortar banking facility, the cost of providing financial services can be dramatically lowered by using digital channels, with the potential to increase their affordability for low-income people.

This meteoric change in the provision of financial services to previously excluded people in the developing world began in March 2007, when Safaricom, Kenya's largest cell-phone provider, launched M-Pesa, the first mobile money transfer service. The word *pesa* means "cash" in Swahili, and the service quickly gained traction as an efficient way for Kenyans to make payments. At the time, only 14 percent of Kenyans owned bank accounts, while nearly 30 percent of the population owned cell phones. With M-Pesa, customers were able to deposit and withdraw money from a network of banking agents that included cell-phone airtime resellers and retail outlets, while partnerships with banks gave them access to a range of other financial services. M-Pesa not only is an innovation that had an extraordinarily fast rate of adoption, but researchers found that within only a few years of its introduction a very large majority of Kenyan users said they would be negatively affected if M-Pesa were no longer available to them.

M-Pesa is also seen as a successful example of a public-private partnership, bringing Safaricom and local banks together with regulators who were open to innovation; they also had critical financial and technical support from the UK development assistance agencies. Today, M-Pesa is used by 96 percent of Kenyan households and the rate of financial inclusion has expanded to 83 percent, driven largely by mobile money services.

Mobile money has exploded across sub-Saharan Africa and the rest of the developing world. South Asia has the highest rate of growth in mobile money accounts and already boasts 34 percent of all accounts registered globally. Indeed, mobile money is ideally suited to the needs of low-income, financially excluded people since it facilitates low-cost, small-scale transactions while providing a safe and affordable store of value for money. Research indicates that there is an inverse relationship between the depth of a country's financial sector and the prevalence of mobile money. Simply put, countries with a higher percentage of people without bank accounts have higher mobile money penetration. Mobile money agent outlets, typically small shops or perhaps even chain stores, nearly tripled between 2014 and 2019 to 7.7 million outlets. And the average agent has seven times the reach of ATMs and twenty times the reach of a physical banking facility.

Critical to understanding how mobile money works and why it is flourishing in places where banking networks don't reach is that mobile money is not linked to a traditional bank account. Mobile money accounts are offered by a mobile network operator. In contrast, mobile *banking* involves the use of an app on a smartphone to access a bank account and perform banking activities such as depositing checks, making balance inquiries, and transferring funds. Mobile banking refers specifically to interactions with a commercial bank through a web portal or cell-phone app; the user can access their bank account to perform certain banking functions such as paying bills, viewing account balances, or transferring money between accounts. Another product linked to a traditional bank account is a *mobile wallet,* an app installed on a cell phone to store credit or debit card and bank account information to make online and in-store purchases.

M-Pesa and other mobile money services provide users with an electronic payment and money storage system that is accessible through mobile telephones. Users are required to register at an authorized mobile money service outlet where they are assigned an account number linked to their phone number, which in turn is linked to the SIM card in their phone. Users deposit into and withdraw cash from their mobile money accounts by exchanging cash for electronic credit at an agent's shop. The agent then receives a commission for each exchange. With this electronic money in their accounts, users can send money to and receive money from other users of the same or another mobile money service through their phones, essentially by sending a secure text or SMS message. They can also use mobile money in their account to pay bills and purchase airtime for their cell phones.

One frequent use of mobile money is a domestic remittance, whereby a family member living in a city sends money to a relative living back home in a rural area. Here's a simple example of such a transfer: a young woman studying in Nairobi and working there as a housekeeper might send money to her grandmother in the village where she grew up to prepare for a family celebration. The young student stops at a small grocery shop on her way home from work and gives cash to the shopkeeper, who is also an M-Pesa agent; the amount is then added electronically to her M-Pesa account. When she gets home, she transfers the funds to her grandmother's M-Pesa account number (which is also the grandmother's cell-phone number). The grandmother receives an immediate notification on her feature phone that funds have been added to her mobile money account. The following day, she goes into town to a Safaricom agent and withdraws a portion of the transferred funds in cash and uses the remainder to top up her cell-phone airtime.

THE ORIGINS OF FINANCIAL SERVICES FOR THE POOR

Digital financial services represent just the latest stage in the evolution of expanding access to finance to the greatest numbers of people. For centuries, financial needs have been met by either informal or formal financial services, or some combination of both. Informal financial services are typically provided through moneylenders, pawnbrokers, or savings and credit clubs. A nearly universal informal mechanism that is still relied on by many low-income households throughout the developing world is the rotating savings and credit association, or ROSCA. Stuart Rutherford, a pioneer in the research and understanding of the savings behavior of low-income people, defines ROSCAs as "groups of people who come together to set up and run their own basic personal financial intermediation services." These groups of friends or neighbors each commit to contributing a predefined amount to a "pot," typically on a monthly basis, for a fixed period of time. Each month the proceeds in the pot are distributed to one of the members. ROSCAs exemplify an indigenous solution that springs directly from within a community; members are often drawn from groups who know and interact with each other for many reasons beyond their shared membership—although, as Rutherford notes, they may also come together as strangers for whom "trust is not a commodity that can be imported automatically from some prior set of relationships. It is something that has to be made and remade—and thereby reinforced—over and over again. People stay in ROSCAs because they observe, round by round, that everyone else is obeying the rules."

In recent years the village savings and loan association (VSLA) has emerged as one of the most prolific adaptations of the ROSCA model, particularly in rural areas across Africa and particularly for women. A group of approximately fifteen women from the same village commit to save a specific amount over an annual cycle. Each woman places her cash in a wooden box with three locks, all of which must be opened simultaneously by three different women designated by the group. The group maintains a strict policy that funds cannot be withdrawn before the cycle completes, and a member must pay a monthly service charge if she needs to withdraw her funds in an emergency. In addition, members can approach the group to request a loan up to a fixed percentage of the total pot; interest earnings from these member loans are distributed to the group at the end of the cycle.

For many years, ROSCAs were understood to be, in the absence of other sources of credit, a way for members to amass lump sums to invest or make larger purchases. On closer study, ROSCA members, whether they are in Bangladesh, Mexico, or Kenya, place higher value on these groups as an effective way to discipline themselves to save rather than as a means to borrow. The primacy of savings in the financial lives of low-income people is brought vividly to life in the groundbreaking work *Portfolios of the Poor,* by Daryl Collins, Jonathan Morduch, Stuart Rutherford, and Orlanda Ruthven. Drawing on financial diaries that were kept by 250 low-income families in Bangladesh, India, and South Africa, the authors conclude that even though none of these families had a lot of money, they were able to manage their limited incomes through engaging in a vast array of strategies. The diaries reveal that the concept of "living on $2 a day" is mostly a statistical convenience. The families didn't earn even that small amount as steady, daily income; rather, they might have sudden windfalls one day and earn nothing the next. The irregularity of their income forced them into a pattern of saving when they could and borrowing when they needed to, and they rarely spent every last cent that came in, so that they could put some money aside to build up savings or pay down debt.

According to the diaries, households placed a huge premium on saving since, given their small, unpredictable incomes, they had an ongoing need to accumulate lump sums to pay medical bills or make up-front purchases for their businesses. The diaries indicate that these families stored savings at home, joined savings groups or clubs with others, and borrowed from everyone: neighbors, family members, employers, loan sharks, and even microfinance institutions (MFIs) if they were an option. This drive to amass significant sums often led the families to make seemingly irrational decisions such as borrowing in order to save, or paying neighbors to "guard" their money. In an environment in which it was difficult to find a safe place to hold savings, families were extremely reluctant to dip into savings they had already managed to accumulate. *Portfolios* tells a story about a family that took a loan from an MFI because it saw doing so as a rare opportunity to gain access to a large enough amount of cash to make a meaningful long-term investment. The monthly repayment amounts, even at high interest rates, were small enough to be manageable, so the family was willing to borrow instead of draw down hard-won savings. The authors also describe a community-based group savings scheme whereby members saved daily for a month and then got all of their deposits back at month's end minus one day's worth of savings, which the money collector kept as his fee. The savings group members reasoned that this arrangement was worthwhile if it enabled them to keep money out of temptation's way.

This invaluable analysis of informal savings plans makes the persuasive case that poor people need financial services more than any other group because of the "triple whammy [of] low incomes; irregularity and unpredictability [of income], and a lack of tools." The success these households had in managing their money was directly linked to their success in increasing their income and improving their families' health and their children's levels of education. But their ability to manage their money was stymied at every turn by the unreliable, expensive, poor-quality financial tools available to them.

The idea of a community-based financial solution has great appeal and represents an innovative way to democratize finance. Nevertheless, it is important not to overly romanticize this informal tool. Since the success of the groups depends heavily on group selection and retention, would-be participants may be extensively screened, and nonperforming participants can be socially ostracized or punished by being excluded from other business opportunities. Some participants have even complained about the use of force by groups to compel the sale of household or business assets to satisfy monthly contributions. Although members set the terms by which the ROSCA operates, the structure, by its very nature, allows for little flexibility, particularly in case of emergency. If you are scheduled to take home the pot in August but your child falls sick in April, you'll have to find some other way to cover that emergency expense. Likewise, the public nature of the ROSCA and the distribution of proceeds encourage disciplined savings, but participants, particularly women, complain about the burden they face during the month they take home the pot. They find themselves inundated with requests for loans and gifts from family members and neighbors. Finally, the community-based nature of the ROSCA limits the amount of capital that a family can amass to whatever money the local participants can contribute; ROSCAs are not designed to mobilize outside resources that might be leveraged toward larger investments.

According to the latest available data, over $500 billion in ROSCA transactions were completed worldwide in 2015, attesting to both the ubiquity and the importance of ROSCAs in the financial lives of low-income people. Jonathan Morduch's book, *The Economics of Microfinance*, explores ROSCAs and their variations at length. While noting their enduring usefulness as an instrument for saving, Morduch also speculates that "imperfect alternative means to save can also explain why ROSCAs stay together." Being able to save in a regulated financial institution would address many of the drawbacks of the group saving method, but most commercial banks actively discourage small depositors by imposing prohibitive minimum balance requirements or avoid taking small deposits altogether.

FORMAL FINANCIAL SERVICES AND THE BIRTH OF MICROFINANCE

At the other end of the spectrum from informal financial services are institutions such as banks, credit unions, and insurance companies, which are usually considered to constitute the formal financial sector. Despite their current status as well-capitalized, regulated institutions, it is important to remember that many formal financial institutions have their roots in community models and traditions. In *Politicized Microfinance*, Caroline Hossein notes that ROSCAs or "informal banks in the Caribbean are a valued African tradition, rooted in the local savings systems of *susus* and *tontines* brought by slaves to the Americas. . . . People of the African diaspora turn to local informal financial groups that they know and trust as a way to harness their own power." Credit cooperatives or credit unions trace their origins back to various nineteenth-century European models that, by the turn of the twentieth century, had spread as far as Japan. In Germany, for instance, they were used to provide finance for agriculture, while in the UK, cooperative building societies came together to finance and build houses for their members. Despite the word "credit" in their name, these early models typically provided a community-based place to save as well as to borrow.

A strict line dividing an informal financial service provider from a formal one can be surprisingly difficult to draw. Informal services typically predate formal financial services, which develop as a country's financial system deepens and matures. But they are not always supplanted by the formal services, and the two models often exist side by side. A study of informal savings methods in Uganda found that 40 percent of female participants in ROSCAs also maintained bank accounts. Like Joyce Wafuko from neighboring Kenya, these women valued the safety and security of keeping their savings in a bank, but also saw the ROSCA as a way to maintain saving discipline. In addition, some informal finance models grow far beyond their indigenous roots by becoming for-profit, commercial ventures. Generations of Indians have invested their money through chit funds, which are a form of ROSCA in which a group of people (called subscribers) contribute monthly for as many months as there are subscribers; an auction or lottery is held to determine which subscriber takes home the monthly pot. The chit fund tradition started and continues to this day as a means for people who know each other to save together in small groups, but since the 1970s, large, commercialized chit fund companies have operated alongside them. One of the largest chit fund companies has an annual turnover of roughly $5 million, and the subscribers, who number in the millions, do not know each other or the chit fund organizers. (Notably, chit funds also represent a riskier alternative to saving in a bank account. Commercial chit fund companies must register to be legal, but the extent and quality of regulation vary from state to state in India, and chit fund account balances are not insured.)

The modern microfinance movement emerged from the context of informal, community-based financial services and represents the next giant step forward in the evolution of expanding access to finance for low-income people. The microfinance "origin story" begins with experiments by Professor Muhammad Yunus in Bangladesh in 1975. Bangladesh was facing devastating poverty from the famine that had swept the country in 1974. Frustrated by the expensive, often corrupt, and largely ineffective poverty reduction efforts of government development banks, Yunus began to lend small amounts of money to groups of very poor people so that they could start their own businesses. He found that not only were these loans repaid in full, but they seemed to offer a genuine path out of poverty. The microfinance model encouraged entrepreneurship and the ability of even very poor people to build a business that could sustain their families without reliance on either formal employment or charity. As it happened, similar models of "banking for the poor" were being tested by nonprofit organizations in other developing countries, such as Banco Sol in Bolivia and SEWA (Self-Employed Women's Association) Bank in India. While there was no single, unified approach, these early microfinance pioneers, including Yunus's own Grameen Bank, started as NGOs rather than as formally licensed, deposit-taking financial institutions, and their modes of operating drew on many of the same techniques and patterns found in informal financial service providers like ROSCAs. The most notable similarity is the use of the group as a mechanism to build trust and repayment discipline.

Unlike ROSCAs, though, most MFIs focused on lending rather than saving. For MFIs all over the developing world that followed the Grameen Bank model (so-called Grameen replicators), savings were an eligibility requirement in order to borrow rather than a distinct product offering. Since NGO MFIs were not legally able to accept customer deposits, they would collect savings from group customers and hold them in a bank account in the organization's name or sometimes in the name of one of the group members. Savings were an eligibility requirement, a way for clients to demonstrate their capacity to make a monthly financial commitment and a way for the MFI to build up a reserve in the event of a default on the loan. Likewise, these deposits could not serve as a source of funding for MFIs to make loans.

With some exceptions, most of the early microfinance lenders used a solidarity group model whereby loans were extended to individuals but the entire group was responsible for repayment. By lending to a group of people known to one another, the MFI effectively transferred the assessment of clients' creditworthiness to the group; like ROSCAs, MFIs operated on the principle that group members would be cautious in selecting potential group members and would allow only those who could repay into their group. MFIs drew on many of the practices seen among informal savings groups, particularly with respect to the "social capital" created by groups that saved and borrowed together. They also experienced astonishingly high loan repayment rates and, for many observers, demonstrated that the poor could be bankable.

Importantly, MFIs also had financial sustainability at the heart of their activities. While many MFIs relied fairly heavily on donor funding in their early years, the intention was always to be run as a sustainable—albeit not profit-maximizing—business. As a result, interest rates had to be high enough—and they were often very high—to cover the costs of operation. While MFIs provided an important alternative to loan sharks or informal moneylenders, the interest rates charged by most MFIs were not significantly lower.

With its narrative of providing a sustainable path out of poverty, the microfinance model soon captured the world's attention. The idea that a financial institution could extend loans to millions of poor entrepreneurs as a business rather than as a charity while maintaining repayment rates verging on 100 percent and achieving staggering financial returns—the return on assets, or ROA, for MFIs typically exceeded 5 percent, while commercial banks struggled to achieve even a 1 percent ROA—was an undeniably exciting one for development professionals and policymakers alike. By the early 2000s, microfinance had become, in the words of Ananya Roy in *Poverty Capital*, "the panacea of choice . . . lauded and deployed by development institutions and theorists of all stripes and varying ideologies as an important antidote to poverty." The excitement, hopes, and (perhaps unrealistic) expectations about the potential for microfinance to change the lives of the poor culminated in 2006 when Muhammad Yunus and the Grameen Bank were awarded the Nobel Peace Prize. In awarding the prize to Yunus, the chair of the Norwegian Nobel Committee said, "Lasting peace cannot be achieved unless large population groups find ways in which to break out of poverty. Micro-credit is one such means."

Although much of the microfinance sector would remain dependent on donor funding, the excitement of "doing well by doing good" didn't escape the attention of the capital markets. Many MFIs were able to mobilize capital for the purpose of on-lending from external lenders in amounts far greater than the resources that would have been available to them from small client deposits in their local communities. In fact, a new type of investor sprang up to finance MFIs. The microfinance investment vehicle (MIV) is an independent investment vehicle, typically a fund, that has 50 percent or more of its assets invested in microfinance. As of year-end 2018 (the latest time for which data are available), there were eighty-seven MIVs publicly reporting operational data (out of a total of 121), with a total of $15.3 billion in assets invested in MFIs. By the end of 2019, this influx of capital had allowed 916 MFIs around the world to reach a total of 140 million microfinance borrowers. As the focus shifted to reaching financial sustainability for many of the largest MFIs, some observers wondered, with Ananya Roy, "whether microfinance, as an asset class, sought after by Wall Street investors, [can] maintain this social purpose? Or will it fuel financial speculation, predatory capitalism, and ever-expanding debt?" The debate over the value or necessity of a trade-off between financial and social returns and the impact of external commercial capital would become a defining issue for the microfinance sector.

Expanded access to financial resources and increasing commercialization resulted in greater regulatory scrutiny of MFIs. Some countries established capitalization requirements and financial regulations specifically tailored to the needs of inclusive finance organizations. In particular, several countries introduced a regulated entity known as a "microfinance bank," which allowed MFIs to accept savings deposits once they had met strict capitalization, solvency, and other regulatory requirements. MFIs were eager to provide their low-income clients with a safe place to save, and many of them that had previously been structured as nonprofit organizations transformed into regulated, formal financial institutions. To meet the new statutory capital requirements, they attracted equity capital both from MIVs and from some mainstream private equity investors.

As the microfinance sector began to change dramatically, two signature events came to epitomize the tension between using commercial capital to reach more low-income customers and the original mission focus of microfinance as a means to reduce poverty: the Compartamos Banco initial public offering in Mexico and the Andhra Pradesh overindebtedness crisis in India.

In 2007, Compartamos, the largest MFI in Mexico, became the first Latin American microfinance organization to issue shares through an initial public offering (IPO). At the time of the IPO, Compartamos was the undisputed market leader in the Mexican microfinance sector with 630,000 clients, 98 percent of whom were women; the small average loan size of $446 indicated that the MFI was reaching a very low-income population. Making small loans to a predominantly female client base was characteristic of the Mexican microfinance sector at the time (and still is today) because of the concentration on group lending. Mexico is Latin America's largest microfinance market, although, unlike its regional peers, Colombia and Peru, the country has not evolved to offer larger individual loans to microentrepreneurs.

There was considerable excitement at the prospect of moving microfinance into the mainstream capital markets, and the IPO was a tremendous financial success: demand for shares was so strong that the deal was oversubscribed by thirteen times by investors in Mexico and internationally. The shareholders who sold into the IPO—international development organizations, the global microfinance NGO Accion, and various Mexican individuals—earned hundreds of millions of dollars. When the dust settled after the IPO, questions emerged about whether Compartamos was *excessively* profitable and whether the organization's high interest rates were in keeping with its social objectives. (Professor Yunus famously said, in response to the IPO, "We came here to fight the loan sharks, not become loan sharks ourselves.")

Compartamos's loan rates of 82 percent were high even for the notoriously expensive Mexican banking industry, although they were not the highest in the microfinance sector. Management was quick to note that the organization's loan loss rates were only 1.1 percent, so their customer base appeared able to afford the loans. In addition, the frequent in-person interactions by loan officers that were at the heart of the group lending model increased administrative costs; management argued that higher interest rates were necessary to cover these higher operating costs. Still, between 2000 and 2006, Compartamos had sustained an average return on equity (ROE) of 52 percent and a much higher profit margin (23.6 percent in 2005) than its competitors and peers. Some analysts argued that the MFI could have brought interest rates down to 65–70 percent and still have achieved an ROE of 15 percent, in line with other Mexican banks. The IPO also provoked debate about the appropriate use of donor funds— Compartamos had received $6.3 million in grant funding from donors both directly and through Accion—and raised questions about whether the organization's new shareholder base would affect the MFI's mission going forward.

The second event took place in 2010 in the southern Indian state of Andhra Pradesh and is a cautionary tale about the perils of government intervention, overindebtedness, and commercialization. Andhra Pradesh is considered to be the epicenter of Indian microfinance. It is home to some of the world's biggest and most successful MFIs, as well as an extensive government-sponsored microfinance program offered through self-help groups as part of a larger poverty reduction effort. Since Indian regulators did not permit MFIs to take savings deposits, they were heavily reliant on banks and other investors for capital to fund the loans they made. The largest of the commercial MFIs, SKS Microfinance, with 5.8 million clients, had attracted mainstream private equity investors; these shareholders provided the company with significant growth capital, for which they expected to receive outsized financial returns. In the ensuing race for growth, Andhra Pradesh's two competing sources of microfinance, commercial and government-led, saturated the market. By late 2010, more than one-third of the 30 million Indian households that used microfinance loans were in Andhra Pradesh and 83 percent of the households were juggling loans from more than one source. At 17.1 million members, the self-help groups dwarfed the MFIs' client numbers, but the government's loan disbursements had begun to slow precipitously and officials frequently blamed the private MFIs for stealing their customers.

Then, in October 2010, a number of female MFI clients committed suicide. Their families said they had done so out of shame and desperation

at their inability to repay their microfinance loans, including the joint lia-
bility obligation they incurred through the group lending model. (While
there is consensus that some suicides did take place, the actual number,
reported as anywhere from eighteen to seventy women, is in dispute and
is widely believed to have been manipulated for the state's own political
purposes.) In response, the state government cracked down on all microfinance activities, effectively shutting the industry down, causing ruinous
losses for the MFIs and forcing low-income households back into the hands
of loan sharks and informal moneylenders. If there is any silver lining to
the Andhra Pradesh crisis, it is that the Reserve Bank of India, the country's
banking regulator, was finally spurred to regulate the microfinance sector.
The Reserve Bank created a new category of legal structure for MFIs, the
nonbanking financial company MFI, which was supervised directly by the
Reserve Bank. In addition, it put guidelines in place for banks that lent to
MFIs, as well as certain mandatory consumer protection measures, including interest rate transparency and penalties for abusive collection practices
and predatory lending.

Perhaps the final blow to the claims that microfinance was a panacea
for poverty came in January 2015 with the release of a compilation of randomized controlled trials (RCTs) by Abhijit Banerjee, Dean Karlan, and
Jonathan Zinman that assessed the impact and limitations of microfinance
on low-income households and businesses across six countries. Broadly,
the studies indicated that, while some entrepreneurs invested more in their
business as a result of borrowing from an MFI, only larger, preexisting
or previously profitable businesses achieved higher profitability. Additionally, the take-up of microfinance loans was notably lower than expected
(only 13–31 percent) when they were offered to the general population
of eligible borrowers. The studies put a lid on the more expansive poverty
reduction claims for microfinance and led to a reassessment of the use of
microloans for entrepreneurial purposes. Nevertheless, they revealed that
microfinance borrowing had spurred higher rates of business ownership
and revenues, increased investments, and led to higher levels of inventory
and assets. And, perhaps most important, they confirmed the conclusion of various financial diaries projects, including *Portfolios of the Poor:*

having access to credit gave low-income people greater control over their financial lives, allowing them to mitigate risks and smooth consumption when needed.

From the earliest days of microfinance, women have made up a substantial majority of the client base. As evidence grew of women's better repayment performance relative to men's, the narrative of women's empowerment through access to finance became a central theme across the sector. However, subsequent research yielded more equivocal results. Some researchers, including Beatriz Armendáriz, Nigiel Roome, and Naila Kabeer, pointed to MFIs in Bangladesh that lent exclusively to women, where microloans were seen to have a "disempowering effect" (including rising rates of intimate partner violence) as men felt their traditional role as the primary breadwinner came under threat. In fact, researchers studying the impact of microfinance on gender-based violence in rural Bangladesh observed that the "highest levels of violence against women were in the village where it was most apparent that a transformation in gender roles was underway." Caroline Shenaz Hossein observed similar outcomes from microlending to the exclusion of men in the Caribbean, noting that "female-focused microfinance programs in Kingston [Jamaica] exacerbate local conflicts between men and women as well as between women."

The six RCTs analyzed by Banerjee, Karlan, and Zinman also found limited impact from microfinance on women's empowerment, with one notable exception. The study of Mexico's Compartamos Banco, which lends primarily to women, found some improvement in women's household bargaining and decision-making power, which the researchers attributed, in part, to the training and other nonfinancial services that the MFI included with the loan. This finding and the results of other recent studies speak to the need to deliberately design financial services to take into account women's needs, lived experience, and cultural milieu, often by including nonfinancial services alongside financial services. In the years since the publication of the research on the potentially disempowering effects of microfinance, many MFIs have come to see that providing loans to women, particularly if men are excluded from borrowing, was not sufficient to make positive material changes in a woman's life, let alone empower her. Chapter 3 explores at length the relationship between access to finance and women's empowerment, underscoring the importance of developing women's capabilities (e.g., financial and digital literacy, negotiation skills) and designing products that strengthen women's control over financial resources.

The years since 2006 have been turbulent ones for the microfinance industry. While no longer hailed as the silver bullet for poverty reduction as it was in the early days, microfinance still plays an important role in the financial lives of many low-income people. However, as the industry has matured, MFIs have begun to face competition from mainstream commercial banks, mobile money providers, and fintech companies. As the possibilities for offering lower-cost access to a wide range of finance services to low-income people expanded, the ease, convenience, and much lower cost of delivery of services brought a number of new players onto the field, eager to serve this new clientele. Seemingly overnight, the game changed from one with a small number of high-cost providers offering microfinance loans to a broader universe of banks, payment providers, and cell-phone companies. Within just eight years of M-Pesa's launch, for example, 271 mobile money services were offered in ninety-three countries around the world.

MFIs have been slow to respond to this changing landscape. Most have not diversified their product offerings and continue to rely on making small loans at very high interest rates. Only 55 percent of the 916 MFIs that publicly report financial data offer deposit services and only 18 percent offer insurance products. In light of the importance of savings to their client base, this seems like a significant missed opportunity. What's more, savings products represent an important competitive advantage over most mobile money providers, which remain focused on payments services.

Likewise, much of the microfinance industry has not kept pace with technological change, and the COVID-19 epidemic accelerated the need for the digital transformation of the microfinance sector. As CGAP's former CEO Greta Bull argues, fintechs and other digital financial service providers may be nimble and have proved they are able to operate at scale.

However, they have not yet shown that they can offer the full range of saving, lending, and insurance services needed by those at the lower end of the economic scale. They are catching up, though, so MFIs must urgently invest in digitizing their own systems and processes or partnering with fintech companies and mobile money providers. Failure to do so risks their ability to grow along with their best clients or, worse, leaves low-income customers vulnerable to digital financial services that are not delivered in a responsible way. Partly in response to the Andhra Pradesh crisis, the micro-finance industry has made huge improvements in pricing transparency, respectful collection practices, preventing overindebtedness, and other consumer protection measures. This focus on responsible financial services should be brought with them into the digital age as soon as possible.

THE COMMERCIAL OPPORTUNITY FOR DIGITAL FINANCIAL INCLUSION

The importance of the nexus of access to technology and access to finance cannot be overstated. The countries that have made the biggest gains in providing access to finance to low-income, unbanked people have done so by placing big, ambitious bets on enabling digital financial services. These countries have adopted a set of technological and policy measures that include (but are not limited to) digital identification, tiered, electronic know-your-customer (KYC) requirements, and broad-based wireless access. But a country that embraces financial inclusion through digital technology but fails to address the gender gap in access to mobile internet technology will exacerbate the gap in access to financial services, possibly leaving women even further behind.

In recent years, several attempts have been made to estimate just how much money is being left on the table as women are left behind by financial service providers. Different methods have been used to project the business to be generated by offering men and women equal access to the same financial services, but they all reach the same conclusion: financial service providers are missing out on a lucrative market opportunity. It should be noted that most of the relevant analysis has included both developed and developing country opportunities, but since the gender gap is even greater in the latter markets, we can still extrapolate meaningful conclusions.

One way is to look at just a single type of consumer banking product. Women are less likely than men to be approved by commercial bank credit departments for mortgages and personal loans. Banks offer a variety of explanations for this disparity, including placing the blame on women themselves by labeling them as more risk averse than men. None of these justifications explains the outright discrimination underlying the credit decisions, particularly since women have consistently higher credit scores and repayment records. Recent research into racial and gender discrimination in lending indicates that there are notably high degrees of bias in this category of loans since they are the most likely to involve a face-to-face, in-person interaction between the potential customer and lending staff. Perhaps even more worrying, though, is seeing these same biases being built into artificial intelligence (AI) and machine learning algorithms. Since 78 percent of AI professionals are men, their biases, unconscious and otherwise, are more likely to be reflected in the calculations that drive decision-making technology. Goldman Sachs's algorithm-based digital lender, Marcus, recently drew attention to these persistent biases when David Heinemeier Hansson, a prominent tech investor, reported that both he and his wife had applied for a Marcus credit card and that he had been granted a credit limit twenty times higher than his wife's, despite her higher credit score. (Goldman was subsequently cleared of bias charges by the New York State superintendent of financial services, who nevertheless noted, "While we found no fair lending violations, our inquiry stands as a reminder of disparities in access to credit that continue nearly 50 years after the passage of the Equal Credit Opportunity Act. This is one part of a broader discussion we must have about equal credit access.")

The gender bias that makes its way into credit decisions, whether digitally derived or not, is costing banks and other lenders a lot of money. If women were granted these mortgages and other personal loans, the credit products that represent the bread and butter of retail lenders around the world, at the same rate as men, the resulting incremental revenue is estimated to be between $32 billion and $65 billion annually. Impressive additional yearly revenues could also be generated by achieving parity in checking and savings account services ($15 billion) and payments ($7 billion.)

There is widespread excitement about the almost limitless potential for digital financial service providers to tap into an unprecedented new revenue opportunity that could ultimately expand financial service providers' balance sheets by as much as $4.2 trillion. McKinsey attributes a 6 percent increase in GDP, or $3.7 trillion, in the emerging markets just to the financial inclusion gains that would be possible through the widespread adoption and use of digital financial services. However, the path to that proverbial pot of gold is a complex one, paved with considerable uncertainty. The ability to operate at large scale is a necessity to achieve profitability, which in turn requires providers to make significant up-front infrastructure investments. To that is added an already challenging regulatory environment that requires the coordination of both financial and communications supervisors; in recent years the regulatory landscape has become even more complex with the emergence of data privacy and cybersecurity concerns. Regulatory decisions such as tariff and fee caps or licensing requirements for agents can have significant implications for operators' ability to scale up profitably.

Finally, the route to greater profitability will almost certainly require an expansion of the types of services and transactions beyond those currently offered by digital providers. This is where it gets really interesting for financial inclusion. At present, mobile money providers derive most of their revenues from so-called cash-in/cash-out or CICO services offered through their agent networks. But going beyond payments and CICO services is where the potential for expanding financial access opens up opportunities for providers to increase profitability and reduce their dependence on customer fees. McKinsey estimates that $4.2 trillion in new deposits and $2.1 billion in loans to an expanded pool of borrowers could be generated digitally by 2025. A growing number of providers are successfully forming partnerships with financial institutions to offer digital credit, saving, and insurance products. Mobile money providers that offer a broader set of financial services have an average 24 percent higher revenue per user than those that don't, and in the war for digital subscribers, these additional financial services are a way to create "stickier" customers through higher activity rates. In 2019, 21 percent of mobile money providers said the majority of their revenues came from business fees rather than from payment commissions, and that figure is likely to grow.

Those mobile money providers that are expanding into the provision of other financial services often do so in partnership with banks. The GSMA noted a significant increase in mobile money providers that offered digital credit, most of them in partnership with regulated financial institutions; a total of $390 million in digital loans had been disbursed by mid-2019. Once again, the M-Pesa experience in Kenya might be instructive. In 2012, M-Pesa joined with Commercial Bank of Africa (CBA), a small Kenyan bank with a relatively affluent clientele, to launch M-Shwari, a savings and loan account. Before M-Shwari, CBA had 40,000 deposit accounts with an average account balance of $20,000. Within five years of the M-Pesa collaboration, the bank's customer base had dramatically changed: it had increased by more than three hundred times and average balances had dropped significantly, hovering around $200. The roles of the two partners are distinct and clear: CBA opens bank accounts, assesses credit risk based on M-Pesa's KYC data, provides funding for the loans, and maintains regulatory compliance. For its part, Safaricom gives CBA access to most of the Kenyan population. Most notably, previously excluded Kenyans now have the benefit of a bank account that offers interest on savings and deposit insurance, as well as small loans disbursed by CBA to their M-Pesa account. When M-Pesa first launched, many assumed it would succeed at the expense of the banks, and indeed, mobile money accounts had exceeded bank accounts within two years of M-Pesa's introduction. Thanks to partnerships with CBA and other Kenyan banks, that relationship has flipped, with the number of bank accounts now exceeding mobile money accounts.

The M-Pesa experience also offers exciting evidence that digital financial services can play an important role in reducing poverty and increasing poor people's economic resilience. Researchers at MIT and Georgetown tracked the rollout of M-Pesa agents across Kenya, then measured changes in per capita consumption and occupational choice for 1,600 households in relation to the density of M-Pesa agents. Consumption is frequently used by researchers as a proxy for the relative economic well-being of a household. Notably, the MIT and Georgetown researchers measured the effects of changes in access or proximity to mobile money agents, not adoption of the service itself. This increase was enough to raise about 4 percent of the surveyed households above the poverty line.

Households where the number of agents located within one kilometer increased by five agents also saw a 6 percent increase in per capita consumption. The impact was even greater for female-headed households, where an increase in agent density accompanied a significantly higher average per capita consumption increase of 18.5 percent and a 22 percent increase in savings. The researchers also found that increases in agent density prompted approximately 185,000 women to shift from subsistence farming to more profitable entrepreneurial businesses or retail sales.

In addition to these profound economic development gains, M-Pesa has undeniably been a great financial success for Safaricom and its largest shareholders, Vodafone and Vodacom of South Africa. For the most recent fiscal year, M-Pesa represented 31 percent of the company's revenues ($743 million equivalent), more than making up for slowdowns in its traditional internet and data businesses. Management expects M-Pesa's contribution to revenue to reach 50 percent soon.

The M-Pesa success story brings us full circle, demonstrating yet again that when a woman's access to financial services is assured and she can control financial resources, she'll run with it. By its very nature, cellphone banking gives women the freedom, the discretion, and the power to maintain their income separately and make choices about how to manage their money. M-Pesa gives them more tools to manage risk and lets them decide whether to save or invest independently of their husbands and other household members—something that is much harder to do when they are transacting only in cash. From this study and others, it becomes apparent that giving women access to convenient, affordable, and confidential ways to manage money changes the ways that money is spent in a household. Indeed, the researchers close their paper by speculating, "For women, the route out of poverty might not be more capital, but rather financial inclusion at a more basic level, which enhances their ability to manage those financial resources that are already accessible. Thus, although mobile phone use correlates well with economic development, mobile money causes it." A bold claim—perhaps even an overreaching one—but a welcome recognition of the important differences in the impact of financial inclusion on women, as well as the need for a broader set of tools than simply access to credit.

For all the progress in financial inclusion that may be directly attributable to digital financial services, it is essential that, having moved on from microfinance, we not replace one panacea with another. In fact, there is already evidence that even digitally active women are more reluctant than men to share data with digital financial service providers, even if it means forgoing better products on better terms. This reluctance should not be dismissed but rather taken into consideration when regulations are implemented and products are designed. Financial inclusion—digital or otherwise—is not a cure-all. But it is an invaluable enabler of all sorts of change in people's lives, removing obstacles to their security and prosperity. So what's continuing to stand in the way of inclusion for the world's unbanked and underbanked women?

2 WHAT'S STANDING IN THE WAY OF WOMEN'S FINANCIAL INCLUSION?

As the widespread use of informal savings groups clearly demonstrates, the lack of a bank account doesn't preclude low-income women and men from conducting financial lives. By the same token, simply opening a bank account or creating a digital wallet (or, worse, having one opened for you) doesn't ensure financial inclusion. Several countries opened bank accounts for recipients of conditional cash transfers without explaining how the accounts worked or that they could be used to save or accept other types of payments, such as remittances. Almost without exception, those who received the government's cash transfers withdrew the full payment and continued to conduct their financial lives in cash through informal financial transactions.

To reap the economic, social, and even psychological benefits of being included in the formal financial system, women and men must go beyond simple ownership of a bank account in order to gain access to safe and affordable ways to make payments and build a safety net to rely on in times of emergency while also being able to save toward long-term goals or borrow to act on opportunities that arise. With digital financial services as the dominant delivery channel throughout the developing world, access to technology and confidence in using it become necessary conditions as well. The importance of closing the gender gap in smartphone ownership cannot be emphasized strenuously enough. That said, increasingly the lack of access to finance or technology is not the biggest barrier women face. Rather, women's own need for skills and awareness, as well as biases and a lack of information (and imagination) on the part of financial service providers and policymakers, looms as an equally significant but ultimately surmountable obstacle.

Women's lack of both financial and digital literacy tops the list of these barriers and accounts for many other underlying impediments as well. Access to financial services is of limited value without the knowledge, skills, and confidence to use them. Women tend to be less aware of the financial options available to them, which contributes both to a lack of confidence in dealing with financial service providers and to a mistrust of them. Unfortunately, this lack of awareness applies not only to the financial products or services themselves but also to the very mechanisms, such as deposit insurance, that have been put in place expressly to protect consumers from predatory or risky practices by financial institutions. Policymakers and financial service providers alike frequently call for more financial education to address this persistent lack of awareness. As a result, efforts to improve financial literacy have increased dramatically in the last decade, but the effectiveness of those efforts has been mixed at best. Numerous studies and randomized controlled trials all point to the same conclusions about the efficacy of financial education to change adults' financial behavior. The research confirms that, while financial education has positive benefits on financial literacy, transforming improved literacy into changed financial behavior is far more elusive. Nevertheless, we have a few clues to what does—and doesn't—appear to work.

Financial education is often delivered by less than engaging instructors in a classroom training environment with a curriculum that is neither relevant nor particularly interesting. And mandatory financial education—a feature of many government-sponsored programs that condition a benefit payment on regular attendance at financial education classes—appears to be particularly ineffective. A few years ago the Mexican government digitized the distribution of benefits payments made under the conditional cash transfer program *Prospera* to its ten million recipients, 92 percent of whom were women. *Prospera* was one of the first conditional cash transfer programs and had achieved impressive outcomes in health, education, and nutrition by conditioning benefits payments on certain "coresponsibilities," such as attending school and showing up for health care appointments. When the benefit payments were digitized and deposited directly into bank accounts accessible through mobile phones, the government added financial inclusion to *Prospera*'s mandate, conditioning payments on mandatory monthly financial literacy training. However, because the training curriculum did not address the recipients' misunderstandings, misperceptions, and fears, the women were largely unaware of the bank account underlying the payment and how they might incorporate that account into their financial lives. Most women simply used the debit card issued with the account to withdraw the entire payment in cash, even though many of them would turn around and save a portion of that cash at home, "under the mattress." In a misguided attempt at security, some women laminated the card, rendering it unusable; others kept the card at home "in a safe place," rather than using it to make purchases. Women frequently cited a concern that if they left the money in the account, the government would think they no longer needed the payments—a critical piece of information that had been missing from the financial literacy curriculum.

With some tweaks to the classroom model, though, financial education has the potential not only to raise awareness of women's financial options but to change their behavior as well. For example, training by peers rather than by professional educators from outside the community appears to be particularly effective. The global nonprofit BSR adapted a highly successful peer-led health and wellness training program that was delivered on factory floors throughout the developing world to impart financial education. The resulting program, called HERFinance, realized impressive gains in awareness and basic financial knowledge among women factory workers in India; for example, after completing the program, four times as many women understood that interest was something that you earned when you saved, not just something you paid when you borrowed. The peer training led to important behavioral changes as well. The women who completed the workplace training demonstrated better budgeting and planning behavior and an increased use of formal financial products and services, particularly savings tools. The women also reported that, as a result of the HERFinance training, they had greater control over their own salaries, leading to more involvement in household decision-making.

One of the key lessons from HERFinance and other financial education efforts is that the effectiveness of a program depends on whether it is linked to direct and timely access to financial products and services through which women can apply what have they have learned. Making the information less abstract and giving women the immediate opportunity to apply the concepts they've learned contributes significantly to lasting behavioral change. The teachable moments, ones that link training to a specific transaction or financial decision that is immediately relevant to the client, enhance the chances for positive behavioral change. A bank in Sri Lanka offered ten-minute on-the-spot financial education at its branches to men and women who were waiting in line to pick up remittance payments from family members working abroad. Within a matter of weeks, not only did the bank see a substantial portion of the remittance payments left in savings accounts rather than being withdrawn in cash, but 30 percent of the people who had been trained made additional deposits of money that they had previously kept under the mattress.

Engaging emotionally with clients through popular media has also proven to be an effective channel for nudging changes in financial behavior. A bank in the Dominican Republic developed a weekly telenovela called *Contracorriente* that had financial education messages embedded within its steamy daytime drama plot. One of the program's story lines featured a character who dreamed of leaving her job cleaning rich people's houses and was saving in order to open her own business by hiding cash in envelopes around the house. She was devastated to come home and find that her husband had discovered her hidden treasure and used the money to throw a big, raucous party for all his friends. When she confided this loss to her best friend, who owned a nail salon, the friend admonished her for not saving in a bank account, which not only would have been safer but also would have paid her interest on the deposit. The bank aired each week's episode in its branches throughout the show's eighteen-week season. Staff from a local NGO offered additional training sessions, also in the bank branches, based on the messaging from the programming with videos that also featured the

Contracorriente cast. In the six months following the airing of the show, the bank saw a 39 percent increase in account openings; even more impressive, 76 percent of the bank's dormant savings accounts had been reactivated. In both cases, women customers overwhelmingly referred to the program and its characters as the principal motivator behind their decision to save.

As more financial transactions move to the digital realm, digital literacy, or knowledge of and comfort with mobile technology, has become a logical, and essential, extension of financial literacy. Indeed, for low-income men and women alike, digital illiteracy is the greatest barrier to their adoption of financial services provided via mobile phone. Higher rates of basic illiteracy and innumeracy make digital adoption particularly challenging for women, difficulties that are exacerbated by a limited understanding of the internet and opportunities to learn on their own. For example, women, already more price sensitive than men for digital services, may not have a clear understanding of how data packages work, leading to a reluctance to explore the functions on their cell phone and experiment with different features and apps for fear of racking up data charges. Women often get "stranded" on so-called app islands like WhatsApp and Facebook without surveying the internet more broadly or applying skills they have learned to other applications, although there is evidence that women's confidence increases considerably after spending time with more functions available on the phone and by learning on their own. Women also tend to learn about the mobile internet through family and friends, so their understanding can be constrained by those sources' capabilities or any restrictive gender norms they observe.

Developers and internet providers are gradually adapting mobile apps to be more user-friendly for those who are less confident and possibly illiterate. Some newer features include the use of local language, simplified content, and expanded use of video and graphic content. A digital financial service provider in Indonesia developed a comic strip to teach female *warungs* (owners of small shops and cafés) how to access supplier credit digitally for their businesses, and in India, the government's COVID-19 relief payments were specifically targeted to women. Several financial institutions enabled account access through interactive voice recognition technology.

Financial and digital literacy implies more than just the knowledge and skills that come from training. It also denotes a capacity to use both technology and financial services with confidence. That confidence is also key to building the trust needed for women to engage with financial service providers. Across the economic spectrum, women require more time than men to build trust with a financial service provider; they tend to ask more questions and take longer to reach a decision on whether to move forward with a financial product or service. Their lack of familiarity with digital technology and concerns about security and privacy magnify women's wariness about formal financial services—so much so that a lack of trust emerges as a significant barrier to women's financial inclusion.

To a much greater extent than men, low-income women express a sense of emotional distance from formal financial institutions, believing that banks are not "for them." Building trust takes time and is rarely the result of a single action but rather takes shape through a series of coordinated interventions. Both men and women are concerned about interest rates and fees, for example, but women tend to ask more questions about how a product or service works, how mistakes will be rectified, and where they can turn for assistance. Research in the US indicates that a woman's trust in a financial service provider can be increased if she perceives the provider to be supportive at an important life moment such as buying a home. Women's greater need to build trust extends into the digital financial services realm as well. TigoGhana, a leading mobile money provider, reports that, on average, women require five to ten interactions with the service, compared to three to five interactions for men, in order to develop trust in and confidence with the service.

Low-income women making their first tentative forays into the formal banking system all too frequently encounter rudeness and even outright hostility from bank personnel. They report feeling lost and bewildered by the forms and required paperwork (particularly if they are illiterate), and justifiably conclude they are not wanted as customers. Interestingly, many of these women mention a "hero" emerging in the form of the bank security guard who notices their frustration and steps in to answer their questions and guide them through the process. They see the security guard as someone more "like them" who can be trusted and who will treat them with respect.

Agent networks established by banks and mobile money providers introduce a touchpoint with a financial service provider that is closer to home and presents greater possibilities for building trust with potential women clients. In many developing countries, commercial banks have established business correspondent or agent networks in retail or postal outlets—convenient places where women perform daily errands. These agents are often in rural areas and provide many financial services without the regulatory burden and financial cost of maintaining a full bank branch. Research indicates that these outlets are particularly effective where digital and financial literacy are low because the agents are able to provide better and more tailored customer service. A survey of customers who relied on Indian banking correspondents for financial services noted that both men and women felt that female agents took more time to build customer trust and confidence and provided hands-on demonstrations of how to use their cell phones and access digital financial services. They also felt that women agents were on par with men agents in terms of speed and knowledge of service. Women customers, in particular, appreciated that agents addressed their safety and security concerns by demonstrating features such as call blocking and privacy settings on their cell phones. As a result, female agents completed more transactions with female customers. To the extent that cell phones threaten traditional gender norms, particularly in the South Asian context, attention to women's security and privacy concerns can become a strategic marketing choice.

Bank of Baroda, India's second largest public sector bank, sought to boost account usage among its urban inclusive finance clientele by basing business correspondents in the community to perform most banking transactions. The bank found that both men and women customers had an increase in transactions of over 20 percent when performed with female business correspondents than with male correspondents. Women correspondents also had significantly higher rates of moving customers from account sign-up to actually making deposits, and they were also better able to cross-sell other financial products to savings account customers.

The real proliferation in financial service agents, however, has been through mobile network operators; mobile money outlets have almost tripled in the last five years. Recalling the critical connection between outlet density and financial inclusion in the case of M-Pesa in Kenya, it is particularly notable that the ratio of mobile money agents per 1,000 square kilometers has expanded from 70 to 148 since 2014. Not only are agent networks the critical front-line soldiers in the march toward financial inclusion, but industry data indicate a particularly strong business case for employing women as agents. Female agents improve the acquisition and retention of both male and female clients and record higher activity rates than their male counterparts. Zoona, a mobile money provider that started operations in Zambia, found that repayment rates by men were consistently higher for digital loans that were extended through women agents. Management believed that women agents were able to establish better lines of communication with customers, combining a "human face" with the efficiency of digital technology, which paid off when the clients' loans came due. When the company expanded operations to neighboring Malawi, it actively recruited women agents through churches, women's groups, and NGOs focused on women. It also launched an innovative "business-in-a-box" franchise model for young entrepreneurs. Zoona provides franchisees with a branded agent kiosk, funds their initial working capital needs, covers losses for the first six months, and offers business training. More than 70 percent of the franchise agents are women.

Some financial service providers are deliberately adopting strategies to build trust with female customers, either working within or respectfully challenging gender norms. For example, an Indonesian fintech company, DigiAsia, is working with midwives to open savings accounts for pregnant women to save for labor and other health services that are not fully covered by the government's universal health insurance plan. Not only are midwives trusted members of the community with whom women have already established a relationship but, mindful of gender norms, they provide women with the opportunity to access digital financial services without sharing a cell-phone number with a male agent. Once the baby is delivered, the mother can continue to use the account, and the midwife's clinic becomes a cash-in/cash-out location for the entire village. Likewise, one of South Africa's first digital banks, TymeBank, has directly addressed distrust of the banking system by making financial services easily accessible in places where people—particularly women—already go. Using a "high-tech/high-touch" approach, Tyme has partnered with a nationwide super-market chain, placing digital kiosks in stores and installing (mostly female) Tyme ambassadors to on-board customers and answer questions.

There is also a positive correlation between the percentage of women agents in a mobile money network and the number of women clients served, a linkage that can be an important contributor to overcoming one of the biggest barriers to women's financial inclusion, namely, social and cultural norms. Attitudes and expectations about women's roles in the home, the workplace, and society profoundly affect the degree to which women have access to and control over financial resources. While societal norms that restrict women's access or mobility are a challenge, they are not an insurmountable obstacle, and women in an agent network or sales force can also provide a pathway into this underserved market. Progress toward greater inclusion can be achieved by working within existing social norms to address market constraints for women. Women aren't really invisible if you know where to look for them; traditional group savings and loan associations, agricultural cooperatives, and religious groups can all be leveraged for greater inclusion.

Telesom ZAAD was the first mobile money provider in Somaliland, one of the world's poorest regions, with annual per capita income ranging between $250 and $350 and nearly 98 percent of the population financially excluded. Men typically work outside the home, while women control most household spending decisions. Most of the men began receiving their salaries digitally, but they would typically cash out the digital payment and give it to their wives to manage the household finances. Telesom realized that reaching women in their role as household financial managers would be essential to achieving the company's goal of encouraging people to keep more money in their mobile accounts and transact digitally rather than cashing out. Having recognized this business imperative, the company introduced a series of measures to attract women customers that addressed barriers to their access from within the conservative Muslim cultural context. Once again, recruitment of female agents played a significant role in driving the registration of women customers. The streamlined process required a photo, though, and women were unwilling to remove their veils in front of men, but agreed to have photos taken by female agents. The company also launched television and radio campaigns that depicted women using the mobile money service and featured the uses for mobile money that were of particular importance to women, especially payments to local merchants and savings. This combination of a robust network of women agents, targeted messaging, and smart, pragmatic process changes led to an increase in women customers from 17 percent in 2010 to 36 percent in 2018.

USING DATA TO UNDERSTAND WOMEN CUSTOMERS

The companies discussed in the previous section recognized that reaching women clients could require different approaches than they had used in the past to reach predominantly male clients—not worse or more difficult, just different. Yet for every financial service provider that is actively seeking ways to serve women clients, countless others persist in the belief that there is not a compelling business case for doing so. The financial service industry has been slower than many other sectors to embrace concepts of customer centricity and analyzing the customer journey when designing their products and services. Legacy banks face increasing threat to their business from fintechs and large tech companies that offer consumers— particularly younger ones—more seamless digital financial options. Rather than using this period of disruption to rethink their business-as-usual approach, though, most financial service providers default to products and services designed *by* men *for* men. The irony is that we have seen time and time again all over the world that, when it comes to financial services, exactly the opposite pattern is the more successful business strategy. Financial products that include the "must have" features required by women to use them are also preferred by men. To give just one example, a Latin

American bank decided to simplify and streamline its small business loan application process to accommodate women business owners who could not access all the supporting documentation the bank typically required. The new process was a hit with both men and women customers and the bank saw an increase in new applications from both men and women, a substantial uptick in repeat business from men, and greatly improved customer satisfaction ratings from male customers.

But banks and other financial service providers don't have to take advice from external third parties, they can just pay attention to what their own internal customer data say. To go to the trouble of collecting data and then not use the data to inform business decisions is illogical and expensive, yet when it comes to women financial customers, it seems to be a fairly common business practice. A study of 110 banks across nineteen Latin American countries indicated that only 14 percent of the banks surveyed disaggregated the data in their credit portfolios by sex; worse still, only six of the banks that did separate their credit data in this way used the information in their managerial decision-making.

Managing customer data—collecting it, disaggregating it, and analyzing it—is at the heart of building a business case for serving women customers. Without data, a business cannot properly size or segment a market or measure the profitability of products targeted to certain customers. Many financial service providers contend that a robust business case for managing data in this fashion doesn't exist, and women-focused initiatives (to the extent they exist at all) remain firmly rooted in a company's philanthropic or corporate social responsibility portfolio. In contrast, a review of broader financial industry customer data reveals that across the economic spectrum, women are good, loyal clients for financial service providers; in developed markets, 61 percent of female customers stay more than five years with a bank, compared with 46 percent of male customers. Women typically have better loan repayment rates than men and are less likely to bounce checks; women also tend to be longer-term, "stickier" savers and to build higher savings to income ratios than men.

How can banks so confidently assert there isn't a business case for serving women if they don't even know who their customers are? One particularly enlightening case involves a large Vietnamese commercial bank that was experiencing unusually high levels of customer turnover in its retail banking portfolio. This bank disaggregated data by gender but did not regularly rely on those data for decision-making; however, the churn in their customer base worried management enough for it to take a second look. The sex-disaggregated client turnover figures revealed a significant disparity between men and women; in fact, turnover was particularly high—90 percent within one year—for some of the highest-volume accounts held by women. Follow-up conversations with some of the former clients revealed further surprises: most of the women customers who had closed their accounts were not typical retail clients but small, informal business owners, many of them generating significant revenues from sales through online platforms such as Facebook. Their principal reason for leaving the bank was that they required a broader range of financial and nonfinancial business services that were not available to them as retail customers.

As this example indicates, ignoring gender-specific data can be costly for banks. With the growing dominance of digital technology as the principal channel for financial inclusion, getting mobile data right is even more consequential. Nonexistent or inaccurate data about women's actual phone usage, combined with women's lower rates of mobile phone ownership, can only further exclude women. Mobile providers typically do not collect gender data at the point of sale—a situation that is further complicated in places where men acquire SIM cards and register phones for their wives and daughters. Fortunately, in the race to add subscribers and increase revenue per user, mobile providers have begun to recognize the value of sex-disaggregated customer data. In fact, the GSMA, the industry association for mobile providers, has designed a machine learning algorithm that allows mobile providers to analyze their customer data in order to generate more accurate projections of the sex of their subscribers. Robi Axiata, a mobile network operator in Bangladesh, was one of the first companies to use the tool; the algorithm is particularly effective in markets, like Bangladesh, where women do not register for a cell phone using their own identification and where there are distinct gender differences in usage patterns. Of the 146 different predictive features used by the model, certain indicators were particularly robust in determining the gender of Robi's users: on average, the duration of women's incoming calls was longer than men's, and women had fewer different contacts. Also, Bangladeshi women's more circumscribed mobility outside the home was reflected in three indicators: the phone's lower radius of gyration on an average active day and throughout the entire period under study, and the number of cell towers that handled a subscriber's transactions. After applying the tool, Robi discovered that 78 percent of its female subscribers had been mistakenly registered as male. Since then, the company has launched two targeted initiatives designed to increase the number of women customers. One of these explicitly recognizes the important relationship between women agents and women clients: the company provides smartphones and startup capital to young women to set up retail businesses selling various cell-phone and mobile money products.

ALL THAT JAZZ: MAKING DIGITAL FINANCIAL SERVICES WORK FOR WOMEN IN PAKISTAN

The ways in which women interact with financial services, the product features that are important to them, and the complexity of the obstacles they face are often quite distinct from men's experience. But addressing these differences and successfully taking them into account in their customers' experience can elude even well-intentioned financial service providers. Take the example of Jazz, one of Pakistan's largest mobile phone operators. In 2007, even as the company was bringing in one million new cell-phone subscribers each month, management recognized the commercial potential of providing customers with digital financial services as well. They tapped Aniqa Sandhu, a seasoned cellular marketing professional, to develop a mobile money offering. Over the next five years, Sandhu and her team encountered numerous regulatory challenges and scrapped two partnerships with commercial banks, until the company eventually chose to establish its own microfinance bank. Finally, in 2012, Jazz launched JazzCash, a digital bank account expressly designed to reach all Pakistanis, including the country's 100 million unbanked men and women. While 35 percent of

Pakistani men owned a cell phone, only 7 percent of women did. But with 133 million registered cell-phone subscribers across the country, digital financial services presented an undeniable opportunity to expand financial inclusion. This bet on JazzCash paid off. By 2016 the company had 12.4 million subscribers to its mobile wallet and Sandhu had been named chief digital officer.

Despite this success, Sandhu couldn't escape the fact that women represented only 12 percent of active wallet users. As she said, "I haven't come all this way just to have women left behind by this innovation." For Sandhu, helping women gain access to financial services was personal: her mother had been widowed at age twenty-five and had made the bold choice to continue to live alone in her Pakistani village as a single mother with three young daughters rather than make the more culturally accepted decision to move into her in-laws' home. Her mother had always stressed the importance of education to Sandhu and her sisters, but she was equally insistent on the need for the girls to be financially independent, pointing to her own experience of "calamity" as evidence of the need to build a safety net. Sandhu maintained close ties to the village where she had grown up and always found it a challenge to send money back to family members to help pay for weddings or school fees. Even if the women in the village owned cell phones, they didn't know how to receive payments independently of their husbands; in fact, many of them asked Sandhu whether they could use their husbands' identification numbers instead of their own. Sandhu wanted these women to have an experience of financial independence, so she often found herself explaining to them how to open a mobile money account on their cell phone and how to use it to send and receive payments.

These impromptu lessons got her thinking—there must be women all over Pakistan that could benefit from mobile financial services, but simply didn't know how to access them. And not just low-income women, either. She had met many educated, middle-class Pakistani women who didn't have the documentation necessary to open a cell-phone account on their own. Registration of a SIM card in Pakistan requires proof of address, such as a rental agreement or utility bill, and a government-issued identification document, such as a passport or voter identification card. Both types of documentation are out of reach for many women in Pakistan; for example, women make up fewer than half of registered voters in Pakistan. It was quite typical in Pakistan for a man to acquire several cell-phone SIM cards in his own name and then distribute them among the women in his family, with the result that a woman couldn't even enjoy the benefits of a unique personal identifier that the phone offered her. Getting women to the point where they could open mobile wallets on their own would represent significant progress toward providing them with a degree of financial autonomy. As a first step, the company launched an awareness campaign targeting women entrepreneurs as part of its social impact initiative, but it didn't run for long. As Sandhu ruefully noted, "those projects are the first to get cut" when budgets get tight since they don't have a direct income-generating impact on the company's bottom line. She knew that corporate philanthropy wouldn't be enough. She had to expand outreach to women, sustainably, from *within* the business if it was going to be taken seriously.

She took her concerns to the CEO of Jazz who encouraged her to develop a woman's product that might boost the number of women using the JazzCash wallet. When Sandhu reviewed the JazzCash customer data, though, she realized that the usage patterns told a slightly different story. Even though they made up only a small percentage of total users, active women clients used the same products in the JazzCash wallet at roughly the same volumes and with the same frequency as men, yielding similar levels of profitability. Once women became customers, they readily used existing products and services such as topping up cell-phone airtime, depositing cash, and paying bills. The company didn't need a new product, one dedicated to women clients. Rather, the real problem lay in how Jazz went about acquiring new women customers.

Sandhu's team stepped back to look at the entire customer experience for women JazzCash users, and they didn't have to look much further than the customer acquisition process to see where the problems might be. New JazzCash customers sign up for an account in one of three ways: by themselves directly on their phones, through referrals from current JazzCash users, or at a JazzCash agent location. Jazz's own customer data showed that a greater percentage of active female customers were on-boarded through referrals from existing JazzCash customers than male customers, so it made sense to try to increase the number of referral messages sent to potential women clients. Interviews with both male and female current and potential JazzCash clients uncovered a number of behavioral differences related to sending and acting on referrals.

The team factored these lessons into a series of test messages sent by SMS text and found that women clients strongly preferred texting messages to other women that had specific references to gender. Using messages mentioning women friends, mothers, and sisters prompted women to send significantly more referrals to other women. Various messages addressing friendship or the female gender were tested at different times of the day, including messages such as *"Hope that JazzCash account has made your life easier. Benefit women around you with this service as well. Dial 787*&# and invite them"* or *"Till now 300,000 people have invited women on JazzCash! Invite women around you to JazzCash mobile account now."* Potential women clients were more likely to accept referrals from women using this more woman-centered language. The female-focused language didn't appear to have any particular impact on the rate of men's sending or accepting referrals. The ability to build trust and a sense of inclusion by using language that underscores the message that banking services are for "people like them" becomes an essential element in winning women's business.

The second approach in revamping Jazz's customer acquisition process dealt even more directly with Pakistani cultural and social norms. Like most digital financial service providers in the emerging markets, Jazz uses agents, mostly small shopkeepers, to introduce new clients to their service. In the case of JazzCash, 95 percent of their 70,000 agents are men. Sandhu had a strong hunch that a potential woman client might be uncomfortable entering a male-owned shop, let alone providing a male agent with her cellphone number in order to open an account. Another series of interviews and focus groups with both men and women throughout the country provided an even more nuanced view of the gender dynamics at work. Even in the most conservative regions of Pakistan every man interviewed owned a mobile phone, while the level of women's ownership ranged widely but never exceeded 80 percent. Although all women said they had access to a phone, many of them shared phones with other family members and used them primarily for calling and messaging; only a few of them had a clear understanding of how mobile money products worked. Nearly all the women reported saving either at home or in community savings groups, although many of these same savers were convinced they didn't have enough money to open a bank account. And while they questioned how they might benefit from a formal account, these women nevertheless looked for ways to protect their confidentiality and assert their autonomy. Most of the women hid their savings from the men in their household. (As one woman put it, "The lady of the house is a thief. If we can't save, then how are we going to survive? If our men give us 100 rupees, we save 20 rupees and tell him that 100 rupees has been spent. . . . That is why we say the woman is a thief.")

The interviews with men revealed a range of cultural concerns and views of women's role in the household and the community that would become central to reshaping the JazzCash product. In more conservative parts of the country, some men expressed resistance to women's moving outside the house, but allowed that if women needed to leave the home to conduct banking transactions, they preferred that their female family members transact with a woman agent. At the same time, several men worried that the women in their family would need more education about the product so they were not taken advantage of by male or female agents. They speculated that it might be better for women to seek help from a trusted source such as a neighbor to transfer funds. Women generally liked the idea of working with women agents and thought it would be easier than working with men, although many expressed doubt that they would obtain permission from their male family members to use an agent.

Armed with this information about their potential client base, Jazz formed a partnership with Unilever, one of the world's largest consumer goods companies with top-selling brands such as Dove, Lipton Tea, and Knorr. Unilever had gone into rural districts throughout Pakistan refurbishing existing shops or opening new ones, providing business training and access to Unilever products through an extended network of one thousand women retailers known as *Guddi Bajis* or "good sisters."

The footprint of the *Guddi Baji* network across rural Pakistan aligned well with JazzCash's expansion plans, and the shop owners were already respected and trusted members of the community, so they seemed ideal candidates to be trained as JazzCash agents. By late 2017, 42 percent of the accounts opened by *Guddi Bajis* were by women customers, compared to agents in the rest of the Jazz network. The company also deployed female brand ambassadors as part of their rural sales force to provide targeted digital and financial literacy training. They repositioned their television and other advertising to emphasize female role models and to showcase the economic benefits of being financially included. By all accounts, the Jazz-Unilever partnership offered a rare "win-win-win" solution for everyone: within the first year, JazzCash had acquired nearly one million female customers performing more than one million transactions per month, worth over $35 million. The *Guddi Bajis* brought in increased revenue through commissions, earning an average of $9.40 per month, compared to the average $5 per month they had made from Unilever sales only, while top performers generated three times that amount.

THE FALLACY OF GENDER NEUTRALITY

As Sandhu's team learned, without collecting and then using gender-disaggregated data, financial service providers have no way of knowing how to find women clients or how to serve them well, leaving them to default to the status quo. And as Caroline Criado Perez says in her award-winning cri de coeur for sex-disaggregated data, *Invisible Women*, "Whiteness and maleness are implicit. They are unquestioned. They are the default." Indeed, a misplaced belief in "gender blindness" may be one of the greatest obstacles to women's financial inclusion. Nowhere is this barrier more evident—or more in need of dismantling—than in the realm of setting financial policies and regulations.

It's worth noting that seemingly gender-blind approaches can have an impact on female employees as well as on their clients. ASA of Bangladesh, the world's largest microfinance institution, had a long-standing operational requirement that loan officers could collect loan payments only by going door-to-door at dusk, when both husband and wife were certain to be home. Many women loan officers resisted the practice, deeply uncomfortable with traveling alone after dark; they typically collected payments during the day, leaving less time to book new loans, which affected not only their collection rates and compensation but also their chances for promotion. Once ASA management changed the practice of nighttime-only collections, they observed that the women loan officers were more successful in collecting from both male and female clients.

Many governments, even those like India's with estimable track records of promoting financial inclusion, insist that their national financial inclusion strategies and policy initiatives are gender neutral. Yet an emerging body of macroeconomic research indicates otherwise. If a policy is described as "gender agnostic," it is far more likely to have been drafted to address an issue as experienced by men without considering how a given course of action might affect men and women differently. Research on infrastructure investment by a team of Turkish economists provides a vivid example. They determined that 20 billion Turkish lira (roughly equivalent to $3 billion) invested in the construction sector would yield 290,000 new jobs, with only 6 percent of them going to women. However, that same 20 billion lira invested in child care and preschool education would result in 719,000 new jobs, 73 percent of them for women. Policies that acknowledge differences in men's and women's lives, particularly with regard to unpaid care work, stand a much better chance of securing more sustainable gains for both men and women.

Policies designed to expand financial inclusion are no exception; however, even the most well-meaning policymaker will be frustrated in her efforts to address the gender gap in financial participation in the face of the nearly total lack of data. Even if countries add explicit gender targets to their national financial inclusion strategies, it will be impossible to set meaningful targets, let alone measure progress against them, without accurate, sex-disaggregated data on women's access to and usage of financial services.

There are two complementary types of data that inform business and policy decisions about financial inclusion, and policymakers can play an invaluable role in expanding their availability: "demand-side" data, which are collected directly from customers, and "supply-side" data, which are reported by banks and other financial institutions, typically as part of the information they are required to submit to regulators and other government agencies. The authoritative global source of demand-side data is the World Bank's Global Findex database. which surveys 150,000 adults from over 140 countries every three years in collaboration with the Gallup World Poll. The Global Findex provides a range of sex-disaggregated indicators on access to and use of both formal and informal financial services. In addition, several countries have launched surveys to gather national-level customer data, which, in principle, should allow policymakers to gain a more nuanced understanding of their own populations. However, only a handful of these surveys distinguish between male and female customer data, which greatly limits their value in testing the efficacy of specific policy initiatives to address gender inequality.

Although there is still a long way to go in accessing sufficient data about women's demand for financial services, it's on the supply side that the most glaring gaps in data persist. While at the national level, regulators require financial institutions to report extensive account-level information, financial inclusion data are far more rarely collected. Rarer still is account-level data disaggregated by sex. The IMF's Financial Access Survey (FAS) is the most definitive source of global supply-side data on financial inclusion and has started to make inroads into this data gap in recent years. After pilot projects in 2016 and 2017, the FAS added several sex-disaggregated indicators to its annual survey, requiring governments to report numbers of household borrowers and depositors by sex. Recognizing the importance of savings as a tool to expand women's inclusion, they have also expanded coverage to include not just commercial banks but deposit-taking micro-finance institutions as well. While these changes to the FAS represent a major step forward, only 60 of the 189 countries surveyed report sex-disaggregated data.

Women's absence from financial data allows policymakers and financial service providers to cling to the false assumption that there is no business or macroeconomic case for women's financial inclusion. This fundamental problem of making—and keeping—women invisible is further exacerbated by the difficulty many women still face in establishing a legal identity.

Legal proof of identity is the key to gaining access to services—including financial services—and exercising both civil rights and privileges, such as the right to vote or to receive government benefits. The World Bank estimates that 1.1 billion people globally still lack a legally recognized form of identification; by now it should come as no surprise that women are disproportionately represented among those without this fundamental tool. The gender gap in access to legal documentation of identity is particularly acute in low-income countries, where 44 percent of women (versus 28 percent of men) lack a national identification card or a similar identification credential. The linkage between lack of identification and financial exclusion in these countries is further underscored by one-third of the population citing "lack of documents" as a reason for not having a bank account. Most countries do not explicitly prohibit women from applying for legal proof of identity such as a national identification card or a passport. However, gender-based differences in laws and regulations in many countries make it far more burdensome for women, particularly married women, to acquire these foundational documents. In several countries, for example, proof of marital status is required to obtain these documents, or a husband's name must appear on the application form or even on the identification card itself. These legal barriers extend to a woman's children as well, both boys and girls, since several countries do not permit women to register their children's birth or obtain a birth certificate for them.

The implications of this lack of proof of identity expand exponentially when we consider that, in an ever more digital world, paper-based identification is simply not enough. Government agencies and companies around the world are increasingly seeking the transparency, cost savings, and efficiency afforded by the digital delivery of goods, services, and entitlements. Those benefits are out of reach for the 3.4 billion people globally whose only proof of legal identity cannot be used digitally—and that's on top of the one billion with no legal form of identification at all.

In response, more than forty national and private sector digital identification programs have been launched, largely in the developing world, to begin to close this gap. These programs have had varying degrees of success and take-up by individuals, but far and away the most successful digital national identification program has been India's Aadhaar system. Launched in 2009, the system has more than a 90 percent penetration rate and provides a unique digital form of identification to 1.2 billion people, greatly expanding access to government benefits transfers and financial services. The technologies most commonly used for the purpose of digital identification include biometrics, smart cards, and mobile technologies, often in combination, and they are becoming increasingly accurate and less expensive. Biometrics uses physical (fingerprints or iris patterns) or behavioral attributes (signatures or keystroke patterns) as credentials, which can then be verified by an issuing authority or a financial institution. Smart cards in various forms use barcode technology (including QR codes) to store numerical as well as biometric data. India's Aadhar, for example, features a twelve-digit identification card that is then verified through a fingerprint scan.

Eliminating the various educational, behavioral, and regulatory barriers that conspire to exclude women from the formal financial system is an undeniably positive objective with clear, measurable economic outcomes. Women's financial inclusion can help to expand inclusive economic growth and reduce the number of people living in extreme poverty and, arguably, should be pursued for those reasons alone. But expanding women's access to and control over financial resources yields benefits that extend far beyond these economic impacts. They reach all the way to an individual woman, how she is perceived by those around her, and how she perceives herself. The very fact of having money in her own name and determining how it will be spent gives a woman choice in other areas of her life as well. It gives her agency. It makes her visible.

3 FROM INVISIBILITY TO AGENCY

In recent years, women's economic empowerment has become the rallying cry and stated objective of countless public and private development initiatives. But even as its popular use—indeed, overuse—has proliferated in recent years, its real meaning has become further obscured. A more precise definition of empowerment and the ways to measure it have long eluded economists, feminists, and researchers. Various constructs and frameworks have emerged, all of which address some element of being able to choose among options; they all speak to a woman's ability to make choices that reflect her own interest and, importantly, to believe she has the right to choose.

Naila Kabeer writes of empowerment as women's ability to make "strategic life choices . . . the choice of livelihood, where to live, who to marry, whether to marry, whether to have children, how many children to have, who has rights over children, freedom of movement and choice of friends that are critical for people to live the lives they want." According to Kabeer, empowerment requires that a woman have a sense of her own *agency* so that those choices are not merely a matter of decision-making but are rooted in a woman's sense of her own self-worth—that she is worthy of having those alternatives. Likewise, she needs access to and control over *resources* to carry out those choices. If a woman depends entirely on other family members for access to financial or other resources, her capacity to make choices is limited. Reliable, affordable, confidential financial services received by the woman herself through accounts in her own name are essential to safeguarding and leveraging her resources. Financial inclusion alone cannot guarantee the capacity to make the full range of "strategic choices," but there is an undeniable connection between a woman's access to financial services and her sense of autonomy, physical security, and self-esteem.

The academic literature has come to acknowledge that a central element of the definition of empowerment is change at either the individual or the systemic level. An academic consensus seems to have formed around definitional elements that emphasize (1) a *process* of moving from one state to another and (2) *agency*, in that the woman herself must be a significant actor in that process of change. Naila Kabeer's definition of empowerment nicely encapsulates these two elements as "the expansion in people's ability to make strategic life choices in a context where this ability was previously denied to them." She then adds the qualifiers that empowerment implies "choices made from the vantage point of real alternatives" and without "punishingly high costs."

A woman's "strategic life choices" extend far beyond the purely economic options that she has available, but her economic empowerment is an essential step toward gaining both resources and agency. The Bill & Melinda Gates Foundation designed a Women's Empowerment Framework that draws on research and data from ninety-five countries representing the greatest part of the world's GDP. Under the Gates framework, a woman is defined as "economically empowered" if she has (1) access to income and assets, (2) control of and benefit from economic gains, and (3) the power to make decisions. The Gates framework also identifies three categories of elements that underpin all economic empowerment: "fundamental enablers," such as education and family planning; "opportunity and inclusion," such as ownership of property and assets; and "equality and security," a category that includes elements such as the availability of social and workplace protections and the alleviation of unpaid work. Financial inclusion falls into the second category and is one of the elements with the strongest linkage to the trifecta of women's economic empowerment. The use of financial services greatly enhances a woman's access to income and assets; for example, a government benefit payment deposited directly into her bank account affords her greater control over how it is spent or saved.

Likewise, a digital wallet maintained on her own cell phone increases her chances of actually benefiting from the money she saves. And her control over those financial assets enhances her negotiating power as household decisions are made.

The process element of Naila Kabeer's definition is trickier to pin down, however. How can we measure the process of transformation a woman undergoes as a result of being financially included? A thorough review of the literature failed to yield a comprehensive framework that captured the transformative change that a woman might experience as a result of her interaction with financial services. In 2015, Martha Chen worked with the Women's World Banking team to adapt an empowerment framework she had developed for USAID in the 1990s to measure the impact of the agency's microenterprise programs. Chen had identified four pathways through which individuals experience change: material, cognitive, perceptual, and relational. Using both quantitative and qualitative measures, Women's World Banking developed a series of questions across each of these pathways to assess whether women were experiencing change—and empowerment—as a result of greater financial inclusion:

- *Material change* measures whether there are any increases or decreases in a woman's income or her earning capacity, and whether she or her household has gained access to additional resources.

- *Cognitive change* measures whether there are any differences in a woman's knowledge or skills, including whether she has expanded her financial or digital literacy. It's also crucial to measure whether she is more aware of financial and other opportunities available to her. Changes in awareness are particularly important to measure since women's own lack of familiarity with financial options is one of the biggest barriers to greater inclusion.

- *Relational change* measures whether a woman plays a bigger decision-making role with greater bargaining power in the household or community. It also measures whether she has reduced her dependence on others for access to resources and whether she is more mobile and able to act independently. Similarly, it assesses whether she increases her participation outside the home, in local institutions or political activities.

- *Perceptual change* assesses whether a woman has gained in self-confidence and has a greater sense of self-worth, while also exploring whether she is able to move beyond her day-to-day existence and begin to plan for the future.

The real-world implications of this academic framework are probably best illustrated by the story of a woman who experienced significant change as a result of being financially included. Managers from a local bank in Paraguay hoping to expand their agricultural loan portfolio decided to visit several of their existing rural clients, all men, looking to better understand their businesses and their needs. On one of these visits, to a soybean farmer named Manuel, the bank representatives noticed a number of chickens and cows, as well as a small kitchen garden. When they asked Manuel about them, he dismissed the question with a shrug, saying, "That's her business," indicating his wife, Maria. Maria was initially hesitant to discuss her business but eventually explained that she sold cheese, milk, eggs, and salsa at a weekly market in a nearby town. After the bankers probed a little further, they discovered that the revenues that Maria generated from these "side activities" represented as much as 70 percent of their household's monthly income.

Maria went on to explain that she came home from the market every week having sold everything she had brought with her; she typically didn't have even a single egg left over when she got back to the house. She knew she could sell more if she had some way to get more cows, more chickens, or maybe a larger plot of land for vegetables—in other words, if she had access to capital to invest in growing her business.

The bankers saw that Maria's eggs and cheese were bringing a much more even, steady cash flow into the household—the direct opposite of the revenues from Manuel's soybeans, which would only be generated twice a year, at harvest times. For the first time, the bankers realized that Maria's thriving business was likely what had kept the family stable and repaying their loan on time for years. This was a pattern that would hold true for most of the wives of the farmers the bankers visited. The loan officers returned to headquarters and designed a loan for this previously invisible market of women farmers, a product the bank called a "side car" loan—a separate loan for the woman to fund her business alongside her husband's, with a repayment plan tailored to the cash flows she was generating.

When the bank's loan officers visited Maria and Manuel six months after she received her first side car loan, Maria proudly showed off the additional chickens and the cow that she now owned. She talked at length about the loan she had received and the additional income that was coming into their household. But the respect she had gained from her husband since she had received the bank's loan was even more important to her than the additional income she was bringing into the family. Manuel's formal recognition of Maria as a contributor had even changed the way she saw herself. In the most profound sense, Maria and her work were no longer invisible.

Through Maria's gaining access to the side car loan, her household experienced significant *material* change, not only in the form of revenue from her expanded sales at the weekly market but also in the additional livestock she was able to acquire. In applying for the side car, the loan officers worked with Maria to formalize a business plan with projected revenues and expenses and a payment schedule for her loan. These additional budgeting and business management skills represented real *cognitive* change for Maria. The *relational* change between Maria and Manuel was particularly dramatic as he explicitly acknowledged for the first time her long-standing contribution to their household's prosperity. But the *perceptual* change in Maria's own self-confidence was perhaps the most striking. On the bankers' first visit, she had not even looked them directly in the eye. For her to lead them on a tour of her business, discussing her plans for the future, only six months later represented a fundamental transformation in the way she viewed her work and herself. This woman, who had literally been invisible to her husband and to the bank, had been empowered in every sense of the word.

EMPOWERMENT, LAND OWNERSHIP, AND PROPERTY TITLE

Maria's control over an asset, the livestock, that she acquired through her side car loan represents an essential element in building women's economic empowerment. Arguably, though, the more important change might have been for her name to be added to the title on the farmland that Manuel owns; notably, women hold title to only 18 percent of the land across Latin America. As one of the essential elements of economic empowerment, acquiring ownership and control over assets is at the front lines of the battle for women's economic empowerment. Gaining title to land or real estate acquired during marriage can be essential to maintaining that all-important combination of agency plus resources, particularly since women's disproportionate share of unpaid household activities often leaves them with fewer assets accumulated after marriage.

One of the first actions taken by Rwanda's postgenocide transitional parliament in 1999 was to allow women to inherit land—a right that was subsequently enshrined in the 2003 constitution. In the immediate aftermath of the genocide, Rwanda's population was 70 percent female. Ensuring that women could inherit land and own it in their own names was critical for the country's food security as well as for the resettlement and continued livelihood of genocide survivors. Rwandan women emerged from this unthinkable horror having overcome a deeply held social norm and gaining an invaluable civil and human right.

Strong property rights that allow women to establish title to property are also essential to unlocking access to finance, especially for female entrepreneurs. Much of the world's financial systems and commercial codes are built on collateral-based lending that enables a lender to acquire a security interest in an asset in return for a loan. As long as women lack the ability to claim assets in their own names, they will be denied full financial inclusion; unsurprisingly, women's asset ownership reverberates throughout the literature on women's empowerment as a recurring stumbling block on the path to equality. By having her name on the title to the land or buildings in which she lives or works means a woman must be engaged in—or at the very least consulted about—the management or disposal of that property, including its use as security to pledge against a loan to grow her business.

As is often the case, women's economic rights and roles in a society are bound up with and largely determined by a country's family and marital law. In particular, a nation's relative progress in expanding women's economic empowerment is strongly linked to the laws governing marital property. Countries that have adopted full or partial community property regimes provide a more level playing field (judicially speaking) for both men and women to use jointly owned assets as collateral to establish and build businesses. Under a full community property regime, assets acquired before or during marriage are treated as joint property regardless of who paid for them. Under a partial community property system, assets acquired before marriage remain the sole property of the acquiring spouse, while those purchased during marriage are jointly owned by the couple. Where these community property regimes exist, lawmakers can further strengthen a woman entrepreneur's claim on those assets by promoting—or even requiring—joint titling of assets, which establishes ownership rights for more than one person. Some governments have gone even further by actively incentivizing joint titling, offering discounted registration fees to register property jointly or in a woman's name.

The restitution of six million hectares of agricultural land was central to the Colombian government's peace negotiations with the Revolutionary Armed Forces of Colombia (FARC) to end fifty years of armed civil conflict. The FARC, a communist guerrilla organization, claimed to represent Colombia's rural poor against the country's wealthy landowners. The half century of violence left 220,000 dead, 25,000 "disappeared," and 5.7 million people displaced from their homes. After several failed attempts to reach agreement, the final, successful round of negotiations in 2016 was marked by much greater participation by women: women negotiators made up 20 percent of the government's team and 40 percent of the FARC's delegation, a proportional equivalent to the female guerrilla fighters. Ownership and control of land, particularly in rural areas, was at the center of the conflict throughout its history. In seeking to secure access to property for women affected by the violence (58 percent of the internally displaced population were women), the final peace treaty secured both joint titling and preferential access to land that had previously been controlled by the guerrillas for women heads of household and rural women.

While asset ownership is an essential condition to women's economic empowerment, it is not a sufficient condition. As the Chen framework makes clear, empowerment can only be effected through change on multiple levels. Simply opening a bank account or being the targeted recipient of a government transfer payment does not meet the test of agency; rather, it is the control over how that money is spent that can lead to a woman's empowerment. And as the high rates of dormant accounts attest, full financial inclusion must go beyond just gaining access to a bank account to active usage of and engagement with financial services. There is mounting evidence that without building both financial and digital capabilities—that is, enabling women to undergo the cognitive changes addressed by the Chen framework—women will not have the skills or the confidence for that full engagement.

CAPABILITIES ARE WHAT LAST

The essential role of building capabilities in the process of empowerment is underscored by two pieces of research led by Kabeer; both studies demonstrate the limits that financial tools alone have in effecting all the elements of empowerment, not just the material changes. In a 2010 study titled "NGOs' Strategies and the Challenge of Development and Democracy in Bangladesh," Kabeer and her colleagues do not set out to study the empowerment effects of financial inclusion or microfinance; rather, they explore why Bangladesh has "made remarkable progress on the social front in terms of health and education . . . [but] has performed abysmally on the governance front." Noting that most NGOs in Bangladesh offer some type of microfinance services, either on their own or in conjunction with other social services and training, she bemoans the fact that "organizations focusing on the social mobilization of the poor, once a strong presence within the NGO sector, have declined rapidly."

Kabeer and a team of researchers studied the impact on 1,800 female and male participants who received various types of financial and social empowerment services from six local NGOs. The services offered by these six organizations ranged across a spectrum from financial services to services focused on building poor people's collective capabilities. Among the six organizations, ASA and Grameen are referred to as "minimalist microfinance NGOs," concerned largely with finance-related services, while Proshika and BRAC occupy a middle position, providing a combination of microfinance with social mobilization and legal training, respectively. The last two of the six organizations, Samata and Nijera Kori, place training activities and organizing for social justice by landless people at the center of their activities. Both require members to save in groups and manage investment decisions (interestingly, Nijera Kori encourages members to hold their savings in a bank account); however, both Samata and Nijera Kori are adamantly opposed to providing microcredit to their members for fear of creating dependency.

Kabeer and her team first assessed the impact on participants using sets of indicators, including economic ones, such as acquisition of land and cattle and food security; community participation, such as membership on village committees or in dispute resolution forums; and political participation indicators, such as voting or campaigning in local and national elections. These assessments revealed that Nijera Kori and Samata, the two NGOs with the strongest focus on social mobilization organization, performed well across all three dimensions. While these two organizations might have been expected to have a robust impact in the spheres of community and political participation, they had a surprisingly strong economic impact as well.

Various statistical analyses of these indicators led to fascinating, and indeed counterintuitive, results. Perhaps not surprisingly, the community and political impacts declined along the spectrum toward the minimalist microfinance end. But the economic effects also declined. While Nijera Kori did not score quite as high as Samata on political participation measures, it outperformed all of the others on both the economic and so-called "democracy" indicators. The researchers posit several explanations for these results. For example, the consistently strong economic impacts on Nijera Kori members could be attributed to the organization's voluntary weekly savings program. Nijera Kori uses a "savings-led" approach (rather than a microcredit model) and the savings groups decide collectively how much to save and how savings will be invested; as a result, these group decisions strengthened a broader set of financial management skills than is typically found in individual financial literacy training. Notably, the length of time that a member spent in Nijera Kori savings group had a significant impact on their holdings of productive assets. The increase in assets and the greater skills and awareness derived through membership in the Nijera Kori savings groups fit squarely into the Chen framework concept of material plus cognitive change.

The study also found that, of all the groups, Nijera Kori members "were more willing to bargain for higher wages or a fairer price for their labor and products," suggesting that acquiring the "intangible skills of economic literacy, negotiating capacity and rights awareness" enables economic progress separate and apart from the material financial support. Referring back to Kabeer's definition of empowerment, it is safe to say that only an empowered woman who believes in her own worth would bargain for her right to higher wages and fairer prices. Likewise, the awareness and usage of a new skill that leads to economic attainment are consistent with both the cognitive change dimension of the Chen framework and the kind of relational change that enables women to engage in activities outside their home and to participate in the civic life of their community. In surprising contrast, the members of the more minimalist microfinance organizations, ASA and Grameen Bank, had clearly identified access to credit as their principal motivation for joining the group. But the extension of credit alone wasn't sufficient to enable the borrowers to leverage that financial resource into longer-lasting economic advancement. It's also notable that BRAC, ASA, and Grameen, those organizations at the microfinance end of the spectrum, recruited only female participants. These members registered much lower levels of participation in the *shalish*, the informal village conflict and dispute resolution body, than the organizations where the members worked together in mixed gender groups.

The study's third hypothesis for the strong economic impacts experienced by members of the social mobilization organizations recalls the observations from *Portfolios of the Poor* in chapter 1. Thirty-five percent of longtime Nijera Kori members (the social mobilization group that achieved both higher economic and democracy impacts than the others) were also members of other NGOs. Members had a clear understanding of the relative benefits of the different organizations. The study quotes one woman, a member of both Grameen and Nijera Kori, as saying,

> For us to get hold of three or four thousand takas is not easy. That is why we are members of Grameen Bank. . . . But with NK, we have savings when we need it. . . . And we are united. No one can stop us. If someone comes to beat one of us, we all sort out the matter together. Grameen would not have done this for us. They give us loans and take them back. That is what they are concerned about.

Kabeer and her colleagues conclude by emphasizing the diversity of support that is necessary for the poor women and men in her study to be empowered economically, socially, and politically. They note that "financial services are important if poor people are to cope with crisis and respond to opportunities, but, on their own, do not equip them with the capacity to translate these services into lasting economic progress. . . . Equally, perhaps an over-emphasis on social mobilization without due attention to livelihood issues may promote grassroots participation, but will not overcome the barriers to economic advancement." While the paper's original intent may have centered on governance and the building of democracy, its findings contribute to the growing recognition that empowerment rests on being able to tap into the broader human capabilities of confidence, self-esteem, and the ability to plan for the future.

The second study explores the impact of an asset transfer project on deeply impoverished women in the Indian state of West Bengal. The project replicated a highly successful program by BRAC in Bangladesh in which women received livestock to start their own enterprises and a series of other inputs, including a monthly stipend so that they could focus on growing their businesses, and intensive training and mentoring. The women were encouraged to save regularly through informal savings groups (self-help groups) to establish the habit of saving and to accumulate a lump sum for investment. The study shares extensive interviews with participants and details the effects on the lives of both "fast climbers" and "slow climbers" and the value that each group derived from the various aspects of the project. The most intriguing part of the report, though, relates to a return visit researchers made to the women seven years later, long after the project's formal end. While the researchers are careful not to attribute the women's circumstances, whether positive or negative, to the project, they offered one very significant insight: "When the fast climbers spoke of the project's contribution to their lives, they did not speak only of the material support that they had received in terms of assets, stipends, savings and loans, but also of the ideas and knowledge they had acquired, the personal mentoring of project staff and the new relationships they had forged through the SHGs." In a subsequent interview, Naila Kabeer noted that perhaps the single most important outcome of the project was that the women had learned to stockpile rice when prices were low so that they didn't have to buy when prices were high. Plainly put, Kabeer noted, "The cows and goats had died. The capabilities were the only things that lasted in these women's lives."

DIGITAL FINANCIAL SERVICES AND WOMEN'S EMPOWERMENT

Most of the research related to the empowerment effects of access to finance draws from women's experience with traditional, cash-based microfinance, To date there has been relatively limited inquiry into the impact of broader financial inclusion, much less digital financial services. Indeed, much of the literature hypothesizes that norms affecting women's behavior or their preferences for certain product attributes prior to the introduction of digital financial services will extend into the digital sphere. For instance, we know that in the nondigital sphere, time savings are highly valued by women, and we see women's rates of financial inclusion increase to a greater extent than men's when their proximity to a bank branch also increases. It stands to reason that the time savings and greater convenience afforded by digital financial services could have a significant impact on their usage of such services, but these topics remain to be studied.

A few insights regarding women's empowerment are nonetheless beginning to emerge from this still nascent field of research, particularly with regard to enhancing women's mobility and their preferences for privacy and confidentiality in financial transactions. A randomized controlled trial conducted in the northern Indian state of Madhya Pradesh measured the effects of digitally depositing a federal "workfare" wage directly into a bank account that had been opened in a woman's own name rather than sending wages to a household account, typically held in the husband's name. Additionally, half of the women who received a bank account were also provided with some basic financial information about the account and the bank that provided it, while the remainder received only the account. At follow-up fifteen months later, researchers found that the women who had received the training and the account were much more likely to be employed outside the home, either by remaining on the payroll of the government employment program or through another private sector employer, and they received substantially higher wages. These women also reported being more economically active outside the household than their peers and made more purchases with their own funds, rather than with money given to them by family members. Importantly, the women who received both the account and the financial training reported greater mobility. This was a particularly notable development since nearly all of the women engaged in the study had reported that they needed to get permission to leave their home or village; many of them were required by their families to have a male chaperone accompany them on errands, including visits to the bank.

Another field experiment involving a government-sponsored unconditional cash transfer program to drought-stricken households in Niger provides some insight into the ways in which the privacy afforded by a mobile money transfer can help women work around gender norms. The program was targeted to women, who were divided into three groups. One group received cash in individual envelopes at a distribution center, often in a village at considerable distance from their homes. The second group received their payment in individual envelopes of cash that they picked up at a village distribution center, but they were also given a cell phone that was enabled with a mobile money wallet. Women in the third group were given a cell phone and payments were made directly into the mobile wallet. These women received a "beep" on their mobile phones signaling that the payment had been transferred to their wallets; they could take their phones to a mobile money agent in their village and cash out. The women in this last group reported that, after receiving notification of the transfer, they would wait until the evening to tell their spouses that the funds were available. They would discuss how the funds would be used in the privacy of their own homes, where they would have greater bargaining power about spending decisions, rather than in a public setting, where gender norms may have compromised their negotiating leverage.

There were various indications that in the households where the women were able to bargain in private, they also had a greater say in financial decisions. These households had significantly greater dietary diversity than those in the other two groups, and the children, in particular, were better nourished. Also, nearly all the women in the first two groups were accompanied by a male family member to pick up their transfer payment, while more than half the women in the mobile money group traveled alone. They were also more likely to travel to weekly markets to sell grains, indicating they had greater involvement in their family's economic activity. The control over the cash transfer—even if just for a few hours—made all the difference in their ability to influence how the money would be spent since, as we saw in the second test condition, merely owning a cell phone did not appear to alter the power dynamic between a woman and her spouse.

DOES FINANCIAL INCLUSION MAKE WOMEN MORE OR LESS VULNERABLE TO VIOLENCE?

All of the studies referenced in this chapter measured women's economic empowerment by tracking indicators such as greater intrahousehold bargaining power or control over income earned. Yet much of this literature raises a "shadow side" of these same indicators, questioning whether increasing women's economic autonomy, particularly in ways that challenge prevailing social and gender norms, might put women at greater risk of gender-based violence at home and in the workplace. Research on the linkage between women's access to finance and gender-based violence has been limited to date, and again has largely focused on microcredit. Owing to the sensitivity of the topic, some of the studies have suffered from data collection and other methodological challenges, resulting in contradictory or inconclusive findings.

A recent evaluation of the relationship between financial inclusion and gender-based violence across 112 countries worldwide highlights the complexity of the relationship, ultimately concluding that women's financial inclusion "may be an important lever in reducing women's risk of intimate partner violence (IPV), but both IPV and financial inclusion exist in the context of social, cultural, and normative barriers and enablers." The study found that in low- and middle-income countries with a high national prevalence of male controlling behaviors (e.g., bullying, stalking, or isolating women from others), women were at an *increased* risk of violence as a result of greater financial inclusion. In these countries marked by high spousal control, women experienced both higher levels of labor force participation and lower levels of cash earnings and unequal employment practices. These findings recall the earlier discussion of the "disempowering effect" of microfinance whereby the exclusion of men threatens traditional gender norms, leaving women more vulnerable to intimate partner violence. For these women, financial inclusion may exacerbate underlying gendered power struggles, resulting in a heightened risk of intimate partner violence. The study's authors stress that expanding women's financial inclusion and broadening economic opportunities cannot be seen as a one-dimensional "silver bullet" solution but must be part of a multidimensional effort to enhance women's status within the society. They also acknowledge the potential for cell-phone-based mobile banking to address women's constrained mobility in countries with very restrictive gender norms while pointing to the gender gap in cell-phone ownership and usage.

One of the best-known studies that combines financial access with other targeted training is the Intervention with Microfinance for AIDS and Gender Equity, or IMAGE, study in South Africa, which combined microfinance for women with training on HIV prevention, violence, cultural beliefs, and livelihoods skills. After two years of the program, a randomized controlled trial showed a 55 percent reduction in reports of physical or sexual violence, as well as improvements in all nine of the study's indicators of empowerment among those participants in the treatment group who received both the loans and the training. Levels of intimate partner violence remained unchanged in the control group. The study's empowerment indicators included measures of self-confidence and autonomy in decision-making and an enhanced willingness to challenge gender norms and participate in collective action such as a march or rally related to HIV awareness.

One cause for the decline in violence in the treatment group was increased self-confidence and a sense of financial security on the part of some of the participants, enabling them to leave a violent relationship. Several of these participants acknowledged that they had received critical support from others in deciding to leave. Without losing sight of the ever-present risk of backlash, particularly in environments where gender roles may be shifting, women's financial inclusion can reduce financial dependence on men and provide women with the resources needed to leave abusive relationships. Indeed, there is evidence suggesting that a woman's power to leave an abusive relationship derived through legal rights and economic autonomy may itself be a deterrent to further violence.

A few years ago, Women's World Banking participated with a team of researchers from Princeton University in a research project with a bank in Colombia; the original research objective was to explore whether having a confidential savings account in her own name would change a woman's behavior in the face of gender-based violence. Over the course of the study several other objectives were added, including identifying the impact of bundling health services with the savings account and the efficacy of different types of SMS messages sent to the account holder. With the original objective obscured, the Princeton team ultimately deemed the results inconclusive. However, a few months after the official end to the project, the president of the Colombian bank's charitable foundation disclosed a fascinating, if anecdotal, result. She said that the bank had begun to notice a distinct pattern in the accounts of some of the women who had participated in the project: when their savings account balance reached 300,000 Colombian pesos (roughly equivalent to US $100), a number of women would flee their homes with their children. And many of these women sought help at the bank branch where they maintained their accounts. In response, the bank had formed partnerships with local women's shelters and schools. It also provided small grants to help the women relocate and had begun to offer digital skills training so that the women were able to seek higher-paying jobs.

Addressing violence against women took on even greater urgency during the COVID-19 pandemic. The UN has identified gender-based violence as a "shadow epidemic" alongside COVID-19, noting that calls to helplines increased fivefold in some countries as rates of reported intimate partner violence escalated. The combination of lockdowns, social isolation, and heightened economic insecurity made many more women vulnerable to violence in their own homes. Although a few far-sighted governments increased funding for women's shelters throughout the pandemic, others instead shifted funding for programs that support victims of gender-based violence to COVID-19 relief initiatives. This tragic misstep left women at even greater risk and ignored the full scale of the health impact of the pandemic.

A woman's control over financial accounts that are held in confidence and in her own name can create a buffer of safety around her, either preventing abuse or providing the means to flee abusive situations. This is as true for women in the United States as it is for the South African women in the IMAGE study and the clients of the Colombian bank. Indeed, financial abuse is a hallmark of domestic violence in the United States: 99 percent of the 7.9 million women in the United States who are victims of intimate partner violence each year also suffer some element of financial abuse as well. Financial abuse includes a broad range of tactics and controlling behaviors that limit a victim's access to assets and finances, including restricting or jeopardizing her ability to obtain and keep a job.

In recent years the #MeToo movement has emerged as a campaign to publicize allegations of sexual assault or harassment committed by powerful or prominent men. While a great deal has been written on the economic impact of the #MeToo movement, very little has been written about the interplay between women's financial independence and sexual harassment. But women around the world share a bond with regard to financial autonomy and the choices they are empowered to make, a bond that extends seemingly as far as Hollywood. At the time of the first published reports of Harvey Weinstein's sexual predation, actress Brit Marling wrote of her experience being trapped, like countless other women, in a hotel room with Weinstein. She opens the article by recalling something her mother had told her when she was a child: "To be a free woman, you have to be a financially independent woman." She recounts her introduction to the harsh realities of Hollywood as a town that "functioned inside a soft and sometimes literal trafficking of young women. . . . The storytellers [were] the people with economic and artistic power." She decided to make the difficult transition from actor to writer, recognizing that "the only way for me to navigate Hollywood with more agency was to become a storyteller myself." Face-to-face with Weinstein, "this man, this gatekeeper, who could anoint or destroy me," she was "able to gather myself together—a bundle of firing nerves, hands trembling, voice lost in my throat—and leave the room." Reflecting on her experience, she concludes that "I was able to leave Weinstein's hotel room that day because I had entered as an actor but also as a writer/creator. Of those dual personas in me—actor and writer—it was the writer who stood up and walked out. Because the writer knew that even if this very powerful man never gave her a job in any of his films . . . she could make her own work on her own terms and thus keep a roof over her head."

Empowerment is, at its heart, the freedom to make one's own choices. Money in a woman's pocket and under her control allows her to choose to write her own story. And sometimes that includes the choice to walk out the door.

II MAKING THE BUSINESS CASE

Across the globe, an eager market of 1.7 billion people, roughly 980 million of them women, are looking for convenient, reliable financial services they can afford. At the same time, legacy financial service providers are under competitive pressures and scrambling to reinvent their business models. Even before COVID-19, banks everywhere were facing the earnings impact of a low interest rate environment that now seems likely to continue into the foreseeable future. Loan loss provisions by the industry as it emerges from the pandemic are projected to exceed those taken at the time of the global financial crisis. COVID-19 is also driving banks to shift more of their business to digital platforms, both in response to customer preference and as a way to lower costs and increase productivity. In recent years, faced with increased competition from fintech companies, many banks forged partnerships with them and benefited from innovative financial solutions and new ways of working with clients. However, the next wave of competition promises to be more of a tsunami as "big tech" companies like Google and Facebook enter the financial services sector. Not only are these companies more agile than most banks in their operations, but they have better, more extensive data on the same customers that banks are struggling to hold on to. And they know how to use that data to tailor products and messages to customer needs and preferences.

McKinsey's *Global Banking Annual Review* for 2020 forecasts that it will be two to four years before the banking sector gets back to pre-COVID-19 revenue levels. The report observes that the banking industry as a whole is well capitalized and will be able to ride out anticipated loan losses resulting from the crisis. Nevertheless, the industry will sustain an estimated $3.7 trillion drop in revenues. The report notes that these losses, combined with the existential threat to their customer base from big tech, will require banks to overhaul their traditional business models. The McKinsey review concludes with recommendations to banks to rethink their approach to risk in lending operations, invest in a range of changes to the customer experience, and bring "purpose to the fore" by engaging more deeply with environmental, social, and governance issues.

By interesting coincidence, in its May 2020 COVID-19 update, the *Edelman Trust Barometer 2020* recorded trust in the financial services industry at "all-time highs" in the developed and developing country markets surveyed. This surprising reversal—financial services were listed as the least trusted of all industries in the 2020 Barometer results released just four months earlier—was a direct result of the actions financial service providers took at the outset of the pandemic. They were now hailed as "economic first responders" as they mobilized to provide immediate relief in partnership with governments.

In this moment of reinvention, when the future is very much up for grabs, there is a compelling argument for banks to capitalize on these new levels of trust and actively embrace financial inclusion. If "business as usual" will result in $3.7 trillion in lost revenue, what does the industry have to lose by becoming more inclusive? The commercial impact of full financial inclusion has never been reliably estimated, but if the industry were merely to serve women at the same level as men, the impact on revenues could be enormous. Closing the gender gap in retail banking alone could yield $40 billion in additional revenue. If banks did nothing more than level the playing field for women entrepreneurs by providing them with business loans at the same rate as it does men, that change alone could represent $30 billion in new net interest income.

The COVID-19 crisis has given this potential strategy a head start as more low-income families enter the formal financial system in order to receive government social protection payments. At Bank of Baroda, one of the largest distributors of the Indian government's COVID benefits, 18 percent of low-income women were still able to make at least four deposits in the first six months of the pandemic despite severe reductions in income, and they did so motivated by guaranteed access to credit. Similarly, the Indonesian government was able to rapidly redirect its largest conditional cash transfer program (Program Keluarga Harapan, or PKH) to COVID-19 relief, since payments were digitally deposited into bank accounts that had already been opened for the 9.2 million beneficiaries when the program launched in 2017. To respond to the economic crisis that accompanied the health emergency, Indonesia expanded the PKH program to 10 million beneficiaries (opening additional bank accounts) and increased both the amount and the frequency of transfers. Many women responded by saving the enhanced benefits as a safety cushion. The crisis has accelerated the financial inclusion of millions; the challenge and the opportunity for the financial system is to keep them in the system and continue to serve them once the immediate crisis has passed. Governments and financial service providers concerned about postpandemic resilience can use the momentum from their successful, collaborative crisis response to build a more permanently inclusive financial system.

Part II presents the business case for financial service providers to invest in women's financial inclusion. It explores the ways in which farsighted companies are adapting their products and services to reach previously excluded customers—and making money while doing so. In keeping with McKinsey's recommendation for financial service providers who seek to thrive in the post-COVID landscape, these financial service providers are "collaborating with the communities they serve to recast their contract with society."

4 MAKING THE BUSINESS CASE FOR BUILDING WEALTH

The desire to keep her money in a place that is safer than under her mattress is often the motivation for a woman to seek her first engagement with a formal financial institution. But the act of saving—either to handle an emergency, or to ensure that her priorities, such as her children's education, aren't ignored, or to achieve a long-held aspiration or goal—carries a deeper resonance throughout women's lives. For many adolescent girls, at the moment in their lives when they are the most vulnerable to decisions being made for them about their future, a savings account can be one of their few sources of autonomy. As the adults in their lives are deciding whether they will be able to continue their education or go to work or marry, the money they have saved in their own names can give them a seat at the table. Having a safe place to save and having control over how money is spent are twin, recurring themes running throughout the lives of women and girls.

One such story centers on a focus group of young girls, aged ten to thirteen years, in Kibera, Africa's largest slum, just a few miles from Nairobi's city center. The girls spoke passionately about having a savings account in their own name, outside their parents' control, so that they could contribute to the payment of their own school fees and continue their secondary education. They already understood that an account with as little as $10 in it would give them bargaining power when their parents objected to the expense of further schooling. Likewise, they saw a savings account as a much better way to ensure their financial autonomy when the only other alternatives were working or entering into early marriage, essentially a transactional sexual relationship. This is often the only route open to young women, one they had likely seen their older sisters and cousins forced to accept. One of the most talkative and insightful girls in the group was about ten years old. Like most of the girls, she was dressed in her school uniform: a red V-neck sweater over a bright blue cotton dress with a white Peter Pan collar, black knee socks, and a pair of black sneakers. She was an excellent student, but she was concerned that her parents would not continue to fund her education once she had finished primary school and would instead require her to start working. She wanted a savings account so she could control how the money she earned collecting fabric scraps for resale was spent. (To put her earnings in context, a schoolgirl would likely earn less than $1 a day for the scraps she sold.) She explained that she would still help with family emergencies and monthly expenses, but the savings account would also allow her to protect some of that money for school fees.

Keeping girls in school, particularly if they are able to avoid child marriage and early pregnancy, is one of the highest-yielding development investments possible. Every additional year of schooling that a girl is able to complete has exponential benefits for her health and lifelong economic well-being, and for that of her future children. Studies show that a girl will earn up to 25 percent more for every year of secondary school she completes. Child marriage greatly reduces the likelihood of girls completing secondary school while greatly increasing their chances of bearing children before the age of eighteen; those children, in turn, are at greater risk of dying before the age of five. Millions of girls throughout the developing world must run a gauntlet thrown up by the people in their lives that see more value in marrying them off or putting them to work than in letting them stay in school.

A surefire way to cap the return on investment in a girl who succeeds in staying in school is to let her graduate without the financial tools to chart her own course. One head of a large charitable organization devoted to girls' secondary education in Africa spoke of the essential role that financial education and saving money can play in making sure that girls reap all the benefits of their hard-won educations. The organization had worked with nearly seven thousand schools across Africa to educate over three million girls from the primary grades through secondary school. Their model entailed not only supporting a girl with tuition, uniforms, and school supplies but also building a support system around her, creating parent groups and training teacher mentors. However, that support didn't extend to the very real challenges of remaining financially independent after leaving the nurturing environment of the school. In some countries the organization watched their graduates marry within a year or two of leaving school because they couldn't support themselves. The curriculum included some basic financial education, but it wasn't linked to any practical, real-time uses of the new concepts being taught, such as opening a savings account or developing a budget. The classroom lessons remained abstract and never came alive as tools for the girls to use once they had graduated. The organization also teamed up with a microfinance institution to provide the girls with microloans to start businesses after graduation, but they were thrust into these entrepreneurial roles without business skills, startup capital, or other resources. Not surprisingly, their attempts at starting a business were largely unsuccessful, and the girls ended up burdened by debt they couldn't repay.

The NGO head was now weighing whether to provide the girls with a savings account when they entered the school. She reasoned that this might allow the girls some breathing room and the possibility of a broader set of choices once they left the nurturing environment of the school. The organization's generous donors would make initial deposits for the girls to open accounts in their own names with a local bank and then match any deposits the girls or their families made over the course of their secondary education. All this would be accompanied by a more rigorous financial education curriculum that used the teachable moment of the account opening to give the girls the greatest chance of absorbing the material.

It's worth noting here that even though the girls enrolled in this type of program are often desperately poor, they always seem to have small amounts of money that they are eager to save. Whether from selling scraps of fabric like the young schoolgirl in Kibera or hawking newspapers in morning traffic in Santo Domingo, girls do earn money that they could be putting away toward a goal. In fact, depending on the country and cultural context, girls often have strikingly different attitudes toward the money they earn. In the Dominican Republic, for example, the first girls invited to open a savings account at Banco ADOPEM also helped the bank pick a name for the account; the overwhelming favorite was *Cuenta Mía,* or "My Account," and the girls almost universally declared they would be saving toward their education. One eight-year-old announced that she would be saving to become a gastroenterological surgeon, since that was the kind of doctor who had saved her grandmother's life, and her parents couldn't afford to pay for the many years of required medical training. In contrast, the daughters of the clients of India's SEWA Bank were adamant that they were not saving for themselves but to contribute to their families.

DIAMOND BANK'S BETA ACCOUNT: BUILDING TRUST THROUGH SAVINGS

Savings accounts represent the backbone of anyone's financial life and provide a gateway to all other financial tools. To achieve gender parity in this most basic financial instrument, 245 million more women around the world would need to gain access to an account, generating annual incremental revenue estimated at $15 billion. While this opportunity may be lucrative, bringing millions of previously unserved customers into a market comes with special challenges. Is there anything that the banking sector can learn from the traditional informal savings groups about how to attract and retain this new customer base? One innovative bank in Nigeria was eager to find out.

At Idumota, one of the oldest and largest markets in Lagos, everything imaginable is available for purchase, from fresh produce to textiles and wristwatches. But Idumota is best known for two things: it's the place to go for bulk products such as groceries, health and beauty products, and office supplies, all sold at very low prices; and it's one of the main distribution hubs for videos produced by "Nollywood," Nigeria's booming film industry, which releases roughly fifty new films each week. The winding paths of the market are lined with thousands of one- and two-story shops with merchandise piled high on the counters and shelves and roll-down grates that close at night, but Ime Akpan Isaace runs her business from a small table protected by just an umbrella overhead. From that table, Ime sells the slightly bitter, spinachlike okazi leaves that are used to make a traditional southern Nigerian soup called Afang that is served at weddings, to celebrate the birth of a child, or to welcome an honored guest to your home. On the table is a wooden chopping block, a rectangular stone to sharpen her knife, and two baskets, one filled with uncut okazi leaves and the other with expertly sliced okazi ready for sale.

For years, Ime had worked alongside her husband in another section of the market, but this stall represented Ime's first full-time venture of her own; she started her business three years ago with $31 that she and her husband had painstakingly accumulated under their mattress at home. She buys okazi from a wholesaler before dawn every day, arriving at the market around 6:30 a.m. and staying until she is able to sell all of the leaves, usually around 3:00 or 4:00 p.m. Half of Nigeria's more than 206 million people live below the international poverty line of $1.90 a day; Ime earns the rough equivalent of $100 per month, depending on how many days she comes to market and whether it is a holiday period.

Ime had recently opened her first bank account—the BETA savings account introduced by Diamond Bank, one of Nigeria's largest banks. Diamond Bank designed the BETA account (which means "good" in pidgin English) specifically to reach market traders like her. Diamond was established in 1990 and, over the years, had built a strong reputation as an international bank serving large Nigerian and foreign corporates, but its retail operations were limited to an affluent customer base. The bank was one of the first in Nigeria to invest in technology to improve the efficiency and service quality of its existing retail offerings for its high-end clients. When the Nigerian Central Bank began to emphasize financial inclusion as a priority, Diamond Bank's management thought there might be a way to adapt the technology to serve unbanked and underbanked clients as well. In 2013, nearly two-thirds of Nigerians had no access to financial services and the government was eager to expand financial services to more low-income people. Nigeria was a pioneer in introducing a tiered KYC system in a deliberate attempt to bring more people into the formal financial system. Know-your-customer or KYC requirements are mandatory processes that financial institutions everywhere use to establish the identity and suitability of potential customers, often as a means to guard against money laundering and the financing of terrorist activities. These procedures can be costly for financial institutions to maintain, particularly for low-balance clients, many of whom are unlikely to have the required proof of identification and other documentation. For some clients, providing even a home address can be challenging. In rural areas, streets and roads are often unmarked, and homes, farmland, and other properties may not have numbers, leaving millions of households without a verifiable address. Without this basic identifier, they are often denied government services such as water, postal, and electricity delivery, while opening a financial account remains out of reach.

A risk-adjusted, tiered KYC system such as the one introduced by the Nigerian Central Bank allows for flexible account opening requirements subject to certain caps and restrictions on the size of account balances and the services provided. A market trader like Ime could open a tier 1 bank account by providing only her name and date and place of birth; the bank was not required to verify the information, but the account balance was limited to approximately $230 and could only be used for deposits and withdrawals. No payments or funds transfers were permitted. A tier 2 account would allow her to maintain a slightly higher balance (roughly $275) and make transfers, but the bank would have to incur additional costs to check the personal information she provided against official databases. Nevertheless, the cost reductions made possible through cell-phone technology combined with more streamlined KYC regulation led Diamond Bank's retail banking team to seriously explore entering the inclusive finance market.

Diamond's senior management made some important early decisions about whom to target and the product they wanted to offer this new client base. The bank already had branches inside or very close to many open-air markets similar to Idumota across Nigeria where they served medium-sized and larger businesses. Their initial customer research indicated that traders, particularly women, who operated much smaller businesses from inside the markets might be interested in services from a well-established bank. Perhaps the bank's most significant decision, though, was to enter this market by offering a savings account rather than starting with a lending product.

Throughout West Africa, group savings schemes, called *ajos* in southern Nigeria or *tsu tsus* in francophone Africa, feature a group coordinator or collector who regularly visits men and women in their homes or businesses to collect and hold small deposits. While the schemes differ slightly from country to country and even between northern and southern Nigeria, an *ajo* is comprised of a group of friends or colleagues who each save a previously agreed-on amount of money each month. They choose a coordinator from among themselves to collect their money and hold it in safekeeping for a fee. At the end of each month, the coordinator gives all of the money saved to one of the group members, and this process continues, month by month, until all members have received the pot once. In customer interviews the traders placed great value on the convenience offered by the *ajo* coordinators' doorstep collection, but the women expressed a strong desire to make more frequent, even daily deposits, and everyone bristled at the fees charged by the coordinator.

The customer interviews also indicated that the women felt a pervasive "emotional distance" from the bank; these women repeatedly expressed concerns that the bank "wasn't for me." Many of them were apprehensive that there would not be anyone from the bank who "spoke their language," in both literal and figurative senses. The women worried that the bankers and the materials related to the product would be in English rather than their own pidgin Nigerian dialect. They were also uneasy that the account would be complicated to use and they wouldn't understand how it worked. The women were particularly skeptical that there would be hidden fees and conditions that would let Diamond Bank take advantage of them. Their concerns about not being understood were not unfounded: Diamond's management was surprised by the reluctance among staff from the branches located near the markets to take on this new clientele. One of the bank's retail executives recounted his experience of a visit to a market branch. He had decided to step outside the gated car park before going inside and had walked across the road to talk to one of the women traders, whose stall was located a few feet away. He was impressed by the monthly turnover the woman was generating from a seemingly modest fruit and vegetable stall, but when he asked the branch manager whether he had ever considered banking the woman's business across the road, the manager replied, in all sincerity, "What woman's business are you talking about? There's no such business across the road." These women and their businesses were literally invisible to that branch manager.

Diamond launched the BETA savings account with all of these insights in mind, recognizing that the product's success would rest on the bank's ability to build trust with market traders like Ime. They took the women's concerns about language to heart and used simple, nontechnical language to explain all the account's features. (The BETA marketing materials all featured the pidgin tagline "No Wahala, No Cost, Plenty Awoof," which effectively translates as "No Hassle, No Fees, Plenty of Free Stuff"). They integrated—and expanded on—the *ajo's* door-to-door collection practice by recruiting a group of young men and women, mostly secondary school graduates from the community, called BETA Friends. The BETA Friends could be seen from anywhere in the crowded markets across the country, dressed in shockingly bright green t-shirts, caps, vests, or aprons. The bank's original plan was for the Friends to provide account opening services at the trader's place of business, introducing her to the various account features available on her cell-phone and the ATM card and providing some basic financial education to new customers. Because of the importance that potential customers had placed on convenience in the interviews, the bank had assumed that customers would eventually migrate to the cell phone or ATM to access their accounts. However, the human connection proved to be at least as powerful as the convenience of technology. The Friends quickly became the choice of most BETA customers to make their deposits. In fact, nearly 70 percent of savings deposits into BETA accounts were made through BETA Friends. While BETA account holders—particularly women—valued the convenience of the technology, the human relationship was essential for building trust and customer loyalty. In addition, the BETA product team mentioned a trend they were starting to see in the

BETA Friends collection data. Even though the product was specifically designed for women traders, the uptake and usage rates were largely the same between men and women. Men customers with female BETA Friends appeared to save at a higher rate than those with male Friends. (One young female BETA Friend was particularly amused by a male trader who told her that he was saving to buy a helicopter in order to whisk her off to dinner in a different part of the city!)

Ime's table is just a few yards down Denton Street from a Diamond Bank branch, but she had never thought it was worthwhile to open a bank account because she couldn't spare the time to stand in line at the branch and wasn't familiar with how an ATM works. Thanks to the daily visit to her stall by her BETA Friend, she has been able to deposit the equivalent of $6 every day that she is in the market. To put that achievement in context: it took Ime and her husband three years to save $31 to open her business, and she is now clearing as much as or more than that on a weekly basis. Ime attributes some of her success in saving to the fact that she looks forward to seeing her "Friend" and doesn't want to disappoint her by not depositing anything. She explains that before she had a BETA account, she would frequently reach the end of the month without having saved enough to afford school fees for all of her seven children. Saving at home under the mattress, or even with the less frequent collections by the *ajo*, made it too easy to spend the money on other things. As Ime put it, "The money slips through your fingers."

Ime is just one of literally millions of women, who, once introduced to banking services, become loyal clients and avid promoters of the financial institutions that serve them. By offering a convenient savings product similar to the *ajo* system these customers were already using, the bank made it possible for the market women to build trust with the bank and allowed Diamond Bank management (especially the bank's Risk Committee) to better understand the risks associated with serving this new customer segment. With an existing informal savings model already in place, the market traders had established savings patterns through traditional money collectors; on average, they were already saving an impressive 60 percent of their income through informal means.

The BETA account represented a remarkably effective entry into the financial inclusion market for Diamond Bank. In fact, when Diamond Bank was subsequently acquired by Access Bank, Africa's largest bank, in 2019, its presence within this growing market segment was cited as one of its most valuable assets. However, evaluating the empowerment effect of the program through the lens of the Chen framework introduced in chapter 3 isn't as straightforward. In the five years following the introduction of the BETA account, Nigeria's economy substantially worsened, with GDP growth dropping from a rate of 6.67 percent in 2013 to 1.92 percent in 2018. This slower economic growth was accompanied by a 42 percent increase in inflation, which caused many BETA clients to question the utility of leaving money in a bank account only to see its value erode. Not surprisingly, the prevailing economic climate severely affected BETA clients' ability to experience positive *material* change. Nevertheless, some important indicators of empowerment are worth calling out. While the number of daily depositors declined substantially over the period, their degree of resilience through hard times was notable. Many of the clients who maintained an active BETA account saw their business profits increase and were able to make substantial investments in their businesses from their BETA account balances. These active clients also felt more able than inactive clients to gather sufficient funds to cover an emergency sum of one year's income. In fact, several respondents identified having a safe place to accumulate emergency funds, particularly one that was safer than the *ajo*, as their motivation for opening or maintaining a BETA account. The difficult economy took its toll on customers' nutrition levels and expenditures on health care and medications; however, more of the BETA customers reported that all of their children were in school than had been the case before they opened the account. Perhaps the most noteworthy changes were in the realms of *relational* and *perceptual* change. While Nigerian women are generally actively engaged in household and business decision-making, the women who maintained an active BETA account reported significantly greater involvement in making decisions on how to use their business's profits and in making household purchases.

As the BETA account experience indicates, providing low-income women with a safe, reliable, convenient place to save can be an effective way to attract them as clients and provide a lifeline to their families. A regular savings habit is critical to low-income families with fluctuating earnings. The concept of "living on $1.90 per day" is merely economic shorthand for establishing an international poverty benchmark; rarely do these households receive a regular, daily income of any kind. Within these low-income households as well as those in developed countries, there is a clear pattern of women providing the safety net for their families. Women in the UK save an average of 41 percent of annual wages, compared to 23 percent for men, while Chile has seen women's savings accounts grow at three times the rate of men's savings accounts in the past decade, and this behavior holds true for both single and married women. In the case of the BETA customers, Diamond Bank found that women were far more active savings clients than men, with over half making daily deposits. Male customers, on average, had 22 percent higher balances than women, but they made significantly more frequent withdrawals, using BETA as a transactional business account. Women, on the other hand, largely through the visits from the BETA Friend, accumulated balances in their BETA accounts over time. In fact, Diamond quickly came to value these dependable, "stickier" savings from women. Within a few months of the product's launch, the bank had changed the commission structure for BETA Friends to incentivize opening more women's accounts.

WOMEN'S PROPENSITY TO SAVE AND THE OBSTACLES THEY FACE

Women's tendency to save is, of course, nothing new—informal group savings mechanisms that draw on social capital have been around for centuries, as we saw in chapter 1. Despite the popularity of these informal savings schemes, women are often attracted to formal savings as a means to keep the sums they have accumulated intact and directed toward concrete goals. Unlike the group savings model, however, a bank account gives them access to funds in case of an emergency without having to take out a loan or wait for their proportional distribution from a group pot. Formal savings also offer greater confidentiality and security. Under the deposit collector model, there are countless tales of the collector disappearing with the group's money.

In developing countries, 11 percent of people—fully one quarter of all savers—reported that they had saved through some mechanism other than a formal financial institution account—either through a savings group, a physical asset such as gold jewelry or livestock, or even with cash under the mattress. Interestingly, this group consisted of some savers who used only these informal means (approximately 7 percent of the total), with the remainder using both formal and informal means of saving. That represents close to 500 million people in the developing world who are actively accumulating savings balances outside the formal financial system. Financial diaries maintained over the course of a year by three hundred low-income Kenyan families showed that saving was the most frequent financial transaction performed by these households, and particularly by women, who placed a significantly greater emphasis on saving over borrowing. By year's end, the median household had saved a whopping 129 percent of monthly income in financial assets compared to borrowing 53 percent of monthly income. That's an extraordinary demonstration of demand for a safe place to save, and yet only 9 percent of those savings were held in formal financial institutions. Notably, only a relatively small portion of those savings were held in liquid form so that they could be easily withdrawn in the case of emergency. At the same time, many of these households used a rotating savings and credit association (ROSCA) as their principal mechanism for investment, although the sums they could access were relatively modest. It is clear that both women and men throughout the developing world derive considerable value, both economic and social, from these informal financial relationships. Unlike these informal systems, though, formal financial service providers committed to serving low-income customers can offer the tools to maintain short-term liquidity needs without the saver sacrificing long-term investment goals.

There is now a substantial base of research on the motivations for and impacts of savings by the poor. For many low-income women, saving behavior is in large part driven by the degree of financial independence and bargaining power they have in the household, and there are notable differences in saving behavior between women and men. One field experiment among 142 married couples in Kenya gave either the husband, the wife, or both a 50:50 chance to receive a small windfall once a week for eight weeks; both spouses knew the outcome of each week's selection. The husbands and wives were all day workers, household income averaged $2.42 per day, and both were members of informal ROSCAs. Throughout the experiment, husbands spent their windfall on goods they consumed themselves (e.g., cigarettes and alcohol) in the weeks they were chosen. In contrast, there was no significant increase in expenditures by the women, and the data indicated that they saved the windfall either in cash at home or in a ROSCA. The study confirms years of observation and anecdote: when presented with additional income, women tend to save it rather than spend it on personal items.

Women's need to shield their savings from the demands of family members and neighbors is also borne out in the literature. Researchers gave free ATM cards to 1,100 randomly selected holders of Family Bank of Kenya's "Mwananchi" (meaning "citizen" in Swahili) account. The cards would lower withdrawal fees by 50 percent and allowed for greater convenience since banking transactions could take place outside branch operating hours. This new product feature appeared to be an immediate success: within the first six months, deposits had increased by 45 percent and withdrawals had doubled. On closer examination, though, the account data showed that all of these gains took place among joint and male-owned accounts only. For women, the ATM card was not seen as providing a cost saving or greater convenience; rather, it served to inhibit their financial autonomy. Prior to the card's issuance, the Mwananchi account provided a secure place outside the home for a woman to protect her savings from her husband's demands; she could refuse his requests for funds by saying the withdrawal fee was too expensive or it would take her too much time to travel to the bank. Once the ATM card was introduced, however, it was much harder to refuse him, or he could just take the card and make the withdrawal himself. There was a particular irony in this outcome since women in the part of Kenya where the experiment took place were reported by both men and women to be the household's primary saver. Women, who should have been the target customer of this product feature, were driven away instead because their need for greater security and confidentiality was ignored in the design.

Intrahousehold dynamics dominate the academic research on women's saving behavior and are critical to our understanding of the barriers to their accessing the formal financial system. There are other factors at play, though, which can also provide insight into designing bank accounts that serve low-income people's needs. Around the world, fully two-thirds of unbanked individuals mention having too little money as a reason for not having a bank account, while another quarter cite transaction costs such as account opening fees and minimum balance requirements and distance to a financial service provider as major impediments. Reducing or even eliminating these costs at the outset appears not only to increase uptake of savings accounts but to have long-term benefits as well. A study among low-income households in Indonesia found that a relatively modest one-time subsidy, ranging from $3 to $14, at the time of account opening, could increase take-up by nearly 300 percent. Perhaps more important, though, two years later those households that had received the higher subsidies were significantly more likely to use the bank accounts for various financial activities.

Another study, once again in Kenya, tracked the saving behavior of a group of bicycle taxi drivers (all men) and market traders (nearly all women). Both groups saved in ROSCAs rather than in a bank, and most of the participants agreed with the statement "It is hard to save at home." Both men and women reported that account opening fees and minimum balance requirements were the principal stumbling blocks to opening an account at a bank. In addition, the only bank in the village where the study took place made its services particularly inconvenient, offering no ATM or any other way to conduct banking activities outside the nine to three opening hours and actually charged a steep fee to withdraw savings. Researchers paid the account opening fee and provided the amount of the required minimum balance, which the study participants were not allowed to withdraw. With those initial costs covered—and with a substantial disincentive to take money out of the account in terms of time and withdrawal fees—the differences between the men's and the women's behavior were quite stark. The women traders not only had very high rates of usage of the account, they also substantially increased investments in their businesses, in some cases by as much as 56 percent. The bicycle taxi drivers used the accounts far less often and did not increase their total savings or investments in their business. The authors of the study declined to speculate on the men's behavior beyond noting that the women seemed to experience the barriers to saving (convenience, time, and costs) far more significantly than men and that lifting those constraints while protecting the women from the demands of family members had a far greater impact on women's ability to save and invest.

Digital financial services, with their lower transaction costs, greater convenience, and, in many cases, lower KYC requirements, hold promise to address many of these barriers to saving, particularly for women. Not only has Kenya's pioneering mobile money service M-Pesa lifted one million people out of poverty, it has also improved their resilience to unexpected reductions or irregularities in household income. Many low-income households are dependent on a wide network of friends and family for loans and gifts as an integral part of their emergency safety nets. Studies have shown that users of mobile money are able to put out the call for help to a broader network and receive payments in a much more timely and efficient way than those households that must rely on in-person cash payments. As a result, M-Pesa households were able to maintain their level of spending on food and other goods and services even in the face of health emergencies or agricultural losses. In contrast, households that did not adopt digital payments were forced to decrease consumption levels by 7 percent in response to these income shocks. Digital payments yield similarly improved financial outcomes even in some of the poorest countries in the world. In Burkina Faso, users of mobile money are three times more likely to save for health and other emergencies than non-users. As discussed in chapter 3, in Niger, government benefits payments that were deposited directly into women's cell-phone accounts gave them greater control over how the money was spent; consequently, their families had more diverse diets and were more likely to grow cash crops than women who received the benefits in cash.

Although academic research on the impact of combining cell-phone technology with traditional financial services is still in a nascent stage, both early studies and anecdotal evidence offer an important cautionary tale. Ime and the other market traders in Lagos valued the convenience of using their cell phones to perform financial functions, particularly as a way to verify that their money had been safely deposited in their accounts. But to make the transition from saving with the *ajo* (even with the risk of losing their money) to placing their trust in Diamond Bank, they needed the bank to have a human face as well. The BETA savings product had very high take-up rates, but the number one reason given by those individuals who closed their BETA accounts was not seeing their BETA Friend frequently enough. When designing financial products to be delivered through digital channels, service providers would do well to remember the importance of retaining human touchpoints. Researchers in the Philippines studied a bank that introduced mobile banking to a sample of roughly three hundred low-income account holders. Prior to the change, clients deposited savings and repaid loans at regular in-person meetings with peers and an account officer in their villages; they could make withdrawals from a bank office in town. The bank decided to enhance customers' convenience by shifting all payments and withdrawals to mobile transactions made through a corner store in their village for a small fee. In all cases, the transactions were more convenient for customers, with time savings of 30 percent and 70 percent for deposits and withdrawals, respectively. What were the results of all this newfound convenience? A significant decline in usage of all financial services by this customer base! Even long-time savers broke well-entrenched habits and stopped transacting with the bank. For those living closest to the new transaction points (i.e., those who experienced the greatest gains in convenience), deposit balances fell by 28 percent on average, the frequency of both deposits and withdrawals fell by 15 percent, and loan usage fell by 5 percent. Follow-up interviews determined that these results were almost entirely driven by the loss of peer interaction from the village meetings, as well as by a sensitivity to fees.

THE VALUE OF PRODUCT BUNDLING

The experience of traditional savings models and the results from a growing body of research point to some "do's and don'ts" as well as some "must-haves" for financial service providers when designing products to serve low-income clients. Savings products are rarely considered the big money-makers for banks, particularly those accounts where clients are saving relatively small amounts at irregular intervals. With all the potential pitfalls, the small margins, and customer resistance to transaction costs that come with serving this client base, financial service providers would be rightly concerned about this market's commercial viability. While for some financial service providers, subsidizing client deposits or eliminating account fees may seem like a bridge too far, this kind of nudge offers an important philanthropic or partnership opportunity with donors or governments eager to achieve inclusion goals. It's critical to bear in mind that organizations serving these low-income customers equitably as well as profitably share several characteristics with respect to their culture of client service and customer protection, always recognizing the importance of building and retaining trust. They also have tended to approach product design in similar ways, recognizing the basic savings account as a gateway product that can be successfully bundled with other products and services.

As Diamond Bank evolved its BETA account, it would become a great example of product bundling. Within five years of the product launch, Diamond had opened nearly 700,000 BETA accounts while offering various ancillary products throughout that period. Recognizing that many BETA account holders were accumulating savings over time in their accounts, the bank decided to offer a BETA Target savings product. The BETA Friend would discuss the client's goals, and together they would develop a savings plan on a mobile app. Unlike "basic" BETA, the Target account required a fairly hefty opening balance and a minimum maintenance amount, but it paid higher interest rates, depending on the account balance. Diamond also developed a thirty-day digital loan that was offered, documented, disbursed, and collected entirely through the client's cell phone and her BETA account. The bank used the client's savings behavior to develop a credit rating and secured the loan using a portion of her BETA savings balance as collateral.

A frequent motivator—both stated and unstated—for some low-income people to participate in informal savings groups is the ability to borrow from those groups. However, savings groups typically have strict limits on members' borrowing, and loans made out of the groups' collected savings are insufficient to accumulate a lump sum. The opportunity that banks offer to borrow larger amounts, along with a safe, confidential place to save, can be a powerful draw. That combination has emerged as a factor in the success of one of the fundamental pillars of the Indian government's financial inclusion efforts. The government created the Pradhan Mantri Jan-Dhan Yogana (known as the Jan-Dhan, or PMJDY bank account) in 2014 as a basic no-frills account that can be opened at any retail bank in India. With 15 million new bank accounts created on the day it was announced, the program entered the *Guinness Book of World Records* for the most bank accounts opened on a single day and is generally considered a tremendous success in terms of account opening. Today there are 361 million PMJDY accounts that in aggregate hold a total deposit balance of $14 billion. Still, banks have struggled with inactive accounts and zero balances, and nearly 31 percent of these accounts have seen little to no use. At the time of the PMJDY launch, two additional benefits were also announced: free accident insurance of a little more than $1,300 and a debit card with an overdraft facility up to roughly $130. However, the government has not strictly monitored compliance with the program for anything other than account openings, and consequently, few banks have made this credit feature available to low-income clients.

Bank of Baroda, India's second largest public sector bank, has 36 million PMJDY accounts, for a 15 percent market share, and the overwhelming majority of these accounts are held by women. The bank found that roughly a quarter of account holders were "high savers" and had established a regular pattern of savings, maintaining average annual balances of approximately $200. The remainder used the account infrequently, if at all; to break even, the bank needed account holders to maintain at least a $7 balance, so Bank of Baroda was incentivized to drive more activity. A closer look at the customer data revealed an interesting behavior pattern: once a woman in the bank's urban branches reached a level of engagement at which she was making six deposits per year, she appeared to have established a solid savings habit and was able to maintain a steady deposit balance. In response, the bank created a campaign to welcome and recognize women's small savings deposits; once a customer had made four deposits, the bank named her a "Jan Dhan Plus" customer and made her instantly eligible for a credit facility to incentivize even deeper engagement. The Jan Dhan Plus product is still in the early stages of rollout, but indications of higher account activity are promising.

Bundling an asset accumulation product such as a savings account with a loan can also be a risk mitigation strategy for financial service providers. A leading microfinance lender in Colombia found that its loan portfolio quality could improve by as much as three percentage points if women had either an active savings account or a health insurance policy in addition to their microloan. If a woman had a financial safety net in place so that she was not forced to choose between repaying her loan and paying the doctor to treat her sick child, chances were much greater that the bank would see its loan repaid.

Payments, particularly when made through digital channels, offer another product bundling opportunity for banks, particularly for people new to the banking system. One quarter of the people in developing countries receive government benefits or wages directly into an account; a roughly similar number are paid their wages by a private sector employer into an account. The vast majority of those payments are immediately cashed out to pay living expenses—including the payment of utilities, school fees, and remittances sent home to family members. On top of that, 15 percent of the people living in developing economies—including 210 million women—receive payment for agricultural goods in cash. The business opportunity for banks to help recipients keep this money within the system and facilitate digital payments electronically is enormous. With 585 million women around the world paying for utilities and 252 million women paying school fees all in cash, there must surely be a way for mobile network operators and payments companies to leverage these flows into greater access to a broader range of services.

Payments sent by migrant workers living abroad to family members at home represent a significant source of capital inflow for many developing countries and a critical source of household income to millions. Global remittance payments reached a record high of $554 billion in 2019. In low- and middle-income countries, these receipts represent more than both foreign direct investment and development assistance, and in thirty countries remittances make up 10 percent or more of GDP. Remittance payments also provide another opportunity to bring low-income recipients into the formal financial system. If other financial services such as insurance premiums or loan repayments are linked to these flows, they can provide even greater financial security for senders and recipients and open up additional business lines for the financial institutions that serve them.

Migrants sending money home have strong preferences over how their money is spent by recipients and are particularly concerned about how much is saved. At the other end of the transaction, recipients' priorities may differ; they typically use their bank accounts simply to collect and then cash out remittance payments. Hatton National Bank of Sri Lanka designed a product that recognized the dual objectives of senders and receivers. More than 1.5 million Sri Lankans work in the Middle East and the Gulf States, over half of them women. While these women clearly understand the important role they play in supporting their families by sending home a portion of their wages, many also express the desire to save for their eventual return to Sri Lanka for retirement. All too often they found that their families had not honored their wishes to save a portion of their remittances and had spent the entire amount on consumption, leaving them nothing to retire on. Hatton created an account that would ensure that these women's wishes were honored: the bank would distribute a designated portion of the remittance to family members and save the balance toward the woman's longer-term goals. The bank also designed on-the-spot financial literacy training for receiving family members; this training resulted in significant increases in recipients' savings balances.

The agency, autonomy, and freedom of choice that a savings account can confer on a girl cannot be underestimated; neither can the downstream developmental impacts that flow from giving her access to that account. Happily, financial service providers don't have to make those investments in human capital at the expense of financial sustainability. With 1.8 billion youth between the ages of ten and twenty-four representing 25–30 percent of the population in developing countries, acquiring a client as a child can be seen as a smarter (and less expensive) customer acquisition strategy than waiting to pursue new clients as adults. Indeed, there is ample evidence that attracting banking customers in their youth leads to unmatched customer loyalty and a higher customer lifetime value, or the "net profit attributable to the future relationship with a customer." Hatton National Bank in Sri Lanka is also one of the world's leaders in youth banking and has run a "classroom banker" program for more than thirty years to make it easy for children to open savings accounts and make deposits at school. Over the years, the bank has built this program into a pipeline of long-term clients and has one of the most impressive client retention rates in the region. The program has also become one of the bank's most effective recruiting tools: many of the children who served as "bankers" in elementary and secondary school have gone on to become successful and loyal bank employees on graduation.

When Banco ADOPEM in the Dominican Republic launched the Mía girls' savings program with 15,000 girls, some as young as seven, the bank expected it to be nothing more than a community development activity. While the girls' accounts never accumulated significant balances, an evaluation of the program five years later nonetheless revealed some interesting impacts on the bank's business. All the family members—both parents and even some grandparents—of the Mía account holders transferred their banking business to ADOPEM as a direct result of the bank's engagement with the girls. As a group, the Mía families held larger savings balances in the bank and had better loan repayment rates than the bank's average client. If the family was a remittance recipient, the payments transferred through the bank tended to be higher. Perhaps most notable, the customer retention rate of the Mía girls and their families was 82 percent, compared to the bank's already high average rate of 77 percent.

Youth savings programs don't have to be loss leaders, particularly if they incorporate cost-saving digital features. A few years after introducing the BETA account, Diamond Bank developed an innovative youth savings proposition that follows young people—and their parents—throughout the years of their education. The Diamond Future account was marketed to new and existing adult clients of the bank as a flexible targeted savings plan designed to enable parents to secure their children's future. The account also had a "Kiddies" feature so that primary-school-age children could save alongside their parents. Interestingly, the largest account balances were accumulated in accounts where mothers and daughters were saving together. At age thirteen, the children saving alongside their parents, as well as new youth clients, were able to open their own "Cool Teens" account, while parents continued to save through Diamond Future. Youth clients accessed their accounts through a digital gaming platform known as "Dreamville" where they could design financial plans, save, update their financial knowledge, and chat. When a child reached age eighteen, her parents' Diamond Future account matured; if the student was an existing client and she decided to proceed to tertiary education, she was eligible to migrate from the "Cool Teens" platform to a "SWAG" ("Student With A Goal") account. This account was also available digitally and was tailored to facilitate loans for higher education and professional training, as well as continued saving. The profitability of the long-term Diamond Future account effectively subsidized the other elements in the program that served to attract new, younger clients to the bank.

Access to a safe place to save is central to achieving the promise of financial inclusion for women and for financial service providers. The security and confidentiality of a savings account protect the resources that allow women to make positive changes in their families' lives, such as more nutritious diets or better educational outcomes. Greater control over those resources, in turn, enhances a woman's bargaining power and her role in the community, allowing her to make those strategic life choices that are at the heart of empowerment. For financial service providers, savings products are an ideal route to enter the financial inclusion market, building trust with customers and greater understanding of their needs and preferences, and, eventually, bundling or cross-selling other products and services together with savings accounts. Savings, along with financial literacy, can be a first step toward inclusion for a girl or woman and the acquisition of a lifelong client for a financial service provider.

5 MAKING THE BUSINESS CASE FOR ACCESS TO CAPITAL

A savings account can be the instrument of a woman's agency, providing her with the means to control resources and extend her influence over household decisions; by shoring up her own resources, a woman builds a safety net for herself and her family. Credit, on the other hand, represents an opportunity for a woman to tap external resources, to go beyond her own assets and build something bigger. Women's financial inclusion assumes greater security for low-income women in the face of myriad risks, but it must also capture the possibility of prosperity for the woman herself, as well as for the financial service providers who partner with her.

To do this, a persuasive business case for providing financial services to low-income women must include the opportunity to extend credit. Savings accounts are an indisputably important threshold product for low-income women, providing them with a safe place to build both a financial safety net and a sense of trust in an institution they may not have considered to be "for them." For the bank, mobilizing deposits provides a reliable source of local currency liquidity that can be a lifeline during periods of financial crisis, when external funding typically dries up. But lending is the way banks make their money; net interest income makes up well over half of most banks' net profit. Being able to demonstrate the earning potential from lending to an underserved customer base is essential to putting forth a credible business case, and lending to women can be among the most convincing arguments. Since women customers are often more open to cross-selling, when banks bundle credit with other products, such as a savings account or insurance, the resulting customer lifetime value of a woman client can be higher than that of a man. In much the same way that Diamond Bank in Nigeria built credibility as a trusted partner for women business owners by first offering the BETA savings account before adding a credit feature to the product, an investment in this customer base should be seen as a long-term gambit that is optimized through the provision of credit.

The discussion of access to capital is also the point at which financial inclusion most clearly dovetails with the opportunity for inclusive growth. Micro, small, and medium-sized enterprises, or MSMEs, are powerful contributors to economic growth and job creation around the world and particularly in developing countries. In fact, research indicates that the size of a country's MSME sector is positively related to its overall economic growth. However, unless and until the disparity in women's and men's access to finance is addressed, there is significant evidence that further growth will only exacerbate existing economic inequality.

There are an estimated 320 million formal MSMEs in the developing world, where they contribute on average two-thirds of total permanent full-time private sector employment and up to 40 percent of GDP. In developing countries, small companies have the highest rate of employment growth, followed by medium-sized firms. A direct line runs between those companies' capacity to create jobs and their ability to raise funds. Analysis based on the World Bank Enterprise Surveys and other country-level data finds that a business's access to financial services (e.g., having a loan, sales credit, or other external financing) has a significant effect on a firm's capacity to expand its number of permanent employees. And yet these powerhouses of economic growth and job creation are perennially starved of the capital they need to grow. Following the global financial crisis of 2007–2008, banks focused on derisking their portfolios, lending to only the most creditworthy, larger borrowers—or at least those that they (and regulators) perceived to be less risky, with the result that even fewer bank loans were made to smaller businesses.

Before we consider the economic and commercial opportunity presented by the needs of MSMEs for financing, some discussion about what constitutes an MSME is in order. Definitions and classifications are notoriously inconsistent for this segment, with many countries setting their own criteria based on their local context. However, around the world, policymakers, researchers, and financial service providers are beginning to converge around consensus definitions that consider certain enterprise characteristics, namely, number of employees, amount of assets, and sometimes annual business turnover. Accordingly, *micro* enterprises are considered to be those with fewer than ten employees and assets worth less than $100,000; *small* enterprises are those with between ten and forty-nine employees and assets valued between $100,000 and $3 million, and *medium-sized* enterprises are those with between fifty and three hundred employees and assets valued between $3 million and $15 million.

Another important definitional criterion is whether an MSME operates as an informal or a formal business. Informal businesses typically are those that are not incorporated or registered; most likely they do not maintain a legal identity distinct from the individual owner. Moreover, that owner operates the business primarily to support herself and her family. Informal businesses are estimated to make up close to 80 percent of MSMEs in the developing world. These informal firms rely primarily on informal financial services for their financing needs (e.g., friends and family, savings and credit clubs, moneylenders.) While it is believed that much of the sector's demand for financing stems from these enterprises, the paucity of reliable, cross-country data on the number of informal MSMEs, let alone their financing needs, makes an accurate calculation of the financing gap extremely difficult, if not impossible.

Even without trying to track informal MSMEs, determining the number of formal businesses and their financing needs is a challenge. In a perfect world with universally available, transparent information to evaluate credit risks, the supply of financing by banks would equal the amount of funding demanded by businesses. In the real world, however, MSMEs routinely cite lack of access to capital as one of their biggest obstacles to growth, while banks claim that MSMEs are too risky and lack audited financial statements and other information that would allow them to assess creditworthiness. It's safe to assume, then, that there is a meaningful disparity between demand for funding (what a business would have asked for) and supply (what a bank would have been willing to lend if it could assess credit risk). While no international governing body aggregates data on the number or financing needs of informal enterprises, the SME Finance Forum, housed at the International Finance Corporation (IFC), has emerged as a reliable clearinghouse for tracking the funding needs of formal MSMEs. The forum estimates that 41 percent of formal MSMEs have unmet financing needs totaling $5 trillion—an amount that is 1.3 times the amount of lending currently being done.

According to the SME Finance Forum, women-owned businesses constitute 23 percent of formal MSMEs. However, they are disproportionately represented among the companies facing capital constraints, making up fully one-third of businesses that are unable to tap the financing they need to grow. In many countries, women entrepreneurs are not only less likely to be able to take out a loan than their male counterparts but, when they do secure loans, the terms of borrowing are often less favorable. Women are frequently subject to shorter-term loans, higher interest rates, or heavier collateral requirements than men. Despite these disadvantages, women's repayment rates on MSME loans are directly comparable to men's; when the IFC analyzed its own MSME loan portfolio it found that 4.5 percent of loans to both men and women are overdue at ninety days.

THE ROLE OF GOVERNMENT IN EXPANDING MSMES' ACCESS TO CAPITAL

In recent years, as developing country governments have sought to expand economic growth and job creation, some have recognized that providing access to capital for MSMEs, especially for women-owned businesses, can allow more people within the society to benefit. Governments can lead the way in creating a well-regulated enabling environment for financial service providers to operate in, particularly by addressing the most pervasive and frequently mentioned obstacles to banks' provision of credit to MSMEs.

Modernizing a country's credit infrastructure, particularly with regard to secured transactions, can have a profound impact on MSMEs' access to capital. Inadequate collateral is a significant obstacle to gaining access to credit for small businesses. Data suggest that the number one reason why bank loan applications are denied is unacceptable or inadequate capital; while it does not appear that women are rejected for loans more often than men, they are less likely to apply for loans in the first place, citing concerns about their lack of collateral. But what if the problem isn't so much a lack of assets but that a country's legal framework isn't set up to allow the assets that businesses *do* own to be used as collateral? Movable assets such as equipment, inventory, and accounts receivable represent about 78 percent of the capital stock of small businesses in the developing world, while immovable assets such as land or buildings represent only 22 percent. Unfortunately, those proportions are almost the mirror opposite of what banks in developing countries accept as security against loans: land and buildings form 73 percent of the assets used as collateral by developing country banks. This misalignment results in what economists call "dead capital"—assets that could be leveraged for badly needed growth capital.

A growing number of developing countries are moving to reform the legal and regulatory environment for the use of movable collateral. Central to an effective reform process is ensuring that creditors can transparently establish their rights to the movable collateral. This is typically done through the establishment of a collateral registry, which provides publicly available information about who owns or has a security interest in an asset. In a study of seventy-three countries that have established a collateral registry or related collateral reforms, researchers found that access to credit expanded by eight percentage points; interest rates declined by an average of three percentage points and loan maturities were extended by six months. The strongest impact of these positive changes was felt by small businesses.

Expanding the range of assets that businesses can put to work to gain access to finance can also lead to the development of a more diverse set of financial instruments and the creation of new institutions that are particularly well suited to serving MSMEs. For example, a farmer could finance the purchase of a tractor using the tractor itself as collateral, either through a traditional bank loan or perhaps through an equipment leasing company.

Likewise, a supplier could finance its short-term working capital needs by either pledging receivables for a loan or selling them to an intermediary known as a factor or a factoring company. Let's say a small garment business lands a contract with a government agency to provide uniforms. Since governments are reliable but often slow payers, the business owner could sell a factor the receivable from the government agency and the factor would pay the small business the face value of that invoice, minus a commission and fees. The business owner would have an immediate cash injection to cover payroll and other expenses and the factor would collect payment directly from the government. Typically, asset-based lenders, such as factors, will provide borrowers with more cash more quickly and with fewer strings attached than banks, although a factor's fees may be higher than bank interest rates.

The other component of a healthy, inclusive credit infrastructure that could greatly facilitate banks' move into the MSME market is the credit reporting system. Banks and other financial service providers rely on information collected by credit bureaus and registries to determine a borrower's capacity to repay; alongside physical collateral that lenders use to secure loans, this information is often referred to as "reputational collateral." Research indicates that in developing countries, a lender's ability to obtain third-party information about a borrower's creditworthiness can play a more significant role in increasing credit to small and medium-sized enterprises than strengthening that lender's rights in a secured transaction. There is ample evidence linking effective credit reporting systems with increased credit at lower cost for small businesses. In fact, one study in Latin America showed that where credit bureaus collected and distributed both positive and negative information (i.e., both proof of timely repayment and evidence of late payments or defaults) and 100 percent of the country's banks participated in the registry, lending to the private sector increased by at least 47.5 percent.

But in many developing countries these types of information-sharing institutions either don't exist or don't collect the information that women—particularly low-income women—are most likely to have. According to *Women, Business and the Law*, 139 of the 189 countries surveyed either have no public or private credit registry or have one that does not cover more than 5 percent of the adult population. In economies where women are less likely to have access to property to pledge as collateral, the ability to demonstrate a history of successful payments—to retailers and utilities, as well as to financial institutions—can be an important stepping-stone to access credit. When the US included utility and telephone payment histories in credit scores, the share of adults who were considered "unscorable" dropped from 12 percent to 2 percent and the greatest beneficiaries were low-income Americans, members of minority communities, and younger and elderly Americans. Loan acceptance rates for those earning less than $20,000 annually jumped by 21 percent. Promoting or creating information-sharing institutions such as credit bureaus and registries and then ensuring that they capture information about smaller transactions and microfinance loans are an especially important way for women to establish credit histories.

ONE BANK'S JOURNEY TO SERVING MORE WOMEN-LED BUSINESSES

Sometimes in response to these government efforts and sometimes for their own competitive reasons, commercial banks have gradually begun to address this underserved market. A smaller but growing subset of banks has created dedicated women's MSME business initiatives. One such bank is Kenya Commercial Bank (KCB), the largest bank in Kenya, with $6.3 billion in assets and 282 branches throughout the country. The bank attempted to attract MSME customers over the years but, like the other banks in the Kenyan market, had not really made a concerted effort to design a distinct product tailored to the needs of this customer segment, let alone a proposition that targeted women-owned MSMEs. By 2016, though, Kenya's financial landscape had changed dramatically. Most notably the dominance of M-Pesa, the mobile phone-based money transfer system, and the accompanying rise in digital financial services had shifted the ground for large banks. Serving women-owned MSMEs offered a clear opportunity for KCB to differentiate itself in an increasingly crowded market.

The bank analyzed the business landscape for MSMEs and confirmed that the market was ripe for a dominant player. None of Kenya's forty commercial banks had emerged as the leading financial service provider to the country's 300,000 to 400,000 registered MSMEs. In addition, the Kenyan government had identified the growth and improved competitiveness of these companies as critical to achieving its goal of moving the standard of living for the majority of Kenyans above the international poverty line by 2030. The government was particularly eager for the nation's banks to address the consistent complaint of women-owned businesses that a lack of external funding was the greatest obstacle to their growth. Policymakers also recognized that support for women-owned businesses could contribute to another of its strategic priorities: increasing women's labor force participation. Women-led businesses are more likely to hire other women; for 45 percent of women-led firms in Kenya, most of the employees are women, compared with just 24 percent of men-led firms.

KCB's market analysis identified two principal constraints to ensuring these companies' access to adequate financial resources. The first was the limited use of lending methods that allowed bankers to assess a company's creditworthiness, leading to an overreliance on collateral. The second, related constraint was a lack of understanding on the part of the bank's loan officers about the specific needs of MSMEs and how they differed from the lending needs of retail or corporate customers. To hear directly from the business owners themselves, the bank held a series of focus groups at the offices of a local market research firm in Nairobi. Staff from the market research firm led the discussions, while representatives from KCB's business lending division paid close attention. The focus groups comprised both men and women MSME owners, some of whom were existing KCB clients and some who banked with KCB's competitors. Each of the business owners had completed secondary education and their businesses were all formally registered, maintained premises outside their owners' homes, and had between ten and 120 employees. They ranged in age and business segment from Esther, who, at thirty years old, had saved money from her job at a large foreign bank to build a residential real estate business, to sixty-two-year-old Julius, who was eager to retire and turn over his successful paint manufacturing business to his two youngest children once they finished college. A series of conversations conducted over the course of two days highlighted the challenges faced by small business owners regardless of gender and some of the issues of special importance to entrepreneurial women.

In the first, all-female group, Anne started the conversation off by talking about her printing business. She had worked as a secretary for several years and saved so that she was able to buy equipment and materials "bit by bit." "My first printer cost me 50,000 Kenyan shillings [about $500], but from that time it has grown to much more and today I have about $20,000 worth of machines. . . . I have a lot of machines, digital and large format . . . and I acquired them all through loans."

Margaret jumped in, with a surprised look on her face, "Really? I didn't know anything about loans when I started my business! I was making money selling auto parts, distributing them together with brake fluid and other engine oils in different places. . . . After a while I started selling small trucks, and then six years later, I bought my first ten-wheel truck from my savings. One of them costs $60,000 to $70,000 and I currently own four trucks." Margaret's husband had worked in construction materials and joined her in the business after she acquired that first truck, and together they started transporting concrete and other building materials. They went to KCB together for her first loan when she wanted to purchase a second truck, but she was disappointed that KCB had not been supportive of her ambitions the following year when she wanted to purchase a third. (KCB's lending guidelines preclude back-to-back loans.) She went to another bank, which loaned her the money, and, while she keeps her business accounts with KCB, she also borrowed from the other bank for her most recent purchase, saying, "I went to the other bank because they were more helpful than KCB. With business you have to keep growing your money."

The reliance on savings to start businesses was a consistent theme among the women in the focus group and is supported in the literature as well. In countries where informal transfers from friends and family are the most common sources of startup funding, women are often less likely to be recipients of these loans; if they do receive them, the loans are typically very small and may be extended through their husbands rather than directly to the women. In fact, most of the women from the focus groups in Nairobi said matter-of-factly that they could not ask friends or family members for money if they wanted to maintain any semblance of financial independence. (This need to rely on savings to start a business comes into focus when juxtaposed with what we know about women's fierce desire to keep their savings confidential and protected from requests for loans from friends and family.)

And it contrasted sharply with the men's experience—all of the men interviewed had received money from friends, family members, and even clients. For example, Samuel, a thirty-nine-year-old HVAC contractor, said (in an all-male group) that he had left the business where he had been employed for three years and started his own business with "funds from my friends." He went on to say that, after he had started his own business, his first client (who was neither a friend nor a family member) had lent him $2000 against a postdated check. When he tried to repay the loan, this client told him, "No, keep it and buy more equipment."

Both men and women shared a healthy skepticism about banks and were equally concerned about interest rates on loans, hidden fees, and the need to understand all the terms and conditions attached to bank products before signing. And while both men and women participants grumbled about the need to pledge collateral against the loans, there were deeper issues of ownership and independence at play for the women. Blanche, who, in partnership with her husband, uses bank loans to buy old houses and refurbish them for sale, referred to "tough love" when the subject of loan collateral came up. She complained that title "is registered in the husband's name so that [women] do not have land. You have to have a good relationship with your husband. It is 'tough love' if you have been with him all the years; even if you are bored with him, you have to stay!" Several of the women noted that since they did not have title to land in their own names, they had been able to get loans only after they had purchased equipment and, in fact, the equipment seller had made a referral to the bank, which then used the equipment as collateral. Likewise, nearly all the women had made sure to have their cars or trucks registered in their names and not their husbands' so that they could use the vehicles as security for business loans.

The discussion of collateral opened up the conversation to an even deeper discussion of personal autonomy. Emily, a thirty-nine-year-old event planner, volunteered that she sought out opportunities where "you can act as a woman on your own. I do flowers on the side, that has nothing to do with my husband. That money is not enough for my business, but it helps me to buy things for my children." And Blanche seemed to speak for many in the group when she stressed how important it was to "have your salary, you do your savings, it goes to your account and no one touches that. When I am tired of my 'tough love,' then I can have my savings. That is my voice, that is my strength."

Several of the Kenyan banks, including KCB, offer business club membership to their SME clients, organizing networking events, training classes, and even trade trips to China and Dubai, where several of the focus group participants sourced supplies and inventory. Members in KCB's Biashara Club (meaning "Business" in Swahili) had their own dedicated service desk in each branch, and the ability to bank without standing in line was the membership privilege most valued by women and men alike. However, the women placed a decidedly higher value on the training and networking opportunities, whereas the men were far more concerned about whether membership would enable them to get larger loans. As one of the men put it, "[You can] offer me . . . like one hundred trainings in a month, [but if you] don't support me financially it's like zero work." In contrast, Emily, the event planner, enthusiastically embraced the networking opportunities afforded by the club: "For me, networking is everything. That is how we are where we are." She went on to describe how she and several women she had met through the club had brought her business to the next level by joining together to offer their catering and other event services as a package.

All of the entrepreneurs emphasized that customer service, whether through the clubs or in other ways, was a critical factor in their decision to maintain a relationship with a bank. To a much greater extent for the women than for the men, though, the level of customer service and the treatment also called up issues of identity and autonomy. Underscoring her desire for independence, Emily told us that "I expect good service, they should talk to me nicely, confidentially. We want to do things that our husbands do not know about. I don't want them telling my husband, 'Oh, I saw [her] at the bank today.'" But perhaps, Anne, who runs a larger, more complex printing business, with the Kenyan government as one of her customers and fifteen full-time employees, best expressed the desire for respect in saying, "I am the boss and I want to be treated like the boss I am."

The participants' unvarnished impressions of the bank and its competitors, as well as their aspirations for themselves and their businesses, were eye-opening for the KCB staff. One of the younger loan officers shook his head, saying he felt as though he had been shown a little "tough love" after sitting in on Blanche's group. Armed with analytical data and the candid feedback from the focus groups, the leaders of KCB's MSME business division set out to reinvent the bank's approach to doing business with this customer segment. They made a critical strategic choice up-front in deciding to approach the MSME business with an explicit gender focus. First, they addressed the customers' clearly expressed desire to have a dedicated person within the bank who would serve as a point of contact for all their business and personal needs. The bank transformed MSME bankers from one hundred branches into relationship managers, by providing training on how to establish and maintain long-term relationships through topics such as communicating effectively, selling and cross-selling, and the importance of follow-up.

Revamping the Biashara Club provided another way for relationship managers to deepen their connection to clients, but they quickly realized they had no way to track a customer's membership status and activities. Their decision to restructure the bank's Customer Relationship Management (CRM) system would turn out to be one of the most eye-opening elements of the entire initiative and challenged many preconceived ideas about the bank's women clients. With better customer data available, the relationship managers discovered that women club members were more likely to own their business than male members and to have larger businesses, employing more than ten people.

Through a deeper engagement with Biashara Club members, relationship managers also learned of the significant demand from both men and women for more structured technical training courses on subjects they considered critical to running a successful business but had had no formal education in. In response, KCB partnered with the African Management Institute (AMI), a local business training organization, to deliver a six-month blended training program that combined in-person and online engagement that enabled clients to implement new practices and improve their managerial skills.

KCB's management had heard loud and clear that customers found the bank's collateral requirements a particular pain point. In fact, an over-reliance on collateral was at the center of the bank's credit approval process, which essentially consisted of two steps, neither of which involved an actual analysis of the business's capacity to generate enough cash to repay the loan. The bank would first review the turnover in the business accounts that the client held at the bank to determine the size of the loan. Then it would assign a collateral requirement, which for MSMEs was typically set at twice the value of the loan. In effect, the bank wasn't evaluating an enterprise's ability to make timely payments throughout the life of the loan; rather, it was betting that, if the borrower couldn't repay, the bank would be able to seize the property pledged as collateral and sell it to cover the unpaid loan amount. In 2017 Kenya had undertaken an extensive overhaul of the laws governing the use of collateral to secure credit facilities. Yet even with these reforms in place, realizing the value of collateral to settle an unpaid loan was a lengthy and often arduous process. This lending practice severely limited the bank's understanding of the true size and potential of a client's business and was arguably less efficient and more expensive than adopting a lending method that analyzed the cash generated by a company's operations.

As part of the effort to expand their MSME business, KCB dramatically overhauled its credit assessment and approval processes. All relationship managers were trained in a cash-flow-based lending method that required them to go into their clients' businesses to get a genuine understanding of the business dynamics the owner was facing. They were trained to assess and understand risk rather than to rely solely on collateral to mitigate repayment risk. KCB established credit panels at the branch level to ensure that a rigorous assessment had been done before loan applications were submitted to headquarters. And, once again, the bank made a critical operational change to improve the collection and reporting of data. Recognizing that "what gets measured, gets done," KCB took the step every commercial bank dreads—modifying its core banking system—to disaggregate its customer data by gender in order to accurately measure the success of the program.

KCB's management embraced the MSME initiative, investing significant amounts of money, time, systems, and other resources in its success. Nevertheless, several months after the project was launched, results were decidedly lackluster. Even though the project was known internally as the "Women's Proposition," there was not an appreciable increase in the number of loans to women-owned MSMEs—or male-owned MSMEs, for that matter—although customer satisfaction had improved, thanks to the deeper engagement with relationship managers. Branch managers felt that the project was just one more so-called "priority" from headquarters and had not assigned it any particular urgency or precedence among the other initiatives and mandates they were asked to deliver on. To underscore the importance of the Women's Proposition, KCB management decided to roll out what would be the most impactful part of the project.

The bank conducted gender sensitization training in the one hundred pilot branches. Today, training sessions of this type are ubiquitous in the financial services sector and beyond; attendance tends to be mandated by the Human Resources Department, and programs often have a distinct "tick the box" quality. Not surprisingly, research on the efficacy of such diversity programs, particularly those targeting a more inclusive workplace, is inconclusive. Most study results indicate that programs either do nothing to change attitudes or behaviors or conclude that there is insufficient evidence to determine what does work and under what conditions. All that said, the training at KCB had a profound and measurable impact on the bank's outreach to women clients; loans to women-led businesses increased by more than 150 percent in the branches where the training was offered.

In those branches, loans to women-led businesses increased from 22 percent to over 50 percent of the MSME portfolio.

The daylong gender training session considered the difference between sex and gender, and then explored how gender affected financial behavior in the Kenyan context. For example, men were more likely to borrow from multiple sources and accept offers from several financial institutions; women, on the other hand, tended to shop around for a financial service, asking many more questions, but were more likely to be loyal clients. The trainers clearly outlined management's rationale for the MSME program and presented the business case for the focus on women. They also called on KCB's proud history as one of the country's oldest Kenyan-owned financial institutions, noting that women represented 50.1 percent of the Kenyan population but only 25 percent of KCB's customer base. They gave concrete examples of how preconceptions about gender affected banking practice; for example, the presumption that more women owned food and textiles businesses resulted in men not being offered services applicable to those kinds of businesses, such as financing to support a food manufacturer's new contract with a large supermarket or distributor. The curriculum also provided important context about why collateral was so onerous for women-led businesses by explaining the property rights afforded women under the Kenyan constitution and how those rights were substantially more restricted under customary law as practiced in Kenya. The relationship managers saw clearly, many for the first time, how the limits on women's ownership, management, control, and inheritance of assets and property affected KCB's ability to serve women-owned businesses.

Relationship managers who participated in the gender sensitization training attributed its success to several factors. Most notably, they felt the training was deeply grounded in the business opportunity in serving women-led businesses and clarified for many of them why the bank had reprioritized its commitment to this customer base. The fact that the Women's Proposition was not a new product or service but rather a new approach to reaching a valued but underserved customer segment resonated with many of the relationship managers, and they felt they had been given tools and tactics to win these customers' business. They also appreciated that the targeted gender workshop was offered alongside training in sought-after business skills such as cross-selling, marketing products, and communications training.

Throughout the launch and rollout of the program (in 2017–2019), an external evaluator conducted a total of 568 interviews with KCB's MSME customers. Seventy-two businesses surveyed were customers for all three years, while the others changed over time; one-third of the businesses in the sample were women-led. By December 2019 KCB had seen impressive results from its investment in the Women's Proposition, with a substantial increase in loans to women-owned businesses. The experiment in cash-flow-based lending quieted the doubts of even the most skeptical credit officers, many of whom had worried about the impact of expanding into a client segment perceived to be riskier while at the same time reducing the reliance on collateral. Despite these concerns, nonperforming loans in the new MSME portfolio were only 1.2 percent—substantially better than the bank's overall loan portfolio. Likewise, the investments in relationship management and the expansion of tailored Biashara Club offerings increased customer satisfaction scores from 73 percent to 81 percent. The powerful impact of credit on job creation was also evident: businesses that had received loans from KCB increased their number of employees by an average 113 percent, compared to the average 40 percent increase by nonborrowers.

The women who were clients of the KCB MSME initiative differed in some respects from the other women we have discussed in the context of the Chen empowerment framework. They had all completed at least secondary education, and most had been employed by formal businesses or the government prior to becoming entrepreneurs. They were already banked—some with accounts at multiple banks. Perhaps most important, all of them owned registered, formal businesses. In terms of *material* change, the women's businesses experienced modest increases in profit, although there was considerable fluctuation in profitability in the second year, which coincided with election-related unrest in Kenya. During that challenging year, both men and women borrowers reported being grateful to KCB for the long repayment period on their loans, which allowed them to navigate cash flow disruptions. The Biashara Club, particularly the technical training with AMI, was the source of considerable *cognitive* change for many of the female entrepreneurs. At 94 percent, the MSME clients who had borrowed from KCB during the project period had a much higher awareness of the training and networking opportunities on offer. Notably, some of the women who did not have technical business skills when they joined the Biashara Club reported a substantial improvement in their managerial competence after attending the training. The most striking outcome, much as with the women from the BETA program, was in the realm of *relational* change. The evaluators designed an index to measure the extent to which the women participated in decisions pertaining to business growth, finances, employees, and inventory management. A stunning 100 percent of the women entrepreneurs reported that they were active participants in all business decisions by year three of the project, up from 86 percent at the outset.

KCB has now rolled out the various elements of the program to all of its branches, even though the bank's move into the women's MSME market required a significant commitment of resources, involving fundamental changes to the bank's MIS systems, credit processes, staff training, and product offerings. KCB joins a growing number of emerging markets banks that are beginning to recognize women-owned businesses as valuable and underserved clients. The banks that have been most successful with their women's propositions follow an approach similar to KCB's, taking care to align their products and services with women's distinct attitudes, preferences, and values. These banks recognize the importance of nonfinancial services such as training and opportunities for networking, alongside access to finance, as the secret to winning these customers' business. Many of these financial service providers who have successfully established their own women's propositions also participate in the Financial Alliance for Women, a global advocacy organization whose member banks report impressive results from serving this customer base. Alliance members find that women-owned MSMEs' nonperforming loans are 53 percent lower than men's and that micro and small businesses owned by women use the same average number of products as their male counterparts. Not surprisingly, some of these financial institutions have found that their average profit margin on a woman's MSME loan is up to 15 percent higher than loans to male-owned MSMEs.

WHAT'S KEEPING WOMEN-LED BUSINESSES FROM GETTING THE CAPITAL THEY NEED?

With so much evidence of women as good—indeed, better—borrowers than men, and a solid business case for serving women's businesses, does the persistent, disproportionately unmet need for credit on the part of women-owned MSMEs reflect economically irrational behavior on the part of financial service providers? Or is it discrimination?

Disparities in access to formal finance for men's and women's businesses are typically attributed to three, often mutually reinforcing factors: structural and sectoral differences in the types of businesses men and women establish, women's lower tolerance for risk (sometimes coupled with their observed or perceived lack of confidence), and discrimination on the part of financial institutions. First, generally speaking, women's businesses in the developing world tend to be smaller and are often started with less capital than men's, making them appear less bankable to traditional lenders. Seen through the lens of traditional banking credit assessments, loans to smaller companies appear both riskier and more expensive to service. Likewise, women frequently start businesses in the services sector because such businesses can be started and run with less capital. A survey of access to credit for small businesses in sub-Saharan Africa concluded that "firms with female ownership were unconditionally less likely to use formal bank credit than male-owned firms." However, the researchers point out that the gender gap disappears when they control for factors such as the size and age of the business or whether the business has an export orientation or foreign ownership, with the size of the business as the most explanatory variable. They argue that there is no gender discrimination in the allocation of credit to these businesses since men-owned businesses with these same characteristics were also denied credit. At the same time, they also conclude that women must surmount greater obstacles than men to start those businesses in the first place. The relationship among business size, sector, and the amount of startup capital needed becomes inescapably circular: women's businesses in low-capital-intensity sectors begin small because women have lower amounts of startup capital and stay small because their size precludes women accessing to credit to expand.

The second frequently mentioned reason for differences in access to credit for men's and women's businesses is the belief that women are more risk averse than men. An extensive body of literature documents women's preferences for smaller, more stable businesses with slower, steadier rates of growth, requiring less external finance. The research also points to women entrepreneurs' tendency to diversify their activities in order to guarantee a certain level of income, while men are more likely to concentrate their investment in a single high-yielding project. These findings, while consistent across a wide variety of studies and research methodologies, beg the question of whether they are actually measuring women's aversion to risk or instead their awareness and management of risk, particularly in the context of their other family responsibilities. Does diversifying investments across a portfolio of entrepreneurial ventures (i.e., running a bustling restaurant business while also renting out a second-story apartment) indicate that a woman is averse to risk or that she is managing that risk effectively in order to ensure that she can feed, clothe, and house her family or save for her retirement? In Bangladesh, for example, some microfinance institutions observed that women would not begin to borrow to expand their businesses until they had accumulated a certain level of savings; once that risk cushion was in place, the institutions observed that men's and women's requested loan sizes and borrowing frequency were roughly equivalent.

References to women's perceived risk aversion are often cited alongside assertions that women have less confidence than men and are reluctant to ask for what they need. Indeed, there is ample evidence in the literature that women are more likely than men to fall into the category of so-called "discouraged borrowers"—an otherwise creditworthy business owner who self-selects not to apply for a loan for fear of rejection. Goldman Sachs's 10,000 Women initiative tracked the progress of the women entrepreneurs who graduated from their rigorous, highly competitive business training program, which includes several modules on leverage as a factor in business growth. They found that over 70 percent of the women who applied for loans successfully received them, but in all fifty-six countries participating in the program, the majority of graduates self-selected not to borrow. Additional research documents that in Africa, women entrepreneurs are more likely than their male counterparts to self-select out of applying for credit because of their own perceived lack of creditworthiness.

Evidence of the third explanation for women's more limited access to credit—outright discrimination by lenders—is more mixed and typically comes with a raft of caveats. Over the years, researchers have adapted a theoretical framework originally developed to explain discrimination in hiring practices to study bias in lending. Statistical discrimination in lending occurs when a financial institution uses inferences about the behavior of people with certain demographic characteristics such as race or gender as proxies for the likelihood of default on a loan. The other framework, so-called "taste-based" discrimination, takes place when the terms of a loan are negatively influenced by the lender's preference or "taste" to discriminate against certain groups, even if it is financially disadvantageous to the lender. Much of the research concludes, as did the sub-Saharan Africa study mentioned above, that neither statistical nor taste-based gender discrimination exists for women-owned businesses because enterprises with the same characteristics (particularly those of the same size) face equivalent obstacles in accessing external finance whether they are owned by men or women. Digging deeper, however, reveals a more nuanced picture of how discrimination in lending unfolds.

A number of studies indicate that while women-owned businesses may not be rejected for loans more than businesses owned by men, the terms on which those loans are granted, such as interest rate, tenor, or the requirement of a guarantor, can differ significantly. A recent experiment among 334 loan officers from a bank in Turkey revealed that both male and female loan officers were likely to make loan approval for a woman-owned business conditional on the presence of a guarantor—even when an identical loan application is submitted with only the gender of the entrepreneur changed. In studying the roots and practices of discrimination, the literature consistently refers to the complexity of understanding roles, motivations, and behaviors and how they affect the decision to grant a loan and on what terms. Some recent studies point to the way in which discrimination might serve to exacerbate differences between groups through "self-fulfilling prophecies." If lenders believe that women are riskier clients and that their businesses should remain small, they will collect less data on them and invest less in monitoring their actual performance. Behavior that starts out as taste-based discrimination inexorably becomes statistical discrimination.

The academic literature suggests that while there is gender bias in the allocation of credit, there is also the possibility of both systemic and individual change. One study that looked at bank lending to entrepreneurs in twenty-six countries across Europe found that female-managed firms had a lower probability of receiving a loan than male-managed firms. If the women's businesses received a loan, they were also more likely to be charged higher interest rates than male-managed firms of similar size and creditworthiness. However, the authors note that the degree of discrimination was highly correlated with the level of development of the financial sector. Where financial regulation was more mature, especially with regard to collateral, bankruptcy, and other laws that ensured women's equal access to property rights, there was far less scope for discriminatory behavior.

Unconscious bias at the individual level also plays a demonstrable role in the allocation of credit, but there are hopeful indications that, as seen with the training program at KCB, it need not be a permanent barrier. One study examined the impact that being assigned to a same sex or opposite sex loan officer had on both the terms of a borrower's first loan and his or her access to finance over time. The researchers concluded that when a variety of observable factors were controlled for, the playing field was substantially leveled. For purposes of the study, roughly half of a bank's small business borrowers were assigned a loan officer of the opposite sex for their first loan transaction. A majority of the loan officers were female, while an even larger proportion of the borrowers were male. The loan officer's professional experience working with clients of the opposite sex and the degree of competition within his or her own working environment (i.e., small branch versus large branch) as well as within the local banking market had a notable impact on loan terms and conditions. If a loan officer was relatively less experienced in working with customers of the opposite sex and worked in a small branch or a county with little competitive pressure from other banks, an opposite sex borrower was far more likely to be charged a significantly higher interest rate and to receive less attractive terms for the loans (e.g., smaller loan size and shorter tenor). While 65 percent of first-time clients in good standing applied for a second loan, clients assigned to opposite sex loan officers were much less likely to apply for a second loan, either choosing to limit their access to finance or starting over with a new bank. The researchers' analysis included statistical tests to determine whether this bias could be attributed to loan officers' preference for borrowers of the same sex or disfavoring those of the opposite sex. They concluded that it was purely "unfavorable treatment of out-group borrowers because of initial prejudice about the other group." But they also note that this initial "taste-based" discrimination "fades away with gender-specific learning on the job."

These findings are consistent with the study of the Turkish bankers referenced earlier. The researchers point out that, while Turkey boasts a mature, competitive banking sector and has few legal obstacles to women's entrepreneurship, it is also a country with very conservative gender norms. For purposes of this experiment, male and female loan officers and supervisors were asked to assess actual, previously processed first-time loan applications from "gender-neutral" companies (no beauty parlors or construction companies that might give away the gender of the borrower) carrying a fictitious male or female entrepreneur's name. As previously discussed, when an application was presented from a woman entrepreneur, the loan officer was up to 30 percent more likely to condition approval on a guarantee for the loan than when the same application had been presented with a man's name attached. The requirement for a guarantee was concentrated among less experienced loan officers in more junior positions—the ones who, in real life, made the initial screening decisions. As a result, there was a greater likelihood that a woman borrower with a strong business proposition but no guarantor would be denied access to credit. The benefit of using real loan applications is that we can see how the loans had actually performed, and this is where the business cost of discrimination becomes apparent. The requirement of a guarantor was concentrated among good loans that in real life had not carried the extra security of a guarantee and had been repaid on time. In addition to increasing the possibility of losing the business altogether, adding a guarantee to a loan makes it more expensive to the client, and adds monitoring and servicing costs for the bank. Gender discrimination was literally costing the bank money.

Both studies reached a comparable finding that offers cause for hope and perhaps provides guidance on the way banks can act on their professed interest in expanding access to finance to women-owned businesses. Both studies found that biased lending behavior disappeared as loan officers gained greater experience. In the Turkish bank experiment, the participants who were at the superintendent level did not place stricter requirements on women's loan applications; likewise, in the earlier study, researchers found that once loan officers gained sufficient experience working with clients of the opposite sex, they no longer imposed discriminatory loan terms. Once a loan officer had processed more than nine loans with opposite sex borrowers, which typically took about a year and a half to complete, the loan officer no longer showed evidence of discriminatory behavior. As we saw with the KCB branch staff who received the gender sensitization training, gender bias was very real and perhaps unconscious, but it was not static.

The studies were also strikingly similar in noting gender bias on the part of both male and female loan officers. Another recent contribution to the literature on gender bias in the allocation of credit—in this case a review of the loan approvals and repayment performance of close to half a million loans by one thousand male and female loan officers across several Spanish banks—illuminates this finding further. In assessing loan applications, all loan officers received the same in-house credit scoring information and an internally generated recommendation to approve or reject the application based on the bank's credit policies. It was left to the loan officer's discretion whether to accept the recommendation or claim an exception. Women loan officers followed the recommendations produced by the internal system more frequently than men, and loans approved by female loan officers had delinquency rates 15 percent below those approved by their male counterparts. Before chalking up this result to gender stereotyping about women "following the rules" or suggesting that women are more risk averse than men, the researchers took a deeper look at the incentives for and against compliance. Indeed, acting on the recommendations of the internal risk assessment process was a rational decision by women because their careers were more severely penalized for mistakes. Over the course of her career, if a woman was responsible for a high proportion of delinquent loans—particularly if she had approved those loans as exceptions to the recommendation by the credit assessment system—she was much more likely to be demoted or fired than was a man with the same level of performance. The loans that were included in this study were made between 2002 and 2013. After the financial crisis of 2008, the banks, working with Spain's financial regulators, eliminated the option for loan officers to override the risk system's recommendation. Perhaps not surprisingly, the gender difference in subsequent loan performance was also removed, and male and female loan officers performed similarly.

TECHNOLOGY TO THE RESCUE?

As with so many of the knotty issues impeding the development of a more inclusive financial system, technology has the potential to break the logjam preventing MSMEs' access to capital. Companies known as fintechs sit at the intersection of financial services and technology and cover the gamut of digital financial services from payments to asset-backed lending. While not all fintech companies are necessarily driving explicitly toward greater financial inclusion, the sheer volume and diversity of data generated through digital technology have reduced the cost of providing credit and widened the circle of companies eligible for loans.

The explosion of digital lending (and resulting overindebtedness) to low-income consumers throughout Africa in particular has made many apprehensive. Much greater supervision and consumer protection efforts are needed to ensure that these loans are disbursed transparently and responsibly and that low-income households are not put into even greater distress. However, these concerns should not obscure the exciting developments that fintech companies have started to make in the realm of MSME credit. Digital technology can drive down the cost of each step in the lending process, from sourcing capital to credit assessments to collections, with the potential to increase lending to these companies. While the various fintech business models are still nascent, there is also great potential for technology to enable women-owned businesses to circumvent the barriers to accessing growth capital.

The dearth of available data on MSMEs' creditworthiness through credit reporting agencies makes traditional credit assessment methods costly and inefficient for banks, particularly for relatively small loans. Using alternative sources of data such as phone and utility payments to make credit decisions—especially if those payments are made through a cell phone—can be a boon for women. These technological disruptions can be particularly powerful in countries where credit reporting systems exclude the kinds of information that allow women to demonstrate their creditworthiness. With access to all of a potential borrower's smartphone data, including payments, SMS and text history, GPS data, and personal contacts, lenders can construct algorithms to predict ability to repay; some even include a business's social media ratings as an indicator of customer satisfaction. The popularity of some of these models has begun to wane in the US and other developed markets because of concerns regarding data privacy, but in many developing countries where MSMEs face greater capital constraints, use of these models—together with data privacy protocols—is growing.

Online peer-to-peer (P2P) lending platforms are emerging as a faster, less cumbersome route to connect women business owners to potential lenders than traditional banks. Through such platforms, borrowers post unsecured loan requests, providing information about their businesses and their plans to use the requested funds, while investors on the platform make lending decisions based on the information provided. For example, Amartha, an Indonesian fintech, extends microloans to rural women entrepreneurs using a P2P platform and a proprietary credit scoring system based on the women's performance with informal financial transactions.

Loans for three, six, or twelve months start at $225 and increase as borrowers build their credit history. Amartha establishes the borrower's creditworthiness, assigns her a credit score, approves her loan application, and then posts the loan request on its online marketplace platform. Individual lenders establish an investment account with Amartha and then choose a loan to fund that is based on a customer profile that includes a credit score, the loan size, and the region where the borrower is located. Amartha handles disbursement of the funds and the investor-lenders receive weekly payments of principal and interest and can monitor the status of the loan online.

Globally, P2P lending totaled $67.9 billion in 2019. While most of this lending took place in the US and other developed markets, this mode of lending is gaining ground throughout the emerging markets and has been particularly beneficial for women business owners. Early research indicates that P2P platforms may not yet be a panacea for women borrowers, though. A recent statistical analysis of peer lending in China revealed that loans to female borrowers carried a lower likelihood of default and a higher expected profit than loans to their male counterparts. However, women borrowers are not rewarded for this superior financial performance with a higher funding success rate. Rather, to be funded, women business owners must demonstrate greater levels of proven profitability than men and pay higher interest rates.

Other fintech companies are addressing the issue of information asymmetries head-on by effectively embedding themselves inside the business. As more MSMEs use online tools for business processes such as ordering, payments, and deliveries, a lender can integrate its technology into the company's systems to design a more flexible repayment schedule that mirrors the company's cash flows. The lender can also schedule automated deductions for loan payments, reducing both the risk of default and the overall cost of the loan, even varying the amount and timing of payments to match seasonal business variations. By using a company's own data and financial performance rather than relying on collateral, these fintechs can make unsecured digital loans an attractive option for women-owned businesses.

Kenya's Kopo-Kopo is one of the best-known emerging markets companies using this business model, partnering with M-Pesa to provide even very small business owners a platform with the capability to accept digital payments. Once the merchant has a ninety-day payments track record on the platform, it is eligible for a cash advance; the business owner selects the percentage of daily sales to dedicate to repayments via the Kopo-Kopo digital platform, and Kopo-Kopo automatically deducts that percentage each time the customer receives a payment, effectively eliminating delinquent loans.

Supplier credit has also seen technological disruption, allowing small businesses to avoid inventory shortages due to lack of funding while expanding the value chains of larger companies. Tienda Pago, a fintech operating in Mexico and Peru, has a particularly innovative approach, partnering with fast-moving consumer goods distributors (e.g., Coca Cola , AB InBev) that supply small shops or *tiendas*. Tienda Pago pays the distributors directly for inventory ordered by the shop owner through its mobile platform. The shopkeeper, in turn, repays Tienda Pago as the merchandise is sold. Although the loans are extended to the shopkeeper in inventory rather than in cash, Tienda Pago reports the shop owner's payment record to the credit bureau, allowing her to build a credit history.

Technological disruption is also making inroads into the traditional asset-based lending market. The new digital factoring business model—such as that used by Lidya, a fintech operating in Nigeria and Eastern Europe—allows MSMEs to upload digital invoices from a larger, more creditworthy company to a factoring platform. In exchange, the MSME receives a cash advance equal to the amount of the invoice minus interest and a processing fee. The factoring company then takes care of collecting the invoice from the larger company and builds a credit history and understanding of the company's cash flows for future lending.

The fintech companies mentioned here are just a few of the companies throughout the developing world that have made MSME finance possible—and profitable—in ways that have eluded legacy banks. In recent years, banks' traditional reticence about lending to MSMEs has been compounded by regulatory pressures to both derisk credit portfolios and hold larger capital reserves against MSME loans. At the same time, the massive influx of data offers lenders unprecedented potential to assess risks and understand the dynamics of even the smallest businesses. The magnitude of the financing gap, particularly for women-led MSMEs, combined with their economic growth and job creation firepower, cries out for a fresh look. Partnerships between the lean digital players that can deploy technology and data without the fiduciary responsibilities of deposit-taking institutions and banks with capital in search of digital business models and badly needed returns offer a tantalizing win-win proposition.

6 MAKING THE BUSINESS CASE FOR MANAGING RISK

Access to a safe place to save and the ability to borrow are understandably the first two pillars of financial inclusion. Savings accounts allow women in particular to accumulate money to improve their family's health, nutrition, and education or to make investments in their businesses or farms. Loans, on the other hand, can provide the growth capital that lifts a business to the next level and creates more jobs. But all of that hope and progress can be wiped out if people do not also have the tools to manage the inevitable risks that all of us face. That's where insurance comes in. At some level we will have failed those billions of underbanked people if we don't ensure that they have some way to protect their gains in the face of a health emergency or a natural disaster. Yet fewer than 20 percent of low-income are people currently insured. The vast majority must still rely on largely inadequate informal risk management strategies that are estimated to be ten times less effective than formal protection mechanisms.

The story of Nandini, a client of one of India's leading microfinance institutions, illustrates both the limits of credit-only microfinance and the tragic shortcomings of informal risk management. Nandini owned a business she'd built literally out of the trash. She collected used bottle caps and then, with a $100 loan from a microfinance institution, bought a machine that would flatten the caps, which she then sold back to soft drink distributors in her city. After several quite prosperous years, Nandini's husband became ill and could no longer work. The money she earned from the bottle cap business wasn't enough to cover his medical costs, and the family was forced to take their eldest daughter out of school so she could work to supplement the family's income. Ultimately, Nandini wasn't even able to repay the balance on her microfinance loan, and the family slipped deeper into poverty. In the midst of all the other calamities she faced, the cash she had painstakingly saved under her mattress was stolen. Without a safe place to save her money and insurance to protect her family from a health emergency—in other words, a full financial safety net—she could not protect her hard-won success.

Low-income people face the same risks—illness, loss of property, and susceptibility to both natural and man-made disasters—as the rest of the population. Yet the symptoms of poverty leave low-income families far more vulnerable to those risks and less able to cope with and recover from a crisis when it does occur. Low-income families live under constant threat of the sudden death of a breadwinner or the destruction of a crop by drought or flood; this uncertainty typically leaves them unwilling or unable to take even small risks or to benefit from income-generating opportunities that might improve their situations. Jayshree Vyas, managing director of India's SEWA Bank, likens poverty to the children's game of Chutes and Ladders: the sudden death or illness of a family member is the risk most likely to unravel a low-income family's progress up the ladder toward prosperity, sending it back down the chute into deeper poverty.

Among the many risks they face, low-income households around the world cite health emergencies as the biggest risks to their financial security. In the face of such an emergency, low-income households resort to different, often detrimental coping strategies. They tend to deplete their savings, sell their assets, decapitalize their businesses (and if the husband and wife each have a business, the woman's is typically liquidated first), borrow from friends or family, or reach out to expensive informal money lenders. As we saw in Nandini's story, when faced with a health emergency, children—more often girls than boys—are taken out of school to earn money for the family in times of emergency, or the family reduces food consumption (again, women and girls make the first sacrifices.) Although women typically earn less income than men and have less ownership and control of property, they tend to be the primary caretakers for their families. As such, they utilize their earnings to improve the care and standard of living of their households—which may be good for their family members, but often comes at the expense of further growth and investment in their businesses. In fact, selling assets in response to health emergencies is the most frequently cited reason low-income women's informal businesses fail.

All of this points to women as an important target market for insurers, but we cannot forget how important the element of trust is for women to engage with a financial service provider. And insurance is notoriously the least trusted financial product: the South Africa–based Centre for Financial Inclusion surveyed customer attitudes about various financial products throughout the developing world and insurance reliably came in dead last. Clearing the hurdle of trust will be essential to tapping this largely unserved market. Additionally, insurance is a complex financial product for people at all income levels to understand; the old adage that "insurance isn't bought, but only sold" has become cliché for precisely this reason. So designing simple products that are easy to understand, enroll in, and make claims against is indispensable to reaching low-income customers. In addition, since premiums paid on insurance products destined for this customer base must be as low as possible, insurers will need to keep costs as low as possible as well.

This juggling act between offering appropriate risk coverage for women and overcoming their lack of awareness, even distrust, of the product is often seen when examining the real-life experiences of women. Hiyam is a client of Microfund for Women, the leading microfinance institution in Jordan, but, more important, she represents a success story for their innovative Caregiver microinsurance product. She had become something of a poster child for Caregiver (known as *Afitna* in Arabic) based on her own experience and referrals she made to other women. Hiyam was well known for running a popular local business selling cold cuts and sausages to her neighbors in Amman, Jordan's capital city. She moved to Amman from Beirut at age seventeen for a marriage arranged by her parents, and as a young woman, she found it difficult moving to a new country alone without a family around her for support. She and her husband, Hasan, moved to different parts of the city a few times before settling in North

Marka, where she and Hasan live with their youngest son, Ahmed. Their three older sons, Muhammad, Tareq, and Mustafa, are all married and also live nearby in Marka.

Early in her marriage, Hiyam wanted to contribute to the household's income, but also put aside some money she could call her own. Since Hasan worked as a butcher, the cold cuts and sausages business seemed like a natural way to bring in some extra money. Soon she could not keep up with the demand for her sausages, and when a neighbor introduced her to Microfund, she borrowed 300 Jordanian dinars (approximately $400) to purchase more raw materials. Her business continued to grow, and she repaid the first loan quickly in order to borrow a larger amount to purchase machinery to increase her productivity. Sure enough, using the grinders and casing machines she was able to produce six kilos of meat in just three days, when it would have taken her fifteen days before.

Then, just as the prospects for Hiyam's family and her business seemed brightest, Hasan had a heart attack. He was rushed to the hospital for emergency open-heart surgery, after which he went through a long, slow recovery. Hiyam recalled that, while Hasan recuperated, the family's savings were wiped out. Not only did the family struggle financially from the loss of his income but her business also suffered as she traveled back and forth to the hospital, caring for Hasan and bringing him meals, which weren't provided by the state-run hospital. (In many developing countries, only direct medical care is provided by the hospital, particularly if they are public facilities. Everything else—food, much of the nursing care, pharmaceuticals, in some countries even the bed linens—must be brought in by the family.) All of these expenses wreaked havoc on Hiyam's family's finances, and the situation deteriorated further when the doctors told Hasan he could no longer work after he was discharged from the hospital. Overnight, Hiyam's contribution to the household became the family's sole source of income.

Once Hasan was home from the hospital, Hiyam began rebuilding her business and was gratified (and relieved) to know that demand for her sausages was still strong. With another loan from Microfund for additional machinery and an expanded kitchen, she looked forward to selling her products beyond her immediate neighborhood. It was clearly a great source of pride that she had kept her business afloat; no matter how tenuous their finances had become, Hiyam had been able to keep her children in school throughout this household crisis. Her role in the home had changed, and the bond with her husband had strengthened, but her responsibilities as both caregiver for Hasan and sole financial provider for the family left her little time to expand her business further. An unexpected health emergency can so easily dim aspirations, as Hiyam shelved her expansion plans, limiting her business to pick-up orders at the apartment.

This is indeed a story of resilience, but setbacks can strike again, and two years later, Hasan suffered a second heart attack. This time, however, Hiyam had an insurance policy from Microfund that was bundled with her loan and that allowed her to cover the cost of Hasan's hospitalization without having to dip into the savings she had painstakingly rebuilt following his earlier illness.

The type of insurance policy that allowed Hiyam and her family to weather her husband's second heart attack with their finances intact is known in the insurance industry as "hospital cash." It's often one of the first types of insurance offered to new client segments because it's fairly easy to understand and it offers the insurance company an opportunity to build trust with clients since claims can be easily verified and settled quickly. There is a truism in the insurance industry that the prompt payment of claims is the easiest way to win clients' trust, so insurers often choose personal accident insurance or hospital cash as an early product offering because they offer the opportunity for more frequent payouts. Additionally, products with more frequent payouts provide more opportunities for contact between insurer and client.

While some countries make social security programs available to the low-income population, these plans are often woefully inadequate. They typically do not cover out-of-pocket expenses on medicines or medical equipment. Travel costs are frequently cited as a reason that low-income people do not seek medical attention, even with government or military coverage of the actual medical care itself. Even in Rwanda, with its exemplary Universal Health Coverage plan, there is strong interest in a

Caregiver-like hospital cash policy because transportation costs often preclude people traveling to receive the care they need. A raft of other, nonmedical costs also accompanies a family member's hospitalization, including loss of income and transportation; in some countries, bribes are all too often required to receive adequate hospital care. These hidden expenses can represent almost 70 percent of the total cost of a hospitalization, exposing low-income families to an even greater risk of falling deeper into poverty.

THE BUSINESS CASE BEHIND CAREGIVER

The organization known today as Microfund for Women was established in 1994 as a pilot program by Save the Children to provide microcredit to women in two Palestinian refugee camps in Amman. It became an independent Jordanian NGO in 1996 and today is the largest microfinance institution in Jordan, with a 34 percent market share and sixty branches throughout the country. The organization provides both financial services and nonfinancial training services to 146,000 clients, 96 percent of them women. It's particularly impressive that in a country with only 12 percent female labor force participation, 73 percent of Microfund's staff and management are women.

The Caregiver policy was considered quite revolutionary at the time Microfund introduced it, requiring extensive discussions with Jordan's insurance regulator, but it has many elements that have come to be standard for successful microinsurance initiatives. In designing Caregiver, Microfund was particularly attentive to three interrelated priorities: the product had to meet women's needs, operating costs for both the insurer and Microfund as distributor should be minimized, and premiums had to be kept low so that the product would be affordable to the broadest number of clients. Microfund bundled an unsecured microfinance loan together with an insurance policy that provided a cash payment (roughly equivalent to a day's earnings for most of its clients, including Hiyam) for each day that any member of the borrower's family had an illness requiring a hospital stay. The policy was mandatory for all Microfund borrowers in order to spread risk among the largest number of people, which lowered premiums and avoided adverse selection. Clients make a single monthly payment that includes their loan installment and a premium payment roughly equivalent to $1.50. Microfund conducted extensive training on Caregiver for both field staff and customers, including a radio campaign and a very popular comic book series that illustrated various scenarios for when the product could be used and how to file a claim.

An important contributor to Caregiver's success was Microfund's partnership with Jordan Insurance Company, a composite insurance company that offers both life and nonlife insurance products. Building trust with low-income clients who are new to insurance is an absolutely essential prerequisite, so mainstream insurance companies frequently partner with organizations that have long-standing trust relationships with clients, as Microfund does, to serve as distribution partners.

Senior executives at Jordan Insurance first met the Microfund team in 2006. Mazen Nimri, then the company's deputy general manager, remarked at the time that he had never heard of the idea of providing insurance to very poor people, and his initial response to Microfund's proposal was that it was crazy. He had concerns that the company could not price a product for low-income women that would be both affordable and still cover the administrative costs of maintaining the policies. He also thought that insurance products would never be accepted by Microfund's client base of low-income women because of their lack of insurance education, and possibly for religious reasons. Nevertheless, he was very impressed by the Microfund team's passion to serve their clients and, motivated largely by a sense of corporate social responsibility, agreed to move forward with a fairly simple product, a credit life policy that would repay a borrower's debt in the event of her death. This is the most common microinsurance product, offered by most microfinance institutions around the world, although it is usually quite unpopular with clients. Even though the client is paying the premium, it's the lender, not the client or her family, who is the policy's beneficiary. Mazen and his colleagues heard the clients' dissatisfaction and worked with Microfund to reshape the product into a term life insurance policy that still ensured that Microfund's loan would be repaid if the borrower passed away, but it also paid an additional amount to the borrower's survivors. They also added a "living benefit" that paid a lump sum to the borrower in the event her spouse died while her loan was still outstanding. Jordan Insurance has written more than $1.6 billion in insurance for Microfund clients since launching the revised policy (called "*Himaya*," or "safekeeping" in Arabic) and today over 300,000 families—close to two million people—are covered, with both organizations sharing the premium revenue.

The willingness of Jordan Insurance to collaborate and make changes to the Himaya product was a major factor in Microfund's decision to approach them about Caregiver. Over the years Microfund had consistently heard concerns from their clients about the adverse financial consequences of a family health emergency or the impact of woman's own loss of income during childbirth. Clients were saving as much as 10–15 percent of monthly income as a reserve against these health-related emergencies. These women's capacity to maintain such significant savings balances indicated that they could handle a financial tool to help them manage these risks. Microfund briefly considered extending a loan to existing customers in good standing to cover these types of emergencies, but soon realized that insurance would be a more efficient way to manage risk. The only real point of disagreement between Microfund and Jordan Insurance was the former's insistence that there be no exclusions—for preexisting conditions or pregnancy—to the policy. Jordan Insurance thought allowing pregnancy-related coverage would be a costly mistake in light of the demographics of Microfund's client base. Microfund, on the other hand, saw it as a critical indicator to clients that the organization had heard their concerns about managing income they lost from their businesses immediately before and after giving birth. In the end, Jordan Insurance came to see the lack of exclusions as a useful way to keep premiums low, since collecting data to monitor exclusions can be quite costly.

Mazen Nimri is quick to point to the level of trust and transparency that built up between Microfund and Jordan Insurance over the years as the most critical success factor in bringing the Caregiver to market. They learned a lot about each other's business and their respective motivations and incentives while they designed and then revamped the Himaya policy together. Mazen mentioned the Caregiver claims process as an example of the unusual degree of trust that existed between the two organizations. Even though Jordan Insurance was underwriting the Caregiver risk, the company delegated the payment of claims to Microfund first for claims of up to three nights' stay (now up to ten nights' stay). This not only keeps administrative costs down, but, through its specialized claims unit, Microfund has established strong relationships with hospitals throughout Jordan and has successfully managed to keep fraudulent claims to less than 2 percent.

For Jordan Insurance, the collaboration with Microfund introduced the company to a new market for which it established a considerable "first mover" advantage and has brought them steadily increasing premium income since the product launched. For Microfund, Caregiver has increased the organization's already high levels of customer loyalty. In addition, in a market where the regulator strictly limits the way that microfinance institutions can generate revenue, Microfund's portion of the Caregiver premium income represents a valuable source of noninterest earnings.

After successfully collaborating with Microfund for over ten years, Mazen Nimri speculated about why Jordan Insurance Company's entry into the microinsurance segment was such a success, saying, "Maybe we had the courage to take risks as a smaller insurer that larger companies won't take." The size of the potential microinsurance market merits another look from those larger insurers, though: the 3.8 billion uninsured low-income customers could generate premium income estimated at $30–$50 billion. As Jordan Insurance and a few other insurers (e.g., AIG Uganda) have discovered, it's not all that difficult to reach scale, particularly by marketing to women, who have a strong preference for enrolling their husbands and children in addition to themselves, particularly for health coverage.

EXPANDING ACCESS TO INSURANCE WITH TECHNOLOGY

As in all areas of financial inclusion, digital financial services are lowering the cost of delivering microinsurance products, in addition to disrupting various steps in the insurance process. The situation on the ground is changing rapidly, but some areas of fruitful technological innovation have included instant customer enrollment via cell phone—a process made even easier as countries introduce a national form of identification, such as the Aadhaar in India, or premium collection by mobile payment. Weather satellites and drone photography have revolutionized claims verification for weather-related agricultural insurance. And the enormous volume of data available through mobile phones allows the analysis of low-income people's behavioral and social data to establish risk profiles far beyond anything previously available through actuarial data. BIMA, one of the pioneers of digital insurance, now offers simple life, personal accident, or hospital insurance coverage on a "pay as you go" basis. PAYG products can be purchased in monthly blocks, and customers can "re-up" without penalty. Based on cell-phone top-up plans, the PAYG insurance product serves to build trust and familiarity with insurance products.

PULA, an insurtech company in Kenya, offers a unique approach to agricultural insurance. It has specifically targeted women, who make up more than 40 percent of smallholder farmers in Africa. The company works with agricultural input providers to bundle an insurance voucher with each bag of seed or fertilizer purchased by a smallholder farmer. The farmer then registers for insurance with a local agricultural dealer, who is typically a trusted source of information and advice. The company monitors rainfall as the growing season starts. If a farmer has a failed planting due to drought, the farmer can claim another bag of seed to replant. At the end of the season, PULA measures yields, and if a farmer's yield is below the average for the area, she or he receives a cash payout. To date, PULA has insured over one million African farmers and is now exploring expansion to other emerging markets.

Beyond their role in microinsurance, women represent an enormous growth opportunity for insurers, particularly women in the ten largest emerging economies. In a groundbreaking report titled *She for Shield*, AXA, one of the world's largest insurance companies, estimates that women in these developing markets will represent half of the global women's insurance market by 2030. There are two principal drivers of this growth. As women throughout the emerging markets gain greater access to tertiary education, enter the labor force, and earn a higher income, they have greater ability to spend on insurance, and they also have a greater willingness than men to pay for insurance to protect themselves and their families from risks they might face. Women all along the socioeconomic spectrum tend to purchase coverage for their entire family. This not only provides insurers with a greater opportunity to cross-sell, it also decreases costs by limiting distribution to a single decision-maker.

The business opportunity for insurers to cultivate this underserved market is clear. Since women are chronically underinsured, just reaching gender parity on a single product, life insurance, would yield $500 billion in new written premiums. But there is also a business case for banks to integrate insurance into their offerings to women clients. Including insurance coverage in a bank's women's proposition—particularly health- or education-related coverage—can increase per customer profitability and savings account balances and lower the rate of nonperforming loans. Women not only seek ways to mitigate business risks, they are typically household risk managers as well. Insurance products that provide women with a claim payment that allows them to make loan repayments or otherwise smooth consumption not only see improvements in the credit quality of their loan portfolios but may also see improved rates of customer retention.

CAN INSURANCE EMPOWER WOMEN?

The Caregiver collaboration between Jordan Insurance and Microfund for Women has been a commercial success. Similarly, having ready access to cash at the time of a health emergency to cover medical costs or make up for lost income can keep a family from tumbling down the chute into poverty. But can we say that women are empowered as a result of their access to this insurance product, and can that empowerment be measured through the changes identified under the Chen empowerment framework? Did the Microfund clients undergo *material* changes to their income thanks to Caregiver? Did they change *cognitively* as a result of learning the mechanics of the insurance product, one of Jordan Insurance's initial misgivings? Did the product affect their *relationships* within the household or community or their own *perceptions* of themselves?

Conversations with Microfund clients and an analysis of five years' worth of customer data indicate that women experienced both tangible material benefits and important changes in confidence and self-perception. Nearly all the women used the cash payout from the insurance policy to repay debt or avoid going into debt as a result of their own or a family member's hospitalization. Families with the Caregiver policy were able to maintain overall consumption levels and were better able to cover health-related expenses such as prescription medicines or medical dietary requirements. Those women who had income-generating businesses either by themselves or with their husbands said that by protecting the money they generated for their families, the insurance policy affected the women's decision-making role within the household. One woman interviewed summed up a perspective echoed by others: "When a woman has money, she's strong in everything. If you have an opinion and your husband has an opinion, you can talk to him. Money is strength." Although several women noted that their husbands treated them better now that they played an active economic role in the household, many also mentioned that this change had not come without complications. As one woman ruefully told us, "He knows I have money, so he will save his own money for himself and will wait for me to get my own money to spend on the house."

Several of the women linked their ability to manage the risk of an unexpected health emergency with a greater capacity to plan for the future. Perhaps no one better exemplified this determination and sense of vision than a woman who had recently used a Caregiver claim to cover household expenses while she recuperated from a cesarean section delivery. With her infant daughter in her arms, she smiled and said to the interviewer, "I plan to keep working. I plan to improve my business. I will open a store."

7 A CALL TO ACTION

One billion women are entirely shut out of the formal financial system, roughly another billion are woefully underserved by that system, *and* another 30 million women-led businesses are without sufficient access to capital to flourish: these are the stark numbers behind the current state of women's financial inclusion. Whether you see these statistics—and the women they represent—as an unmet economic development challenge, an untapped source of inclusive economic growth, or an exciting commercial opportunity, enabling women's access to the full suite of financial services is a daunting challenge. But it is also an achievable one.

Like any truly worthwhile goal, full women's financial inclusion will only be realized by creating a rallying point for a broad set of stakeholders. The changes that are needed and the obstacles that stand in the way of that change are too complex and intertwined for any single actor to tackle alone. Governments will have to shape policies that are solutions-driven and address the differences in women's access to and usage of both technology and financial services. Financial service providers will need to take off the blinders that keep them from seeing women as valued clients while they persist in offering products that are designed for men's needs and preferences by default. That goes for "old-line" financial institutions like banks and insurance companies, but it applies equally to mobile money providers and fintech companies, which are already baking gender bias into their decision-making algorithms. And now that digital technology and the data made available through the cell phone have completely changed the playing field, no woman need ever again be considered too remote or too invisible to be served affordably. The caveat, of course, is whether telecom companies and mobile money providers have the will to get phones into women's hands.

Interestingly, systemic change that can often take decades has been implemented with great speed out of the necessity created by a pandemic. The COVID-19 crisis has provided an unexpected nudge (or perhaps more of a kick in the pants) for many of the players that can be most instrumental in driving the necessary change. This is certainly the case for digitization, where governments have been leading the way with digital COVID-19 relief payments. Some agencies are motivated by the efficiency and transparency that digitization offers, some by the ability to track funds and spending patterns among recipients, and some by the financial inclusion impacts. The case for digital payments was strong before the COVID-19 outbreak, and after social distancing became a universal priority, contactless payments were truly in everyone's interest.

India's COVID-19 relief program provides a particularly enlightening comprehensive case study for the ways in which crisis conditions can be used to accelerate change. India leveraged two important elements of its existing financial infrastructure to provide timely pandemic relief to millions. The first element was a national unique identification number called the Aadhaar number, which can be used to meet KYC requirements to open a bank account; today over 95 percent of the Indian population have an Aadhaar number (obtaining one is voluntary). The Aadhaar was combined with a basic, no-frills bank account, the Jan Dhan account, explicitly designed to serve previously unbanked low-income Indians. When the pandemic first broke out, the Indian government specifically targeted relief payments to low-income women. With digital identification already in place, the government was able to distribute three months of digital cash transfers into the Jan Dhan accounts of approximately 200 million low-income women within one week. Twenty-five million new accounts were opened, primarily by women, to receive these government payments, although a further inclusion opportunity still remains with the roughly 176 million poor women who do not yet have a Jan Dhan account. While owning a bank account represents only one step in the process toward financial inclusion, the speed with which the Indian government was able to deploy relief payments on a large scale, through women, because of their prior investments in the "architecture" of financial inclusion is impressive.

All of us can contribute to building a more inclusive financial system, and we can start by demanding more of the financial institutions to which we entrust our money. If achieving gender equality is important to you, you can insist that your bank, your insurer, or your money manager does its part—or take your business elsewhere. Here's a sample of what each player in this grand, interdependent global coalition can do to make women's financial inclusion not just an aspiration but a reality.

REGULATORS AND POLICYMAKERS MUST LEAD THE WAY

So many of the barriers to women's financial inclusion are systemic and will require a rethinking of the fundamental elements of a country's financial infrastructure in order to see significant results. These changes cannot be addressed, let alone implemented, without the active engagement of policymakers and regulators. The first step they must take is to acknowledge that no policy is truly gender neutral; in practice, policy changes that are dubbed "neutral" typically default to the male perspective. When weighing the costs and benefits of any policy initiative it is essential to measure the likely consequences—intended and otherwise—for both men and women. Prioritizing policy changes that promote women's financial inclusion can have a positive impact on the reach and effectiveness of a much broader range of economic objectives as well. All too often governments sideline financial inclusion as an instrument to achieve social or developmental goals without recognizing its broader macroeconomic potential. Yes, building an inclusive financial system that brings more women into the formal economy can lead to greater economic growth, reduce income inequality, and foster financial stability. But it can also improve the effectiveness of traditional macroeconomic or fiscal policy tools. Let's say that a country's central bank wants to stimulate the economy by lowering interest rates. It stands to reason that the more people operating in the formal financial system that can be touched by those rate changes, the more successful they'll be as a stimulus.

Here are some things regulators and policymakers can do to promote women's financial inclusion.

- *No need to reinvent the wheel.* In recent years, many developing country governments have launched comprehensive, national-level efforts to systematically accelerate financial inclusion. At least fifty countries have completed national financial inclusion strategies, with another twenty preparing to do so; some countries, such as Nigeria and Tanzania, are on the second versions of their national plans. While these national financial inclusion strategies may differ in the targets they set or the populations they seek to include, certain initiatives have been successful in many countries and could provide direction for other nations to follow suit. These include the implementation of simplified "know-your-customer" (KYC) procedures that allow banks and mobile network operators to open financial accounts for customers with minimal documentary requirements and verification of identity. These procedures often accompany the creation of basic or no-frills bank accounts, which provide an easy, low-cost entry into the formal financial system. These basic accounts and simplified opening procedures have been particularly important in the context of COVID-19, along with waived or reduced account fees, to serve the millions of previously excluded people who have opened accounts to facilitate government relief payments.

- *Collect both demand- and supply-side gender-disaggregated data.* One finding in particular resounds across all national financial inclusion strategies: the need for more and better data about who is and who isn't included (demand-side data), as well as data on products and services that are available to them and who is providing them (supply-side data). Further, since many national plans specifically identify underserved women as a target segment, the lack of gender-disaggregated financial inclusion data has emerged as a significant obstacle. Regulators cannot establish measurable financial inclusion goals or track progress against them without an accurate reading of access to financial services.

While global demand-side surveys such as the Global Findex database are an invaluable resource, national-level surveys can provide policymakers with a more nuanced picture of the state of women's financial inclusion in their own countries. On the supply side, regulators should require financial service providers to report on the kinds of products being used and by whom and how frequently; the channels used (e.g., ATMs, branch, cell phone); and the effectiveness of different types of providers (e.g., banks, microfinance institutions, mobile money providers). All these data allow policymakers to design informed and effective policy interventions. This information is essential to develop baselines and then to set and monitor targets. Banks can use the data to improve their product offerings to women. Such a change in regulatory reporting requirements will undoubtedly require a combination of political will and changes to systems, processes, and ways of thinking. But there really is no other way to make informed financial inclusion policy decisions without a clear understanding of the differences in women's and men's financial behavior.

- *Include explicit women's financial inclusion targets in national strategies.* Governments that have made the most progress toward financial inclusion in recent years are those that have held themselves accountable to national financial inclusion strategies with clearly stated targets. However, some of those same governments have started to realize that overall inclusion goals will not be achieved if they don't make concerted efforts to reach women. Nigeria's original national financial inclusion strategy, adopted in 2012, laid out ambitious goals for building a more inclusive financial system; the plan called for broadening access to a range of banking products to the 64 percent of its adult population that was financially excluded but did not set explicit goals for expanding women's access to finance. In 2018, recognizing that women, together with youth, made up a significant majority of those who remained excluded, Nigeria revised its national strategy and has subsequently adopted a broad-based framework of actions and the metrics to track them, all designed to eliminate the gender gap in financial inclusion by 2024.

- *Repeal discriminatory laws.* Although gender norms are slow to change, economic transformation is impossible without a conducive legal framework. Since women's financial inclusion is higher in countries with legal equality between men and women, governments should, at the very least, eliminate financial discrimination if it is enshrined in the legal code. The World Bank's *Women, Business and the Law* report finds that 115 countries prevent women from running a business the same way as men. The slowest pace of reform is in laws pertaining to the management of property and other assets, but 167 countries still have at least one law restricting women's economic opportunity.

- *Ensure universal access to identification documents.* Access to a national identification document is perhaps the single greatest enabler of financial inclusion. At a minimum, a verifiable national identification document is required to open a bank account and forms the backbone of most KYC regimes. Ideally, all people—and particularly women and girls—would also have documentary proof of registration for birth, death, marriage, and divorce as keys to unlocking the ownership and inheritance of land, property, and other assets. Not surprisingly, those are the same documents that allow women to vote and to be counted in a national census.

  Identification and mobile phone ownership, increasingly the passport to financial inclusion, are closely linked; the lack of appropriate identification documents exacerbates and reinforces the gender gap in mobile phone ownership. SIM card registration that requires government-recognized identification documents is mandatory in over 150 countries. According to the Global Findex, the most popular use of identification documents in sub-Saharan Africa is to obtain a SIM card or mobile phone service, but women are 9 percent less likely than men to have the necessary documents.

- *Expand phone ownership and mobile connectivity.* Addressing the gap in smartphone ownership provides a natural opportunity for governments to partner with the private sector, and the telecom industry in particular. With the acceleration of digital financial services in response to COVID-19, governments should consider distributing phones or subsidizing airtime for the poorest populations. They should also take aggressive measures to reduce the high cost of data packages by building the necessary infrastructure to support expanded mobile connectivity and encourage greater competition among mobile providers.

- *Implement longer-term changes to the credit infrastructure.* For a woman entrepreneur, having title to property, even jointly with a spouse, makes it possible for her to use collateral to obtain a bank loan. Additional reforms that include the establishment of a movable collateral registry multiply the types of assets that she can use as security for a loan. If banks can register a security interest in a car or a piece of business equipment, or even in the accounts receivable generated by a business—in other words, assets women are more likely to own than land—it enhances women entrepreneurs' likelihood of receiving bank loans. Banks frequently cite a lack of pertinent information about micro, small, and medium-sized enterprises (MSMEs) as a reason for declining to lend. Governments can support the establishment of public or private credit bureaus that collect microfinance loan repayment data and utility and retail payment track records. Expanding the types of financial data reported to credit bureaus enables women to build a credit history that banks can rely on to perform due diligence. When Afghanistan's credit registry began collecting repayment data from microfinance institutions, for example, banks were able to incorporate this information into their credit approval processes. As a result, loans to women based on credit registry data went from a negligible amount to 20 percent of total loans extended in only eighteen months.

- *Direct digital government social benefits and wage payments to women's accounts.* Digitizing the delivery of government benefits and wage payments is a proven way to promote women's financial inclusion; 80 million women around the world opened their first account to accept public sector payments, and another 35 million became formally banked in order to receive a government salary. There is an opportunity to have an even greater impact on formal financial inclusion since 60 million unbanked women worldwide still receive government social benefits in cash. But the benefits of targeting women as recipients of social welfare transfers extend beyond financial inclusion. Research indicates that more family members benefit when such transfers are paid directly to women; nevertheless, many countries still default to the "head of household," more often the man, as the recipient of such payments.

- *Increase the gender diversity of regulatory bodies.* The banking industry has a well-documented gender diversity problem, with women representing only 16.5 percent of senior management and 24 percent of bank board directors. But their gender performance looks positively robust in comparison to that of supervisory bodies. Only 8 percent of central banks have a female governor, and most do not meet their own internal gender or diversity targets, much less report on them. Women make up roughly 17 percent of supervisory agency boards despite the association of more women on these boards with greater banking sector stability. In this period of intense economic uncertainty, policymakers must be even more concerned with serving those who are most vulnerable. That kind of empathy at the policy level will require inclusive representation and diversity of thought and experience. As Georgetown University law professor Chris Brummer writes about the lack of Black appointees to US financial regulatory bodies, "The actions of financial regulators have repercussions for how and whether the racial wealth and income inequality gaps are addressed. And the absence of African American voices deprives the community from having members present in decisions that not only impact them directly, but are often made in their name." As with diversity and inclusion efforts, simply appointing regulators with different backgrounds who represent different communities isn't sufficient to drive greater financial equality. Female regulators and others from previously excluded groups must be listened to and their recommendations endorsed, so that their lived experience is valued as a resource for developing better policies.

FINANCIAL SERVICE PROVIDERS ARE LEAVING MONEY ON THE TABLE

Financial service providers across the board—from traditional legacy providers such as banks and insurers to newcomers such as fintechs and mobile money providers—have failed to optimize the commercial opportunity in serving women clients. In its latest *Women in Financial Services* report, Oliver Wyman refers to women as "the single largest underserved group of customers in financial services . . . [whose] needs consistently are not being met." The report then goes on to identify at least a $700 billion revenue opportunity that financial service providers are missing *each year* by not serving women customers. To put that figure into context, the money that Oliver Wyman estimates banks, insurers, and asset managers are leaving on the table represents 5–20 percent of total revenue for each of those sectors of the industry and far exceeds the annual revenue of the world's leading financial institutions. The world's largest bank, China's Industrial & Commercial Bank, had 2019 revenues of $123.6 billion; JP Morgan Chase was in the number two position at $114.6 billion. As financial service providers respond to technological disruption and the economic fallout of the pandemic, this overlooked market opportunity is long overdue for serious consideration.

Though low-income women constitute only a portion of that underserved customer group, they represent a loyal client base with an increasingly influential role as buyers for themselves and other members of their households. Many of the adaptations and new ways of thinking that financial service providers embrace in order to serve more affluent women will be equally applicable to women in other income segments. In particular, acknowledging that the design, marketing, and delivery of financial products and services is not gender neutral will open up possibilities to serve all women regardless of their socioeconomic status. Applying a "gender lens" will not only result in products that do not simply default to men's preferences, it can lead to better products for men as well.

Here are some things financial service providers, whether cutting-edge fintechs or traditional banks and insurance companies, can do to realize the commercial potential of women's financial inclusion:

- *Develop a "women's proposition" with buy-in from executive leadership.* Research indicates that women across the economic spectrum are often put off by their interactions with financial service providers. Equally consistent, though, is women's stated desire to build relationships of trust with people within financial institutions; indeed, trust is the single greatest obstacle for women in choosing to engage with a financial product or service. While women clients are not a monolith and customer segmentation for both business and personal banking customers is essential, there are some common characteristics that span segments.

  Organizations that have built successful, trusted platforms for women-led businesses and women retail customers have done so by offering both financial and non-financial services. For instance, women generally want more information than men do and prefer taking more time to decide on significant financial actions. And, across the socioeconomic spectrum, women express less experience, confidence and knowledge than men in making financial decisions. Women are also more likely to have limited access to networks than men, but also tend to engage more deeply than men with those relationships. Paying attention to these types of customer insights, rather than making assumptions about women's preferences or, even worse, slapping a pink "wrapper" on a man's product, can lead financial service providers to rethink the design and delivery of financial service.

  To reinforce the understanding of women-led businesses as a distinct segment with a well-defined value proposition requires buy-in from the board and executive management and clear communication and training for employees about the importance of this customer segment and how best to serve them. The most successful women's banking programs also institute clear accountability to a new or existing business unit and KPIs to track both individual and institutional performance.

- *Collect gender disaggregated data, then use it.* Mandating the collection of gender-disaggregated data is a recommendation for policymakers, but even in the absence of a formal policy, financial institutions should be collecting and analyzing such data on their own as the key to getting inside the heads of women customers. Chances are that financial service providers already have a lot of information about their women clients that they simply aren't using. In this age of big data, there are ample tools for spotting patterns in the way women transact or trends in usage that might diverge from their male counterparts' usage. Using those tools can shape product design and delivery and customer service. It can also influence other managerial decisions, such as the recruitment of women agents or the choice of delivery channel strategies, leading, for instance, to locating satellite services in retail shops frequented by women.

- *Encourage "discouraged borrowers."* A substantial body of academic literature is dedicated to the behavior of the "discouraged borrower," the term for an otherwise creditworthy borrower who declines to apply for credit, assuming their application will be rejected. Virtually all of this research—whether explicitly focused on the gender dimension or not, whether in developed or developing markets—finds that majority female–owned firms are more likely to be among the discouraged group. There is some evidence that there is not a significant gender gap in small business loan applications from owners with relatively little business experience. However, as men and women entrepreneurs gain more business experience, the gap in their willingness to apply for credit widens substantially. Likewise, majority male–owned businesses that have been operational for longer (i.e., they are not startups) also tend to apply for loans more than female-owned businesses of long standing. But here's the kicker: this same research indicates that majority women–owned businesses are no more likely to be rejected for loans than those owned by men. The fact that acceptance rates are the same suggests that if more women applied for loans, more might receive them.

Building an ongoing connection with a financial institution, particularly with an individual relationship manager, appears to be effective in coaxing both reluctant men and women borrowers to take that first step and apply for a loan. And if that relationship is established long before a discussion of credit is even on the table, the financial institution is able to learn more about the enterprise over time, enhancing the chances that an eventual loan application will be approved. Research indicates that men entrepreneurs are more likely than women to build that banking relationship early on by seeking banking services other than credit. For their part, women entrepreneurs can reward those financial service providers who are ready to build those relationships, rather than assuming that a loan won't be granted and self-selecting out of this opportunity for business growth.

• *Build more gender diverse teams.* The importance of gender diversity within the ranks of financial service providers can't be emphasized enough—and neither can the benefits. All financial service providers would benefit from greater gender diversity so that they can take advantage of the full range of perspectives necessary to win with women customers. Women in leadership positions in the banking sector correlate with everything from fewer nonperforming loans to higher profitability and even to greater levels of innovation. Despite the linkage between gender diversity and greater innovation, however, fintech companies in the aggregate have not emerged as a disruptive force for gender equality. Only 14 percent of fintech company directors are women, and nearly 40 percent of fintechs globally have no women on their boards. But diversity and inclusion efforts must go beyond the mere recruitment and retention of people from underrepresented groups. Instead, the different experiences of previously excluded people must be tapped as sources of learning about how to improve a company's core business. Research shows that teams that value a variety of views outperform both homogeneous teams and diverse teams that tamp down differences in favor of group cohesion.

MOBILE MONEY PROVIDERS ARE ON THE FRONT LINES OF INCLUSION

Much of the recent gains in financial inclusion are directly attributable to cell-phone access and the proliferation of financial services delivered through mobile phones and the internet. Conversely, the persistence of the gender gap in access to finance is exacerbated by inequality in access to smartphones. The acceleration of digital financial services in response to the COVID-19 crisis, particularly through digital government relief payments, offers an unprecedented opportunity to expand access to cell phones.

- *Once women have the phones, make sure they use them by employing women agents.* A mobile money provider's agent network is the retail "human face" that drives the successful business model. Offering both "tech" and "touch" is particularly important to women customers; women agents and banking correspondents have proven adept at listening to customers' needs, answering questions related to digital technology or the products on offer and, overall, establishing trust with both men and women.

- *Expand the number of cash-in/cash-out (CICO) points.* Despite the growing reach of mobile money, roughly 90 percent of transactions in the developing world are still completed in cash. To put this figure in context: one-third of transactions in the US are settled in cash, while Sweden is on track to become the first cashless society, with only 12 percent of transactions taking place in cash. The growth trajectory of digital financial services throughout the developing world will still require a sufficient number of CICO points so that people can continue to make cash payments until enough products and services can be paid for digitally. The experience with M-Pesa in Kenya demonstrates that the inclusion impact of digital financial services is directly linked to the proximity of agents. For women, who, because of social norms or household responsibilities, often have less mobility than men, the convenient location of CICO points is an even more significant factor in driving inclusion. In the context of COVID, where social distancing is so vital, the India Post Bank has found an innovative solution: it has equipped postal workers with handheld devices to provide doorstep cash withdrawal based on a customer's biometric ID.

WE NEED MORE RESEARCH ON THE LIVES OF WOMEN, NOT HOUSEHOLDS

The constant refrain from nearly everyone associated with women's financial inclusion is the need for more data, better data, and a deeper understanding of women's financial lives. Researchers have a vital role to play in expanding the evidence base for both the policy and business case for women's financial inclusion, and the impact of expanding women's access to finance. There are two urgent contributions that researchers can make to the fight for women's financial inclusion:

- *Apply a gender lens to all research, using only gender-disaggregated data whenever possible.* If researchers around the globe were to make only one methodological change in the service of expanding women's access to finance, it would be to stop using the "household" as an economic unit. The members of a household—both men and women—experience interventions differently. Without assessing those impacts individually, it is impossible to test with accuracy the effectiveness of a given policy or product feature.

  In fact, breaking out the effects of a research experiment or a government program by gender should extend beyond the household as well. A team at the Brookings Institution recently performed a meta-analysis of studies undertaken to assess the effectiveness of a wide range of entrepreneurship programs (e.g., training, financing, mentorship, technical assistance). The authors found that only a very small subset of the prior research had either addressed women entrepreneurs as a target group or disaggregated the programs' results by gender, leading to the lukewarm conclusion that programs to encourage entrepreneurship had little or no effect on women. The Brookings team expanded the number of programs reviewed, including only those where women entrepreneurs had been engaged, and the effects of the intervention were broken out by gender. This more nuanced analysis revealed training *plus* one of the other interventions was always more effective for women than just training alone. This more "gendered" review also clearly pointed to the impact that women's unpaid care obligations had on the success of any entrepreneurial support. Even entrepreneurship programs that offered multiple forms of support would have limited effect on the growth of a woman's business if they did not also address her child care responsibilities.

- *The seminal piece of research on gender-based violence and financial inclusion has yet to be written.* Over the years, there have been bursts of research activity around this topic, and some excellent, although often inconclusive, work has been produced. In some contexts, women's financial inclusion might be seen as a threat to the man's role, increasing household conflict. In others, women's financial inclusion might increase both women's agency and opportunity. It's a very sensitive topic that requires specialized training and methodology, as well as careful research design. Partnerships between researchers and local, trusted parties are essential to open, candid information gathering.

The extra care and discretion required for this important research should not, however, be a barrier to further work. It is imperative that we gain a complete understanding of the potential that greater access to finance has to expand or narrow a woman's physical and emotional autonomy. To realize all of the benefits of women's financial inclusion, we must fully comprehend how we can first, do no harm. This is a research topic worthy of serious time and attention.

BECOMING A CONSCIENTIOUS CONSUMER OF FINANCIAL SERVICES

A well-known *Harvard Business Review* article on the "female economy" notes that "financial services wins the prize as the industry least sympathetic to women and one in which companies stand to gain the most if they can change their approach." With 84 percent of US consumers expecting companies to stand up for women's rights, users of financial services—women themselves, as well as male allies who recognize the importance of equality of access to finance—can use their clout to reward those financial service providers that are more inclusive. It's easy enough to check whether a bank or insurance company has a gender-diverse leadership, but with just a little more research, the attentive consumer can determine whether a financial service provider is genuinely supportive of women as both clients and leaders. One source for this information is the Bloomberg Gender Equality Index, which measures the gender equality performance of 325 companies around the world, including nearly all global banks and insurers as well as a significant number of local providers in both developed and emerging economies. The Index assesses performance across five dimensions: female leadership and talent pipeline, equal pay and gender pay parity, inclusive culture, sexual harassment policies, and pro-women brand.

Likewise, a woman should exercise her right to work with an investment adviser who treats her with dignity and answers as many questions as she wants to ask. Globally, women control $11.2 trillion in investable assets ($5 trillion in the US alone). Yet wealth management firms seldom tailor their products and services to meet women's needs and investor profiles. In fact, 67 percent of the more than six thousand women interviewed by Coqual in the US, UK, China, Hong Kong, India, and Singapore reported being misunderstood by their financial advisers. And on the occasions when wealth advisers do consider women, they tend to see them as either widows or wives, ignoring the fact that 62 percent of women with a net worth of $500,000 or more have built their own wealth.

Research also indicates that women want their values reflected in their investments, so wealth management firms might also consider encouraging their wealth managers to adopt a "gender lens" investment strategy. A "gender lens" or "gender-smart" approach incorporates gender into investment analysis to uncover missed opportunities; investments typically include companies that are led by women or that offer products and services that are inclusive of and empowering to women. To date, approximately $8 billion has been deployed using a gender lens in both public and private capital markets. There are over fifty publicly traded gender lens investment funds, including Fidelity's Women's Leadership Fund, an equity mutual fund that invests in publicly listed companies that prioritize and advance women's leadership.

WE ARE ALL RESPONSIBLE FOR BUILDING THE FUTURE WE WANT

In addition, to being a more informed and active consumer of financial services, there are a few things that everyone can do to work toward a more inclusive financial system:

- *Start financial education early.* Much of the research on the efficacy of financial education taught in the classroom raises legitimate questions about its value. However, there is a general consensus that teaching children life skills such as budgeting and money management as early as kindergarten can have lifelong benefits. In both developed and developing countries, women, regardless of their socioeconomic status, report being less confident than men when it comes to making personal financial decisions. Ensuring that girls are financially literate and have savings accounts in their own names can start them out on the path to financial health.

- *Work to protect women from financial abuse.* Access to and control over financial resources empowers women in myriad ways; the Chen empowerment framework traces the wide-ranging changes that can take place in a woman's life when she controls financial assets. Financial empowerment affects a woman's material circumstances, her relationships with others, and her self-esteem. It is no wonder, then, that a woman's systematic financial *dis*empowerment by a spouse or partner would have equally far-reaching consequences. By controlling a woman's ability to acquire, use, and maintain financial resources, destroying her credit rating and, often, preventing her from working, an abuser leaves a woman little option but to remain in or return to an abusive situation. While financial abuse accompanies physical abuse in nearly all cases of intimate partner violence, programs for survivors do not always address both facets of the problem. Donations and other financial assistance to those organizations that do help survivors of intimate partner violence through financial empowerment programs are of vital importance. They also serve as a powerful acknowledgment of the transformative effect of financial autonomy on a woman's life and that of her children.

Equality of access to financial services is not a cure-all. Women's financial inclusion will not, on its own, fix all the economic and social problems facing the world today. But just for a moment, imagine what might be possible if all stakeholders—regulators, financial service providers, researchers, consumers—not only did their own part but worked collaboratively toward the goal of financial inclusion. Let's start with the most fundamental element of inclusion, a safe place to save in a savings account. And since we're imagining, let's make sure that this account can be accessed through a smartphone. If a government were to make it a priority for each of its citizens to have a savings account, ensuring that everyone had an individual identification and a cell phone in their own names, and then if that government corralled the nation's banks and cell-phone providers into compliance, the country would see an increase in net savings that could be used for productive investment (think infrastructure) and consumption. All the people gaining access to those savings products and their families would be more resilient in the face of shocks (think pandemics and global warming). The women, in particular, would likely invest in the health and education of their family members, which in turn would lead to higher economic growth because this well-educated population would be able take greater advantage of technological changes. And we know that educating girls pays off in numerous other ways over the course of their lives and their own children's lives. If this far-sighted country made a special effort to ensure that farmers opened savings accounts, they would be able to invest more and increase crop yields, which would improve food security in that country as well. As our hypothetical country's financial system became more robust and inclusive, there's a strong chance that its poorest citizens would see their incomes grow at a faster pace than the country's average. And that means you've taken a big step toward reducing income inequality.

This is just an illustration of the potential behind universal access to a digital savings account. We haven't even looked at what additional crop insurance might do for farmers or how health insurance might insulate families from unexpected loss of income. We haven't touched the job creation and economic growth that would be generated if regulators and banks got serious about closing the financing gap for MSMEs. On their own, the smartphone and identification documents could drive tremendous progress, but when harnessed to a financial account they could do even more. In the end, that is the greatest promise of financial inclusion. Financial services alone may not solve the world's problems, but they ennoble and empower women and men, girls and boys, by putting the tools to improve their lives into their own hands.

Acknowledgments

I want to extend my special thanks to those who played a critical role in making this book a reality. Mariska van Aalst poured her passion for women's equality into helping me shape my random ideas into a successful book proposal. My agent, Jessica Papin, of Dystel, Goderich & Bourret, encouraged me to write a book long before these ideas had coalesced and then served as a formidable champion for the manuscript. Karen Wolny was a patient, insightful collaborator who consistently challenged me to bring my clearest thinking and best writing to the page. Finally, I am particularly grateful to Emily Taber of the MIT Press for her advocacy of my ideas and the stories of the women in this book throughout the entire publication process.

The book draws heavily on the work of Women's World Banking, so I owe a special debt to the organization's founders: the late Esther Ocloo, Mary Okelo, Ela Bhatt, and Michaela Walsh. Thanks are also due to the staff, directors, and funders—both past and present—who have carried the founders' work forward into the organization's fifth decade. My gratitude, too, to Women's World Banking's partner financial institutions and their leaders (including Jennifer Riria, Mercedes Canalda, Muna Sukhtian, Aniqa Sandhu, and Uzoma Dozie) for proving that it's good business to serve low-income women.

My appreciation also goes to Silvia Prina, who, even while guiding me through the growing body of research on financial inclusion, highlighted the need for more data and further analysis of women's experiences, particularly with regard to the relationship between financial inclusion and gender-based violence. I also want to thank Naila Kabeer for taking time away from writing her own book to share her insights on the true drivers of women's economic empowerment. I'm also grateful to Ratna Sahay for her support of this book when it mattered most. Moreover, many of the book's policy recommendations are based on her work on the linkage between women's participation in the financial system and greater financial stability.

The Rockefeller Foundation's Bellagio Center is where this book began its journey. I am grateful to Claudia Juech for awarding me a valued fellowship, and to Pilar Palaciá for making my residency at the center so productive and, possibly, the most perfect month of my life.

And my final thanks go to my husband and stepson whose encouragement, love, and good humor got me through the dread and despair of finishing a book against the backdrop of the year 2020.

Notes

INTRODUCTION

p. xiv   **financial inclusion data have been collected**   Asli Demirgüç-Kunt, Leora Klapper, Dorothe Singer, et al., *The Global Findex Database 2017: Measuring Financial Inclusion and the Fintech Revolution* (Washington, DC: World Bank, 2018).

p. xiv   **it improves outcomes for families and wider communities as well**   Esther Duflo, "Women Empowerment and Economic Development," *Journal of Economic Literature* 50, no. 4 (December 2012): 1051–1079, https://doi.org/10.1257/jel.50.4.1051; World Bank, *World Development Report 2012: Gender Equality and Development* (Washington, DC: World Bank, 2011), http://hdl.handle.net/10986/4391.

p. xv   **$2 trillion in new deposits flowing into the financial system**   James Manyika, Susan Lund, Marc Singer, et al., *Digital Financial Inclusion for All: Powering Inclusive Growth in Emerging Economies* (New York: McKinsey & Co., September 2016), 43–44.

p. xv   **women-led micro, small, and medium-sized businesses**   "MSME Finance Gap," Data Sites, SME Finance Forum, https://www.smefinanceforum.org/data-sites/msme -finance-gap#field-data-sites-tabs-tab-2.

p. xv   **$50 billion in insurance premium income annually**   AXA Group, Accenture, and International Finance Corporation, *She for Shield: Insure Women to Better Protect All* (Washington, DC: IFC and AXA Group, 2015), 4.

p. xvi   **addressing the disparity between men's and women's access to finance**   Goksu Aslan, Corinne Deléchat, Monique Newiak, et al., "Inequality in Financial Inclusion and Income Inequality" IMF Working Paper WP/17/236 (Washington, DC: International Monetary Fund, 2017); Martin Čihák and Ratna Sahay, "Finance and Inequality," IMF Staff Discussion Note SDN/20/01 (Washington, DC: International Monetary Fund, 2020).

p. xvi   **96 million people are expected to be pushed into extreme poverty**   UN Women, "Women Bear the Brunt, as COVID Erodes Progress on Eradicating Extreme Poverty," *UN News*, September 2, 2020, https://news.un.org/en/story/2020/09/1071502.

p. xvi   **contraction in the economy is directly tied to declines in women's labor force participation**   World Bank, *Global Economic Prospects* (Washington, DC: World Bank, January 2021).

p. xvii **suffered 54 percent of global job losses** Anu Madgavkar, Olivia White, Mekala Krishnan, et al., "COVID-19 and Gender Equality: Countering the Regressive Effects" (New York: McKinsey & Co., July 15, 2020), https://www.mckinsey.com/featured-insights /future-of-work/covid-19-and-gender-equality-countering-the-regressive-effects.

p. xvii **on any list of growth-oriented policy options** World Bank, *Global Economic Prospects*.

p. xvii **mobile banking services, are closely related to women's labor force participation** Madgavkar et al., "COVID-19 and Gender Equality."

p. xvii **more of the family benefits from the choices she makes** World Bank, *World Development Report 2012*.

p. xvii **women are loyal, profitable customers for financial service providers** Michael J. Silverstein, Kate Sayre, and John Butman, *Women Want More: How to Capture Your Share of the World's Largest, Fastest-Growing Market* (New York: HarperBusiness, 2009).

p. xvii **showed that broad-based inclusion is possible** Zachary Kazzaz, *Emergency Disbursements during COVID-19: Regulatory Tools for Rapid Account Opening and Oversight* (San Mateo, CA: Glenbrook Partners, 2020).

PART I: WOMEN'S FINANCIAL INCLUSION: CLEARING THE ROADBLOCKS TO EMPOWERMENT

p. 1 **shut out from all formal financial services** Asli Demirgüç-Kunt, Leora Klapper, Dorothe Singer, et al., *The Global Findex Database 2017: Measuring Financial Inclusion and the Fintech Revolution* (Washington, DC: World Bank, 2018).

p. 1 **as a necessary condition for success** Leora Klapper, Mayada El-Zoghbi, and Jake Hess, "Achieving the Sustainable Development Goals: The Role of Financial Inclusion," working paper, CGAP (Consultative Group to Assist the Poor) and UNSGSA (United Nations Secretary-General's Special Advocate for Inclusive Finance for Development) (Washington, DC: CGAP, April 2016), https://www.cgap.org/sites/default/files /Working-Paper-Achieving-Sustainable-Development-Goals-Apr-2016_0.pdf.

CHAPTER 1: THE ROAD TO FINANCIAL INCLUSION

p. 5 **typically from the poorest households** Asli Demirgüç-Kunt, Leora Klapper, Dorothe Singer, et al., *The Global Findex Database 2017: Measuring Financial Inclusion and the Fintech Revolution* (Washington, DC: World Bank, 2018).

p. 6 **43 percent have a mobile money account** Kelsey Piper, "What Kenya Can Teach Its Neighbors—and the US—about Improving the Lives of the 'Unbanked,'" *Vox*, September 11, 2020, https://www.vox.com/future-perfect/21420357/kenya-mobile-banking -unbanked-cellphone-money.

p. 6 **adequately addressing these customers' needs** Demirgüç-Kunt et al., *Global Findex Database 2017*.

p. 6 **"a first step toward broader financial inclusion"** website of the World Bank, "Financial Inclusion Overview," https://www.worldbank.org/en/topic/financialinclusion/overview.

p. 7   **twenty more are in the course of doing so**   Nimal Fernando and Robin Newnham, *National Financial Inclusion Strategies: Current State of Practice* (Kuala Lumpur, Malaysia: Alliance for Financial Inclusion, June 2018), https://www.afi-global.org/sites/default /files/publications/2018-06/National%20Financial%20Inclusion%20Strategies.pdf.

p. 7   **collecting data through the Global Findex database**   Demirgüç-Kunt et al., *Global Findex Database 2017.*

p. 7   **women are more financially excluded than men**   Demirgüç-Kunt et al., *Global Findex Database 2017.*

p. 8   **the unbanked typically achieve lower levels of education**   Demirgüç-Kunt et al., *Global Findex Database 2017.*

p. 8   **women's share of the world's illiterate population hasn't change in more than twenty years**   UNESCO, "Women and Girls' Education—Facts and Figures,"http://www .unesco.org/new/en/unesco/events/prizes-and-celebrations/celebrations/international -days/international-womens-day-2014/women-ed-facts-and-figure.

p. 8   **employment in the formal labor force is a strong predictor of having a bank account** Demirgüç-Kunt et al., *Global Findex Database 2017.*

p. 8   **typically as home-based workers or street vendors**   Florence Bonnet, Joann Vanek, and Martha Chen, *Women and Men in the Informal Economy—A Statistical Brief* (Manchester, UK: Women in Informal Employment: Globalizing and Organizing, 2019), https:// www.ilo.org/wcmsp5/groups/public/---ed_protect/---protrav/---travail/documents /publication/wcms_711798.pdf.

p. 8   **such as food security, health, and education**   World Bank, *World Development Report 2012: Gender Equality and Development* (Washington, DC: World Bank, 2011), http:// hdl.handle.net/10986/4391.

p. 8   **from their fathers' improved financial circumstances**   Bohong Liu, Ling Li, and Chunyu Yang, *Gender Equality in China's Economic Transformation* (Beijing: United Nations System in China, 2015), http://www.un.org.cn/uploads/20180326/2063f2493 b160cd25bb79ce54fe8dcc1.pdf.

p. 9   **All these qualities are present with digital financial services**   Women's World Banking, *Digital Savings: The Key to Women's Financial Inclusion?* (New York: Women's World Banking, 2015), http://www.womensworldbanking.org/wp-content/uploads/2015/08 /Digital-Savings-The-Key-to-Women's-Financial-Inclusion_WomensWorldBanking.pdf.

p. 9   **33 percent disparity between men's and women's use of mobile money accounts**   Oliver Rowntree et al., *The Mobile Gender Gap Report 2020* (London: GSM Association, 2020), https://www.gsma.com/mobilefordevelopment/wp-content/uploads/2020/05/GSMA -The-Mobile-Gender-Gap-Report-2020.pdf.

p. 9   **cultural norms represent greater obstacles for women than for men**   Ratna Sahay et al., "The Promise of Fintech: Financial Inclusion in the Post COVID-19 Era," IMF Departmental Paper No. 20/09 (Washington, DC: International Monetary Fund, July 2020), https://www.imf.org/en/Publications/Departmental-Papers-Policy-Papers/Issues /2020/06/29/The-Promise-of-Fintech-Financial-Inclusion-in-the-Post-COVID-19-Era -48623.

p. 10 **substantially more men purchasing their own devices than women** Rowntree et al., *The Mobile Gender Gap Report 2020.*

p. 10 **"family disapproval" as the principal obstacle to smartphone ownership** Rowntree et al., *The Mobile Gender Gap Report 2020.*

p. 10 **breakdown of long-established "purity" and courtship norms** Giorgia Barboni, Erica Field, Rohini Pande, et al., *A Tough Call: Understanding Barriers to and Impacts of Women's Mobile Phone Adoption in India* (Cambridge, MA: Evidence for Policy Design, Harvard Kennedy School, 2018), https://wappp.hks.harvard.edu/publications/tough -call-understanding-barriers-and-impacts-womens-mobile-phone-adoption-india.

p. 11 **passport to financial inclusion** Shalini Unnikrishnan, Jim Larson, Boriwat Pinpradab, et al., "How Mobile Money Agents Can Expand Financial Inclusion," Boston Consulting Group, February 14, 2019, https://www.bcg.com/publications/2019/how-mobile -money-agents-can-expand-financial-inclusion; Piper, "What Kenya Can Teach Its Neighbors."

p. 11 **as a reason for remaining unbanked** Demirgüç-Kunt et al., *Global Findex Database 2017.*

p. 11 **if M-Pesa were no longer available to them** William Jack and Tavneet Suri, "Mobile Money: The Economics of M-PESA," NBER Working Paper 16721 (Cambridge, MA: National Bureau of Economic Research, January 2011), https://www.nber.org/system /files/working_papers/w16721/w16721.pdf.

p. 12 **driven largely by mobile money services** Jack and Suri, "Mobile Money."

p. 12 **34 percent of all accounts registered globally** Nika Naghavi, *State of the Industry: Report on Mobile Money 2019* (London: GSMA, 2020), https://www.gsma.com/sotir /wp-content/uploads/2020/03/GSMA-State-of-the-Industry-Report-on-Mobile-Money -2019-Full-Report.pdf.

p. 12 **twenty times the reach of a physical banking facility** Naghavi, *State of the Industry.*

p. 13 **purchase airtime for their cell phones** Unnikrishnan et al., "Mobile Money Agents"; WorldRemit, "All about Mobile Money," https://www.worldremit.com/en /mobile-money; GSMA, *Mobile Money Definitions* (London: GSMA, July 2010), https:// www.gsma.com/mobilefordevelopment/wp-content/uploads/2012/06/mobilemoney definitionsnomarks56.pdf.

p. 13 **uses the remainder to top up her cell-phone airtime** Unnikrishnan et al., "Mobile Money Agents"; WorldRemit, "All About Mobile Money"; GSMA, *Mobile Money Definitions.*

p. 14 **"run their own basic personal intermediation services"** Stuart Rutherford, "The Poor and Their Money: An Essay about Financial Services for Poor People," working paper (Manchester, UK: University of Manchester, Institute for Development Policy and Management, January 1999), http://www.globalization101.org/uploads/File/The_Poor_and _Their_Money.pdf.

p. 14 **reasons beyond their shared membership** Michael Aliber, "The Importance of Informal Finance in Promoting Decent Work among Informal Operators: A Comparative Study of Uganda and India," Social Finance Working Paper 66 (Geneva: International Labour Office, 2015).

p. 14　**"everyone else is obeying the rules"**　Rutherford, "The Poor and Their Money," 26.

p. 14　**at the end of the cycle**　CARE, "VSLA 101 / FAQs on Village Savings and Loan Associations (VSLAs)," 2020, https://www.care.org/our-work/education-and-work/micro savings/vsla-101.

p. 15　**to save rather than as a means to borrow**　Beatriz Armendáriz and Jonathan Morduch, *The Economics of Microfinance,* 2nd ed. (Cambridge, MA: MIT Press, 2010).

p. 15　**build up savings or pay down debt**　Daryl Collins, Jonathan Morduch, Stuart Rutherford, et al., *Portfolios of the Poor: How the World's Poor Live on $2 a Day* (Princeton, NJ: Princeton University Press, 2009), 10–14, 24–26.

p. 15　**reluctant to dip into savings they had already managed to accumulate**　Collins et al., *Portfolios of the Poor,* 27–31.

p. 15　**draw down hard-won savings**　Collins et al., *Portfolios of the Poor,* 32.

p. 16　**keep money out of temptation's way**　Collins et al., *Portfolios of the Poor,* 31.

p. 16　**"a lack of tools"**　Collins et al., *Portfolios of the Poor,* 25.

p. 16　**poor-quality financial tools available to them**　Collins et al., *Portfolios of the Poor,* 12.

p. 16　**sale of household or business assets to satisfy monthly contributions**　Armendáriz and Morduch, *The Economics of Microfinance*, 74–76.

p. 17　**over $500 billion in ROSCA transactions were completed worldwide in 2015**　Statista, "Value of Rotating Savings and Credit Association (ROSCA) Transactions Worldwide in 2015, by Country," Statista Research Department, February 2017, https://www.statista .com/statistics/756059/value-of-rosca-transactions-by-country.

p. 17　**"also explain why ROSCAs stay together"**　Armendáriz and Morduch, *The Economics of Microfinance*, 76.

p. 17　**"as a way to harness their own power"**　Caroline Shenaz Hossein, *Politicized Microfinance: Money, Power, and Violence in the Black Americas* (Toronto: University of Toronto Press, 2016), 331–332.

p. 18　**community-based place to save as well as to borrow**　Armendáriz and Morduch, *The Economics of Microfinance*, 80–82

p. 18　**the ROSCA as a way to maintain savings discipline**　Aliber, "The Importance of Informal Finance in Promoting Decent Work among Informal Operators."

p. 18　**account balances are not insured**　Advait Rao Palepu, "Chit Funds: India's Oldest Form of Banking Seeks a New Look," *BloombergQuint*, December 17, 2019, https://www .bloombergquint.com/business/chit-funds-indias-oldest-form-of-banking-is-getting -a-fintech-makeover.

p. 19　**a genuine path out of poverty**　Muhammad Yunus, *Banker to the Poor: Micro-Lending and the Battle Against World Poverty* (New York: PublicAffairs, 1999), 1–3, 61.

p. 19　**without reliance on either formal employment or charity**　Ananya Roy, *Poverty Capital: Microfinance and the Making of Development* (New York: Routledge, 2010), 24.

p. 19　**in the event of default on the loan**　Niclas Benni and Rahul Barkataky, "The Role of the Self Employed Women's Association (SEWA) in Providing Financial Services to Rural Women" (Rome: Food and Agriculture Organization of the United Nations, 2018), http://www.fao.org/3/CA2707EN/ca2707en.pdf; "History of Microfinance, Small

Loans, Big Revolution," Newsroom, BNP Paribas, August 17, 2017, https://group.bnp paribas/en/news/history-microfinance-small-loans-big-revolution; Roy, *Poverty Capital*, 26.

p. 20 **struggled to achieve even a 1 percent ROA** Women's World Banking, network member financial reporting template, 2006–2010.

p. 20 **"an important antidote to poverty"** Roy, *Poverty Capital*, 22.

p. 20 **"Micro-credit is one such means"** Ole Danbolt Mjøs, "Nobel Peace Prize Award Ceremony Speech," transcript (Oslo: Norwegian Nobel Institute, December 10, 2006), https://www.nobelprize.org/prizes/peace/2006/ceremony-speech.

p. 21 **$15.3 billion in assets invested in MFIs** Symbiotics, *2018 Symbiotics MIV Survey: Market Data & Peer Group Analysis* (Geneva: Symbiotics, September 2018), https://symbioticsgroup.com/wp-content/uploads/2018/10/Symbiotics-2018-MIV-Survey.pdf.

p. 21 **140 million microfinance borrowers** Greta Bull, "The Best Laid Plans . . . CGAP's Response to COVID-19 (Coronavirus)," *CGAP Blog*, April 16, 2020, https://www.cgap.org/blog/cgaps-response-covid-19-coronavirus.

p. 21 **"predatory capitalism, and ever-expanding debt"** Roy, *Poverty Capital*, 5.

p. 22 **the MFI was reaching a very low-income population** Richard Rosenberg, "CGAP Reflections on the Compartamos Initial Public Offering: A Case Study on Microfinance Interest Rates and Profits," Focus Note 42 (Washington, DC: CGAP, June 2007), https://www.cgap.org/sites/default/files/researches/documents/CGAP-Focus-Note-CGAP-Reflections-on-the-Compartamos-Initial-Public-Offering-A-Case-Study-on-Microfinance-Interest-Rates-and-Profits-Jun-2007.pdf.

p. 22 **larger individual loans to microentrepreneurs** Women's World Banking, "Individual Lending to Microenterprises in Mexico" (New York: Women's World Banking, 2014), https://www.womensworldbanking.org/wp-content/uploads/2014/10/WomensWorld Banking-Microenterprise-Individual-Lending-Mexico.pdf.

p. 22 **"not become loan sharks ourselves"** Muhammad Yunus, "Lifting People Worldwide out of Poverty," interview, Knowledge@Wharton (Philadelphia: University of Pennsylvania, Wharton School of Business, May 27, 2009), https://knowledge.wharton.upenn.edu/article/muhammad-yunus-lifting-people-worldwide-out-of-poverty.

p. 23 **the MFI's mission going forward** Rosenberg, "CGAP Reflections on the Compartamos Initial Public Offering."

p. 23 **blamed the private MFIs for stealing their customers** CGAP, "Andhra Pradesh 2010: Global Implications of the Crisis in Indian Microfinance," Focus Note 6 (Washington, DC: CGAP, November 2010), https://www.cgap.org/sites/default/files/CGAP-Focus-Note-Andhra-Pradesh-2010-Global-Implications-of-the-Crisis-in-Indian-Microfinance-Nov-2010.pdf.

p. 24 **penalties for abusive collection practices and predatory lending** CGAP, "Andhra Pradesh 2010."

p. 25 **mitigate risks and smooth consumption when needed** Abhijit Banerjee, Dean Karlan, and Jonathan Zinman, *The Miracle of Microfinance? Evidence from a Randomized Evaluation* (Cambridge, MA: MIT, Department of Economics, March 2014), https://economics.mit.edu/files/5993; Abdul Latif Jameel Poverty Action Lab, "Microcredit:

Impacts and Limitations" (Cambridge, MA: MIT, J-PAL, 2018), https://doi.org/10.31485/pi.2268.2018.

p. 25   **men felt that their traditional role as the primary breadwinner came under threat**   Beatriz Armendáriz and Nigiel Roome, "Gender Empowerment in Microfinance," MPRA Paper 31040 (Munich: Munich Personal RePEc Archive, June 2008), https://core.ac.uk/download/pdf/213927434.pdf; Naila Kabeer, "Conflicts over Credit: Re-evaluating the Empowerment Potential of Loans to Women in Rural Bangladesh," *World Development* 29, no. 1 (January 2001): 63–84, https://doi.org/10.1016/S0305-750X(00)00081-4.

p. 25   **"transformation of gender roles was underway"**   S. R. Schuler, S. M. Hashemi, and S. H. Badal, "Men's Violence against Women in Rural Bangladesh: Undermined or Exacerbated by Microcredit Programmes?," *Development in Practice* 8, no. 2 (1998): 116.

p. 25   **"as well as between women"**   Caroline Shenaz Hossein, "Using a Black Feminist Framework: A Study Comparing Bias against Female Entrepreneurs in Caribbean Microbanking," *Intersectionalities* 2 (2013): 51–70, 52, https://journals.library.mun.ca/ojs/index.php/IJ/article/viewFile/697/716.

p. 25   **nonfinancial services that the MFI included with the loan**   Manuela Angelucci, Dean Karlan, and Jonathan Zinman, "Microcredit Impacts: Evidence from a Randomized Microcredit Program Placement Experiment by Compartamos Banco," NBER Working Paper 19827 (Cambridge, MA: National Bureau of Economic Research, 2014), https://www.nber.org/system/files/working_papers/w19827/w19827.pdf.

p. 25   **including nonfinancial services alongside financial services**   Abdul Latif Jameel Poverty Action Lab (J-PAL), "Designing Financial Services and Social Protection Programs to Enhance Women's Economic Empowerment" (Cambridge, MA: MIT, J-PAL, last modified February 2021), https://doi.org/10.31485/pi.3090.2021.

p. 26   **offered in ninety-three countries around the world**   Tavneet Suri and William Jack, "The Long-Run Poverty and Gender Impacts of Mobile Money," *Science* 354, no. 6317 (December 9, 2016): 1288–1292, https://doi.org/10.1126/science.aah5309.

p. 26   **only 18 percent offer insurance products**   *MIX Market* (data catalog) (Washington, DC: World Bank, Center for Financial Inclusion), https://www.themix.org/mix-market.

p. 26   **digital transformation of the microfinance sector**   Jessica Schicks, "Covid-19 Has Made MFI Digital Transformation Even More Urgent: How Can Funders Help?," blog post, FinDev Gateway (Washington, DC: CGAP, June 30, 2020), https://www.findevgateway.org/blog/2020/06/covid-19-has-made-mfi-digital-transformation-even-more-urgent-how-can-funders-help.

p. 27   **digital financial services that are not delivered in a responsible way**   Greta Bull, "After the Storm: How Microfinance Can Adapt and Thrive," blog post, CGAP Leadership Essay Series (Washington, DC: CGAP, October 14, 2020, https://www.cgap.org/blog/after-storm-how-microfinance-can-adapt-and-thrive.

p. 27   **leaving women even further behind**   Better Than Cash Alliance, Women's World Banking, and the World Bank Group, "Advancing Women's Digital Financial Inclusion," report prepared for the G20 Global Partnership for Financial Inclusion, Saudi Arabia, July 2020, https://www.gpfi.org/sites/gpfi/files/sites/default/files/saudig20_women.pdf.

p. 28   **more risk averse than men**   Jessica Clempner, *Women in Financial Services 2020: A Panoramic Approach* (New York: Oliver Wyman, 2019), https://www.oliverwyman.com /content/dam/oliver-wyman/v2/publications/2019/November/Women-In-Financial -Services-2020.pdf.

p. 28   **in-person interaction between the potential customer and lending staff**   Laurie Goodman, Jun Zhu, and Bing Bai, *Women Are Better Than Men at Paying Their Mortgages* (Washington, DC: Urban Institute, September 2016), https://www.urban.org/sites /default/files/publication/84206/2000930-Women-Are-Better-Than-Men-At-Paying -Their-Mortgages.pdf; Marcia Tal, "Taking a Stand against Bias," *FrameWork* (newsletter), PositivityTech, June 5, 2020, https://positivitytech.com/taking-a-stand-against-bias.

p. 28   **calculations that drive decision-making technology**   Ayanna Howard and Charles Isbell, "Diversity in AI: The Invisible Men and Women," *MIT Sloan Management Review* (Winter 2021), https://sloanreview.mit.edu/article/diversity-in-ai-the-invisible-men-and-women.

p. 28   **despite her higher credit score**   Karen Hao, "There's an Easy Way to Make Lending Fairer for Women. Trouble Is, It's Illegal," *MIT Technology Review*, November 15, 2019, https://www.technologyreview.com/2019/11/15/131935/theres-an-easy-way-to-make -lending-fairer-for-women-trouble-is-its-illegal.

p. 28   **"a broader discussion we must have about equal credit access"**   Hartley Charlton, "Investigation Clears Goldman Sachs of Apple Card Gender Bias," MacRumors, March 23, 2021, https://www.macrumors.com/2021/03/23/apple-card-cleared-of-gender-bias.

p. 29   **and payments ($7 billion)**   Clempner, *Women in Financial Services 2020.*

p. 29   **by as much as $4.2 trillion**   Philip Osafo-Kwaako et al., *Mobile Money in Emerging Markets: The Business Case for Financial Inclusion* (New York: McKinsey & Co., March 2018), https://www.mckinsey.com/industries/financial-services/our-insights/mobile-money -in-emerging-markets-the-business-case-for-financial-inclusion.

p. 29   **operators' ability to scale up profitably**   James Manyika, Susan Lund, Marc Singer, et al., *Digital Financial Inclusion for All: Powering Inclusive Growth in Emerging Economies* (New York: McKinsey & Co., 2016).

p. 29   **reduce their dependence on customer fees**   Manyika et al., *Digital Financial Inclusion for All.*

p. 29   **could be generated digitally by 2025**   Osafo-Kwaako et al., *Mobile Money in Emerging Markets.*

p. 30   **that figure is likely to grow**   Naghavi, *State of the Industry.*

p. 30   **$390 million in digital loans had been disbursed by mid-2019**   Naghavi, *State of the Industry.*

p. 30   **the number of bank accounts now exceeding mobile money accounts**   William Cook and Claudia McKay, "Banking in the M-PESA Age: Lessons from Kenya" Working Paper (Washington, DC: CGAP, September 2017), https://www.cgap.org/sites/default/files /researches/documents/Working-Paper-Banking-in-the-M-PESA-Age-Sep-2017.pdf.

p. 31   **households above the poverty line**   Suri and Jack, "The Long-Run Poverty and Gender Impacts of Mobile Money."

p. 31   **more profitable entrepreneurial businesses or retail sales**   Suri and Jack, "The Long-Run Poverty and Gender Impacts of Mobile Money."

p. 31 **revenue to reach 50 percent soon** Dickson Otieno, "Safaricom Full Year 2019 Results Summary: Ksh. 63.4 Billion Net Profits, M-Pesa Revenue Up to Ksh. 74 Billion," Tech-ish. com, May 3, 2019, https://tech-ish.com/2019/05/03/safaricom-full-year-2019-results.

p. 32 **"although mobile phone use correlates well with economic development, mobile money causes it"** Suri and Jack, "The Long-Run Poverty and Gender Impacts of Mobile Money."

p. 32 **forgoing better products on better terms** Sharon Chen, Sebastian Doerr, Jon Frost, et al., "The Fintech Gender Gap," BIS Working Paper 931 (Basel, Switzerland: Bank for International Settlements, March 11, 2021), https://www.bis.org/publ/work931.htm.

CHAPTER 2: WHAT'S STANDING IN THE WAY OF WOMEN'S FINANCIAL INCLUSION?

p. 33 **through informal financial transactions** Bill & Melinda Gates Foundation, World Bank, Consultative Group to Assist the Poor (CGAP), and Women's World Banking, *Digital Cash Transfers in the Time of COVID 19: Opportunities and Considerations for Women's Inclusion and Empowerment* (Seattle: Bill & Melinda Gates Foundation, World Bank, CGAP, and Women's World Banking, 2020), https://www.cgap.org/sites/default /files/publications/2020.Digital-Cash-Transfers-in-Times-of-COVID-19-Opportunities -and-Considerations-for-Womens-Inclusion-and-Empowerment.pdf.

p. 34 **to what does—and doesn't—appear to work** Adele Atkinson and Flore-Anne Messy, "Promoting Financial Inclusion through Financial Education: OECD/INFE Evidence, Policies and Practice," Working Papers on Finance, Insurance and Private Pensions 34 (Paris, OECD, 2013), https://doi.org/10.1787/5k3xz6m88smp-en; Tim Kaiser and Lukas Menkhoff, "Does Financial Education Impact Financial Literacy and Financial Behavior, and If So, When?," *World Bank Economic Review* 31, no. 3 (October 2017), 611–630, https://doi.org/10.1093/wber/lhx018; Lisa Xu and Bilal Zia, "Financial Literacy around the World: An Overview of the Evidence with Practical Suggestions for the Way Forward," World Bank Policy Research Working Paper 6107 (Washington, DC: World Bank, June 2012), https://ssrn.com/abstract=2094887; Tabea Bucher-Koenen, Annamaria Lusardi, Rob J. M. Alessie, et al., "How Financially Literate Are Women? An Overview and New Insights," Working Paper 2016–1 (Washington, DC: Global Financial Literacy Excellence Center, February 2016), https://gflec.org/wp-content/uploads /2016/02/WP-2016-1-How-Financially-Literate-Are-Women.pdf.

p. 35 **information that had been missing from the financial literacy curriculum** Ryan Newton, "Women in Mexico Need More Than Digital G2P to Achieve Financial Inclusion" (New York: Women's World Banking, February 5, 2018), https://www.womensworld banking.org/insights-and-impact/women-mexico-digital-g2p-financial-inclusion.

p. 36 **more involvement in household decision-making** Chhavi Ghuliani and Elissa Goldenberg, "Financial Inclusion in the Supply Chain: An Evaluation of the HERfinance Pilot in India" (San Francisco: BSR, March 2015), https://www.bsr.org/reports/BSR _HERfinance_Evaluation_2015.pdf.

p. 36   **enhance the chances for positive behavioral change**   Kaiser and Menkhoff, "Does Financial Education Impact Financial Literacy and Financial Behavior, and If So, When?"

p. 36   **previously kept under the mattress**   Hatton National Bank, Women's World Banking private client advisory assignment, 2015.

p. 36   **nudging changes in financial behavior**   Gunhild Bert and Bilal Zia, "Harnessing Emotional Connections to Improve Financial Decisions: Evaluating the Impact of Financial Education in Mainstream Media," *Journal of the European Economic Association* 15, no. 5 (October 2017), 1025–1055, https://doi.org/10.1093/jeea/jvw021.

p. 37   **principal motivator behind their decision to save**   Women's World Banking, "Can a Soap Opera Help a Woman Save?" (New York: Women's World Banking, December 22, 2014O, https://www.womensworldbanking.org/insights-and-impact/can-soap-opera-help-women-save-financial-education.

p. 37   **restrictive gender norms they observe**   Oliver Rowntree et al., *The Mobile Gender Gap Report 2020* (London: GSMA, 2020), https://www.gsma.com/mobilefordevelopment/wp-content/uploads/2020/05/GSMA-The-Mobile-Gender-Gap-Report-2020.pdf; GSMA, *Accelerating Digital Literacy: Empowering Women to Use the Mobile Internet* (London: GSMA, 2015), https://www.gsma.com/mobilefordevelopment/wp-content/uploads/2015/06/DigitalLiteracy_v6_WEB_Singles.pdf; Oliver Rowntree, *The Mobile Gender Gap Report 2018* (London: GSMA, February 2018), https://www.gsma.com/mobilefordevelopment/wp-content/uploads/2018/04/GSMA_The_Mobile_Gender_Gap_Report_2018_32pp_WEBv7.pdf.

p. 37   **expanded use of video and graphic content**   Lolita Moorena, Simone Schaner, and Nadia Setiabudi, "Improving Women's Digital Literacy as an Avenue for Financial Inclusion," Abdul Latif Jameel Poverty Action Lab (J-PAL) (Cambridge, MA: MIT, J-PAL, November 23, 2020), https://www.povertyactionlab.org/blog/11-23-20/improving-womens-digital-literacy-avenue-financial-inclusion.

p. 37   **credit digitally for their businesses**   Women's World Banking, *Unlocking Credit for Women-Owned Enterprises in Southeast Asia through Value Chain Digitization* (New York: Women's World Banking, 2020), http://www.womensworldbanking.org/wp-content/uploads/2018/12/2020_Unlocking_Credit_Report.pdf.

p. 37   **interactive voice recognition technology**   Atul Tandon, remarks made during Credit Suisse Financial Inclusion virtual panel discussion, June 8, 2020.

p. 38   **move forward with a financial product or service**   International Finance Corporation (IFC), "Quick Tips for Digital Financial Service Providers to Reach Women," https://www.ifc.org/wps/wcm/connect/6f91a9e4-4b6c-4398-8268-d0bb443fa2db/Quick+Tips.pdf?MOD=AJPERES; Anna Zakrzewski, Kedra Newsom Reeves, Michael Kahlich, et al., "Managing the Next Decade of Women's Wealth" (Boston: Boston Consulting Group, April 9, 2020), https://www.bcg.com/publications/2020/managing-next-decade-women-wealth.

p. 38   **where they can turn for assistance**   IFC, "Quick Tips"; Kantar, *Winning Over Women: A Commercial Imperative for Financial Service* (London: Financial Alliance for Women,

2017), https://financialallianceforwomen.org/download/winning-women-commercial
-imperative-financial-services.

p. 38   **important life moment such as buying a home**   Pooneh Baghai, Olivia Howard,
Lakshmi Prakash, et al., "Women as the Next Wave of Growth in US Wealth Management," (New York: McKinsey & Co., July 29, 2020), https://www.mckinsey.com
/industries/financial-services/our-insights/women-as-the-next-wave-of-growth-in-us
-wealth-management.

p. 38   **trust in and confidence with the service**   Claire Pénicaud Scharwatt and Elisa
Minischetti, *Reaching Half of the Market: Women and Mobile Money* (London: GSMA,
September 2014), https://www.gsma.com/mobilefordevelopment/wp-content/uploads
/2014/09/2014_DI_Reach-half-of-the-market-Women-and-mobile-money.pdf.

p. 39   **who will treat them with respect**   Kate Webster, "How to Understand the Customer
Journey through Cognitive Interviews," interview by Karen Miller, *Women's World Banking Podcast*, May 29, 2019, https://soundcloud.com/user-220762778/how-to-better
-understand-the-customer-journey-through-cognitive-interviews.

p. 39   **call blocking and privacy settings on their cell-phones**   Aakanksha Thakur, Samveet
Sahoo, Prabir Barooah, et al., "Agency Banking: How Female Agents Make a Difference,"
Microsave Consulting, April 5, 2016, http://blog.microsave.net/2016/04/05/agency
-banking-how-female-agents-make-a-difference.

p. 40   **cross-sell other financial products to savings account customers**   Women's World
Banking, "Pilot Evaluation Findings," PowerPoint presentation to Bank of Baroda management, December 2, 2020.

p. 40   **expanded from 70 to 148 since 2014**   Nika Naghavi, *State of the Industry: Report on
Mobile Money 2019* (London: GSMA, 2020), https://www.gsma.com/sotir.

p. 40   **higher activity rates than their male counterparts**   Orla Ryan, "Harnessing the Power
of Agents to Drive Female Inclusion," *Mobile for Development* (blog), GMSA, March
29, 2019, https://www.gsma.com/mobilefordevelopment/blog/harnessing-the-power-of
-agents-to-drive-female-financial-inclusion.

p. 40   **70 percent of the franchise agents are women**   Mondato, "Mobile Money's Secret
Agent," January 25, 2016, https://blog.mondato.com/women.

p. 41   **cash-in/cash-out location for the entire village**   Allison Kahn, "Helping to Birth New
Life—and Financial Possibilities—for Families in Indonesia," Future of Work, Mastercard
Newsroom, October 27, 2020, https://www.mastercard.com/news/perspectives/2020
/helping-to-birth-new-life-and-financial-possibilities-for-families-in-indonesia.

p. 41   **to on-board customers and answer questions**   Women's World Banking application to
Fintech Innovation Challenge 2020, June 19, 2020.

p. 41   **can all be leveraged for greater inclusion**   Pénicaud Scharwatt and Minischetti, *Reaching Half*; IFC, "Quick Tips."

p. 42   **from 17 percent in 2010 to 36 percent in 2018**   "Reaching Half the Market: Women
and Mobile Money—The Example of Telesom in Somaliland," *Mobile for Development*
(blog), GSMA, April 27, 2015, https://www.gsma.com/mobilefordevelopment/region
/sub-saharan-africa-region/reaching-half-of-the-market-women-and-mobile-money-the
-example-of-telesom-in-somaliland.

p. 42   **products and services designed *by* men *for* men**   Jessica Clempner, *Women in Financial Services 2020: A Panoramic Approach* (New York: Oliver Wyman, 2019), https://www.oliverwyman.com/content/dam/oliver-wyman/v2/publications/2019/November/Women-In-Financial-Services-2020.pdf.

p. 43   **improved customer satisfaction ratings from male customers**   Women's World Banking, *Making Women's Work Visible: Finance for Rural Women* (New York: Women's World Banking, November 2014), https://www.womensworldbanking.org/wp-content/uploads/2014/11/Making-Womens-Work-Visible-Rural-Finance-WomensWorld Banking.pdf.

p. 43   **used the information in their managerial decision-making**   Cristina Palihé, "Sex-Disaggregated Supply-Side Data Relevant to Financial Inclusion," Discussion Paper IDB-DP-470 (Washington, DC: Inter-American Development Bank, January 2018) https://publications.iadb.org/publications/english/document/Sex-disaggregated-Supply-side-Data-Relevant-to-Financial-Inclusion.pdf.

p. 43   **compared with 46 percent of male customers**   "Kantar Study Shows U.S. Banks Can Increase Their Share of Deposits by 16.5% through Improving Their Customer Experience: USAA, Regions Bank and Chase Lead in Kantar's New CX+ Index," Businesswire, December 11, 2018, https://www.businesswire.com/news/home/20181211005619/en/Kantar-Study-Shows-U.S.-Banks-Increase-Share.

p. 43   **build higher savings to income ratios than men**   IFC, "Quick Tips"; Customer Service Profiles, "Customer Experience for Women: What Banks Need to Know," last modified February 2017, https://www.csp.com/customer-experience-for-women-what-banks-need-to-know/#.YCr7mi2ZN0s.

p. 44   **business services that were not available to them as retail customers**   Women's World Banking, "Custom Product Bundles Can Deepen Financial Inclusion for Vietnam's Economically Active Women" (New York: Women's World Banking, August 20, 2018), https://www.womensworldbanking.org/insights-and-impact/custom-product-bundles-can-deepen-financial-inclusion-for-vietnams-economically-active-women.

p. 45   **selling various cell-phone and mobile money products**   GSMA *The Gender Analysis and Identification Toolkit: Estimating Subscriber Gender Using Machine Learning* (London: GSMA August 2018), https://www.gsma.com/mobilefordevelopment/wp-content/uploads/2018/09/GSMA-Gender-Analysis-and-Identification-Report-GAIT-August-2018.pdf.

p. 45   **including the country's 100 million unbanked men and women**   Aniqa Sandhu, interviews by Mary Ellen Iskenderian, March 8, 2019, and July 3, 2020.

p. 46   **opportunity to expand financial inclusion**   Women's World Banking, *Nigeria and Pakistan: Two Approaches to Removing Barriers to Digital Financial Services for Women*, case studies prepared for the Bill & Melinda Gates Foundation, 2018.

p. 46   **12.4 million subscribers to its mobile wallet**   Women's World Banking, "Bringing Women into Digital Finance," PowerPoint presentation for JazzCash management, May 2015.

p. 46   **Sandhu had been named chief digital officer**   Sandhu, interviews.

p. 46   **how to use it to send and receive payments**   Sandhu, interviews.

p. 46   **the documentation necessary to open a cell-phone account on their own**   Sandhu, interviews.

p. 47   **a unique personal identifier that the phone offered her**   Women's World Banking, "Bringing Women into Digital Finance."

p. 47   **if it was going to be taken seriously**   Sandhu, interviews.

p. 47   **usage patterns told a slightly different story**   Sandhu, interviews.

p. 47   **how Jazz went about acquiring new women customers**   Women's World Banking, "Bringing Women into Digital Finance."

p. 48   **behavioral differences related to sending and acting on referrals**   Women's World Banking, *Nigeria and Pakistan.*

p. 48   **an essential element in winning women's business**   Women's World Banking, *Nigeria and Pakistan.*

p. 48   **providing a male agent with her cell-phone number in order to open an account**   Sandhu, interviews.

p. 49   **"That is why we say the woman is a thief"**   Women's World Banking, Jazz clients and potential clients, interviews, 2017–2018.

p. 49   **doubt that they would obtain permission from their male family members to use an agent**   Women's World Banking, Jazz clients, interviews.

p. 49   **women retailers known as *Guddi Bajis* or "good sisters"**   Women's World Banking, *Nigeria and Pakistan.*

p. 50   **showcase the economic benefits of being financially included**   Women's World Banking, *Nigeria and Pakistan.*

p. 50   **top performers generated three times that amount**   Women's World Banking, Jazz application for the GSMA Award for the Best Mobile Product, Application or Service for Women in Emerging Markets, 2016.

p. 50   **"They are unquestioned. They are the default"**   Caroline Criado Perez, *Invisible Women: Data Bias in a World Designed for Men* (New York: Abrams, 2019).

p. 51   **women loan officers were more successful in collecting from both male and female clients**   Women's World Banking, internal project findings from the Organizational Gender Assessment of ASA, a microfinance institution in Bangladesh, 2010.

p. 51   **719,000 new jobs, 73 percent of them for women**   İpek İlkkaracan, Kijon Kim, and Tolga Kaya, *The Impact of Public Investment in Social Care Services on Employment, Gender Equality, and Poverty: The Turkish Case* (Istanbul: Istanbul Technical University and Levy Economics Institute, August 2015), http://www.levyinstitute.org/pubs/rpr_8_15.pdf.

p. 52   **sex-disaggregated indicators on access to and use of both formal and informal financial services**   Asli Demirgüç-Kunt, Leora Klapper, Dorothe Singer, et al., *The Global Findex Database 2017: Measuring Financial Inclusion and the Fintech Revolution* (Washington, DC: World Bank, 2018).

p. 52   **efficacy of specific policy initiatives to address gender inequality**   Global Banking Alliance for Women et al., *Measuring Women's Financial Inclusion: The Value of Sex-Disaggregated Data* (New York: Global Banking Alliance for Women, October 2016),

https://data2x.org/resource-center/measuring-womens-financial-inclusion-the-value-of-sex-disaggregated-data.

p. 52   **Rarer still is account-level data disaggregated by sex**   Global Banking Alliance for Women et al., *Measuring Women's Financial Inclusion.*

p. 52   **only 60 of the 189 countries surveyed report sex-disaggregated data**   International Monetary Fund, *Financial Access Survey: 2020 Trends and Developments* (Washington, DC: IMF, 2020).

p. 53   **women are disproportionately represented among those without this fundamental tool**   World Bank, *Identification for Development (ID4D) 2019 Annual Report* (Washington, DC: World Bank, 2019), http://documents1.worldbank.org/curated/en/566431581578116247/pdf/Identification-for-Development-ID4D-2019-Annual-Report.pdf.

p. 53   **lack a national identification card or similar identification credential**   Lucia Hanmer and Marina Elefante, Achieving Universal Access to ID: Gender-based Legal Barriers against Women and Good Practice Reforms (Washington, DC: World Bank, 2019), http://hdl.handle.net/10986/32474.

p. 53   **"lack of documents" as a reason for not having a bank account**   Demirgüç-Kunt et al., *Global Findex Database 2017.*

p. 53   **obtain a birth certificate for them**   Hanmer and Elefante, *Achieving Universal Access.*

p. 53   **with no legal form of identification at all**   Olivia White, Anu Madgavkar, James Manyika, et al., *Digital Identification: A Key to Inclusive Growth* (Washington, DC: McKinsey Global Institute, April 17, 2019), https://www.mckinsey.com/business-functions/mckinsey-digital/our-insights/digital-identification-a-key-to-inclusive-growth.

p. 54   **verified through a fingerprint scan**   White et al., *Digital Identification.*

CHAPTER 3: FROM INVISIBILITY TO AGENCY

p. 55   **to believe she has the right to choose**   Anju Malhotra, Sidney Ruth Schuler, and Carol Boender, *Measuring Women's Empowerment as a Variable in International Development* (Washington, DC: World Bank, June 28, 2002).

p. 55   **"for people to live the lives they want"**   Naila Kabeer, "Resources, Agency, Achievements: Reflections on the Measurement of Women's Empowerment," in *Discussing Women's Empowerment: Theory and Practice*, ed. Anne Sisask, SIDA Studies 3 (Stockholm: Swedish International Development Agency, 2001).

p. 55   **her capacity to make choices is limited**   Naila Kabeer, "Gender Equality and Women's Empowerment: A Critical Analysis of the Third Millennium Development Goal 1," *Gender & Development* 13, no. 1 (2005), 13–24, https://doi.org/10.1080/13552070512331332273.

p. 56   **the woman herself must be a significant actor in that process of change**   Kabeer, "Resources, Agency, Achievements."

p. 56   **"where this ability was previously denied to them"**   Kabeer, "Resources, Agency, Achievements," 437.

p. 56   **without "punishingly high costs"**   Kabeer, "Resources, Agency, Achievements," 460.

p. 56 **strongest linkage to the "trifecta" of women's economic empowerment** "Women's Economic Empowerment: Our Approach," Bill & Melinda Gates Foundation, https://ww2.gatesfoundation.org/equal-is-greater/our-approach.

p. 57 **her negotiating power as household decisions are made** Cheryl Doss, "Intrahousehold Bargaining and Resource Allocation in Developing Countries," Policy Research Working Paper 6337 (Washington, DC: World Bank, Capacity Building Unit, January 2013) http://documents1.worldbank.org/curated/en/701071468155969077/pdf/wps6337.pdf.

p. 57 **material, cognitive, perceptual, and relational** Marty Chen and Simeen Mahmud, "Assessing Change in Women's Lives: A Conceptual Framework," Working Paper 2, BRAC-ICDDR,B Joint Research Project (Dhaka, Bangladesh, 1995).

p. 58 **move beyond her day-to-day existence and begin to plan for the future** Women's World Banking, "Empowerment Framework," proprietary material, 2015.

p. 60 **18 percent of the land across Latin America** Carmen Diana Deere and Magdalena León, "The Gender Asset Gap: Land in Latin America," *World Development* 31, no. 6 (June 2003): 925–947, https://doi.org/10.1016/S0305-750X(03)00046-9.

p. 60 **combination of agency plus resources** Doss, "Intrahousehold Bargaining and Resource Allocation in Developing Countries."

p. 60 **with fewer assets accumulated after marriage** World Bank, *Women, Business and the Law 2018* (Washington, DC: World Bank, 2018), http://hdl.handle.net/10986/29498.

p. 60 **resettlement and continued livelihood of genocide survivors** Elizabeth Powley, "Rwanda: The Impact of Women Legislators on Policy Outcomes Affecting Children and Families," working paper, Division of Policy and Planning (New York: UNICEF, December 2006), https://www.un.org/ruleoflaw/files/Rwanda%5B1%5D.pdf.

p. 60 **acquire a security interest in an asset in return for a loan** World Bank, *Secured Transactions, Collateral Registries and Movable Asset-Based Financing* (Washington, DC: International Bank for Reconstruction and Development, World Bank, November 2019), http://documents1.worldbank.org/curated/pt/193261570112901451/pdf/Knowledge-Guide.pdf; Nidhiya Menon and Yana van der Meulen Rodgers, "How Access to Credit Affects Self-Employment: Differences by Gender during India's Rural Banking Reform," *Journal of Development Studies* 47, no. 1 (2011): 48–69, https://doi.org/10.1080/00220381003706486.

p. 61 **strongly linked to the laws governing marital property** Mala Htun, Francesca Jensenius, and Jami Nelson-Nuñez, "Gender-Discriminatory Laws and Women's Economic Agency," *Social Politics: International Studies in Gender, State & Society* 26, no. 2 (Summer 2019): 193–222, https://doi.org/10.1093/sp/jxy042.

p. 61 **to register property jointly or in a woman's name** World Bank, *Women's Financial Inclusion and the Law* (Washington, DC: World Bank, 2018), http://pubdocs.worldbank.org/en/610311522241094348/Financial-Inclusion.pdf; World Bank, *Women, Business and the Law 2018*.

p. 61 **for women heads of household and rural women** Claire Felter and Danielle Renwick, "Colombia's Civil Conflict," (New York: Council on Foreign Relations, last modified

January 11, 2017), https://www.cfr.org/backgrounder/colombias-civil-conflict; Jamille Bigio, Rachel Vogelstein, and Anne Connell, "Women's Participation in Peace Processes: Colombia," Council on Foreign Relations, December 15, 2017, https://www.cfr.org/blog /womens-participation-peace-processes-colombia.

p. 62   **women will not have the skills or the confidence for that full engagement**   Women's World Banking, *Empowering Women in a Journey Towards Digital Financial Capability* (New York: Women's World Banking, March 2021), https://www.womens worldbanking.org/insights-and-impact/empowering-women-on-a-journey-towards -digital-financial-capability.

p. 62   **"has performed abysmally on the governance front"**   Naila Kabeer, Simeen Mahmud, and Jairo Guillermo Isaza Castro, "NGOs' Strategies and the Challenge of Development and Democracy in Bangladesh," IDS Working Paper 343 (Brighton: University of Sussex, Institute of Development Studies, June 2010), 7, https://doi.org/10.1111 /j.2040-0209.2010.00343_2.x.

p. 62   **"once a strong presence within the NGO sector, have declined rapidly"**   Kabeer, Mahmud, and Guillermo Isaza Castro, "NGOs' Strategies and the Challenge of Development."

p. 63   **for fear of creating dependency**   Kabeer, Mahmud, and Castro, "NGOs' Strategies and the Challenge of Development."

p. 63   **such as voting or campaigning in local and national elections**   Kabeer, Mahmud, and Castro, "NGOs' Strategies and the Challenge of Development."

p. 63   **they had a surprisingly strong economic impact as well**   Kabeer, Mahmud, and Castro, "NGOs' Strategies and the Challenge of Development."

p. 64   **significant impact on their holdings of productive assets**   Kabeer, Mahmud, and Castro, "NGOs' Strategies and the Challenge of Development."

p. 64   **"bargain for higher wages or a fairer price for their labor and products"**   Kabeer, Mahmud, and Castro, "NGOs' Strategies and the Challenge of Development," 40.

p. 64   **acquiring the "intangible skills of economic literacy, negotiating capacity and rights awareness"**   Kabeer, Mahmud, and Castro, "NGOs' Strategies and the Challenge of Development," 40.

p. 64   **apart from the material financial support**   Kabeer, Mahmud, and Castro, "NGOs' Strategies and the Challenge of Development."

p. 64   **where the members worked together in mixed gender groups**   Kabeer, Mahmud, and Castro, "NGOs' Strategies and the Challenge of Development."

p. 64   **were also members of other NGOs**   Kabeer, Mahmud, and Castro, "NGOs' Strategies and the Challenge of Development."

p. 65   **"That is what they are concerned about"**   Kabeer, Mahmud, and Castro, "NGOs' Strategies and the Challenge of Development," 41.

p. 65   **"will not overcome the barriers to economic advancement"**   Kabeer, Mahmud, and Castro, "NGOs' Strategies and the Challenge of Development," 46.

p. 65   **broader human capabilities of confidence, self-esteem and the ability to plan for the future**   Nalia Kabeer, *Gender, Livelihood Capabilities and Women's Economic*

Empowerment: Reviewing Evidence over the Life Course (London: Gender and Adolescence, Global Evidence, September 2018), https://eprints.lse.ac.uk/90462/1/Kabeer__gender-livelihood-capabilities.pdf.

p. 66 **"the new relationships they had forged through the SHGs"** Naila Kabeer, "Randomized Control Trials and Qualitative Evaluations of a Multifaceted Programme for Women in Extreme Poverty: Empirical Findings and Methodological Reflections," *Journal of Human Development and Capabilities* 20, no. 2 (2019): 197–217, https://doi.org/10.1080/19452829.2018.1536696.

p. 66 **"The capabilities were the only things that lasted in these women's lives"** Naila Kabeer, interview by the author, October 27, 2020.

p. 66 **will extend into the digital sphere** Sarah Gammage, Aslihan Kes, Liliane Winograd, et al., *Gender and Digital Financial Inclusion: What Do We Know and What Do We Need to Know?* (Washington, DC, International Center for Research on Women, October 2017), https://www.icrw.org/wp-content/uploads/2017/11/Gender-and-digital-financial-inclusion.pdf.

p. 66 **when their proximity to a bank branch also increases** William Jack and Tavneet Suri, "Mobile Money: The Economics of M-PESA," NBER Working Paper 16721 (Cambridge, MA: National Bureau of Economic Research, January 2011), https://www.nber.org/system/files/working_papers/w16721/w16721.pdf.

p. 67 **a male chaperone accompany them on errands, including visits to the bank** Erika Field, Rohini Pande, Natalia Rigol, et al., "On Her Own Account: Can Strengthening Women's Financial Control Boost Female Labor Supply?," working paper (Boston, MAL Harvard Business School, November 15, 2016), https://www.hbs.edu/ris/Publication%20Files/Rigol%20Female%20Accounts_3f8a5d0f-f76b-4a2e-bae7-363cab93f737.pdf.

p. 68 **gender norms may have compromised their negotiating leverage** Jenny C. Aker, Rachid Boumnijel, Amanda McClelland, et al., "Payment Mechanisms and Anti-Poverty Programs: Evidence from a Mobile Money Cash Transfer Experiment in Niger," *Economic Development and Cultural Change* 65, no. 1 (October 2016): 1–37, https://doi.org/10.1086/687578.

p. 68 **power dynamic between a woman and her spouse** Aker et al., "Payment Mechanisms and Anti-Poverty Programs."

p. 68 **focused on microcredit** Lucia Hanmer and Jeni Klugman, "Exploring Women's Agency and Empowerment in Developing Countries: Where Do We Stand?," *Feminist Economics* 22, no. 1 (January 2016): 237–263, https://doi.org/10.1080/13545701.2015.1091087.

p. 69 **social, cultural, and normative barriers and enablers** Lotus McDougal, Jeni Klugman, Nabamallika Dehingia, et al., "Financial Inclusion and Intimate Partner Violence: What Does the Evidence Suggest?," *PLoS One* 14, no. 10 (October 2019), https://doi.org/10.1371/journal.pone.0223721.

p. 69 **leaving women more vulnerable to intimate partner violence** Beatriz Armendáriz and Nigiel Roome, "Gender Empowerment in Microfinance," MPRA Paper 31040

(Munich: Munich Personal RePEc Archive, June 2008), https://core.ac.uk/download/pdf/213927434.pdf; Naila Kabeer, "Conflicts over Credit: Re-evaluating the Empowerment Potential of Loans to Women in Rural Bangladesh," *World Development* 29, no. 1 (January 2001): 63–84, https://doi.org/10.1016/S0305-750X(00)00081-4.

p. 69 **gender cap in cell-phone ownership and usage** McDougal et al., "Intimate Partner Violence."

p. 70 **rally related to HIV awareness** Julia C. Kim, Charlotte H. Watts, James R. Hargreaves, et al., "Understanding the Impact of a Microfinance-Based Intervention on Women's Empowerment and the Reduction of Intimate Partner Violence in South Africa," *American Journal of Public Health* 97, no. 10 (October 2007): 1794–1802, https://doi.org/10.2105/AJPH.2006.095521.

p. 70 **deciding to leave** Kim et al., "Understanding the Impact of a Microfinance-Based Intervention."

p. 70 **a deterrent to further violence** McDougal et al., "Intimate Partner Violence."

p. 70 **deemed the results inconclusive** Margaret E. Tankard, Elizabeth Levy Paluck, and Deborah A. Prentice, "The Effect of a Savings Intervention on Women's Intimate Partner Violence Victimization: Heterogenous Findings from a Randomized Controlled Trial in Colombia," *BMC Women's Health* 19, no. 17 (January 2019), https://doi.org/10.1186/s12905-019-0717-2.

p. 71 **women were able to seek higher-paying jobs** CEO of Fundación WWB Colombia, discussion with the author, 2018.

p. 71 **COVID-19 relief initiatives** UN Women, "The Shadow Pandemic: Violence against Women During COVID-19," News and Events section, https://www.unwomen.org/en/news/in-focus/in-focus-gender-equality-in-covid-19-response/violence-against-women-during-covid-19.

p. 71 **the means to flee abusive situations** Anita Raj, Jay G. Silverman, Jeni Klugman, et al., "Longitudinal Analysis of the Impact of Economic Empowerment on Risk for Intimate Partner Violence among Married Women in Rural Maharashtra, India," *Social Science & Medicine* 196 (January 2018): 197–203, https://doi.org/10.1016/j.socscimed.2017.11.042.

p. 71 **jeopardizing her ability to obtain and keep a job** National Network to End Domestic Violence, "About Financial Abuse," https://nnedv.org/content/about-financial-abuse.

p. 72 **"keep a roof over her head"** Brit Marling, "Harvey Weinstein and the Economics of Consent," *Atlantic*, October 23, 2017, https://www.theatlantic.com/entertainment/archive/2017/10/harvey-weinstein-and-the-economics-of-consent/543618.

PART II: MAKING THE BUSINESS CASE

p. 73 **looking for convenient, reliable financial services they can afford** Asli Demirgüç-Kunt, Leora Klapper, Dorothe Singer, et al., *The Global Findex Database 2017: Measuring Financial Inclusion and the Fintech Revolution* (Washington, DC: World Bank, 2018).

p. 73 **enter the financial services sector** McKinsey & Co., *McKinsey's Global Banking Annual Review 2020: A Test of Resilience* (New York: McKinsey & Co., December 9,

2020), https://www.mckinsey.com/industries/financial-services/our-insights/global-banking
-annual-review#.

p. 74   **environmental, social, and governance issues**   McKinsey & Co., *McKinsey's Global
Banking Annual Review 2020.*

p. 74   **provide immediate relief in partnership with governments**   Edelman, *Edelman Trust
Barometer 2020* (Chicago: Edelman, 2020), https://cdn2.hubspot.net/hubfs/440941
/Trust%20Barometer%202020/2020%20Edelman%20Trust%20Barometer%20
Global%20Report.pdf?utm_campaign=Global:%20Trust%20Barometer%202020;
Edelman, *Edelman Trust Barometer 2020 Spring Update: Trust and the Covid-19 Pan-
demic* (Chicago: Edelman, 2020), https://www.edelman.com/sites/g/files/aatuss191/files
/2020-05/2020%20Edelman%20Trust%20Barometer%20Spring%20Update%20
Financial%20Services.pdf.

p. 74   **$40 billion in additional revenue**   Bank of New York Mellon and United Nations
Foundation, *Powering Potential: Increasing Women's Access to Financial Products and Services* (New York: BNY Mellon, 2018), https://bnymellonlive-bypass.cphostaccess.com
/_global-assets/pdf/our-thinking/powering-potential.pdf.

p. 74   **$30 billion in new net interest income**   Jessica Clempner, *Women in Financial Services
2020: A Panoramic Approach* (New York: Oliver Wyman, 2019), https://www.oliverwy
man.com/content/dam/oliver-wyman/v2/publications/2019/November/Women-In
-Financial-Services-2020.pdf.

p. 75   **guaranteed access to credit**   Women's World Banking, "Pilot Evaluation Findings,"
PowerPoint presentation to Bank of Baroda Management, December 2, 2020.

p. 75   **safety cushion**   Sophie Theis, Giudy Rusconi, Elwyn Panggabean, et al., *Delivering on
the Potential of Digitized G2P: Driving Women's Financial Inclusions through Indonesia's
Program Keluarga Harapan* (New York: Women's World Banking, August 2020), https://
www.womensworldbanking.org/wp-content/uploads/2020/08/August2020_G2P
_Report.pdf.

p. 75   **"to recast their contract with society"**   McKinsey & Co., *McKinsey's Global Banking
Annual Review 2020.*

CHAPTER 4: MAKING THE BUSINESS CASE FOR BUILDING WEALTH

p. 78   **protect some of that money for school fees**   KWFT Focus Group, Women's World
Banking youth savings research, 2012.

p. 78   **every year of secondary school that she completes**   Shannon Hodge, "Six Ways in
Which Educating Girls Benefits Their Wider Community," The Circle, August 30, 2017,
https://thecircle.ngo/six-positive-impacts-educating-girls; "Girls' Education" (Washington, DC: World Bank, last modified March 8, 2021), https://www.worldbank.org/en
/topic/girlseducation.

p. 78   **greater risk of dying before the age of five**   World Bank, "Educating Girls, Ending
Child Marriage" (Washington, DC: World Bank, August 24, 2017), https://www.world
bank.org/en/news/immersive-story/2017/08/22/educating-girls-ending-child-marriage.

p. 79   **ended up burdened by debt they couldn't repay**   CAMFED CEO in off-the-record interview by the author, June 12, 2014.

p. 79   **the greatest chance of absorbing the material**   CAMFED CEO, interview.

p. 80   **but in order to contribute to their families**   Ryan Newton and Anjali Banthia, "Bright Like a Star: The Promise of Savings for Girls in India," International Banker, August 11, 2014, https://internationalbanker.com/banking/bright-like-star-promise-savings-girls-india; Women's World Banking, *Building a Sustainable Youth Savings Proposition: Lessons from Banco ADOPEM* (New York: Women's World Banking, January 2015), https://www.womensworldbanking.org/wp-content/uploads/2015/01/WomensWorldBanking_BuildingSustainableYouthSavingsProposition_LessonsBancoADOPEM.pdf.

p. 80   **annual incremental revenue estimated at $15 billion**   Bank of New York Mellon and United Nations Foundation, *Powering Potential: Increasing Women's Access to Financial Products and Services* (New York: BNY Mellon, 2018), https://bnymellonlive-bypass.cphostaccess.com/_global-assets/pdf/our-thinking/powering-potential.pdf.

p. 81   **expertly sliced okazi ready for sale**   Ime Isaac Akpe, Diamond Bank client, interview by Women's World Banking researcher, 2012.

p. 81   **usually around 3:00 or 4:00 p.m.**   Akpe, interview.

p. 81   **below the international poverty line of $1.90 a day**   World Bank, *Poverty and Equity Brief: Africa Western and Central—Nigeria* (Washington, DC: World Bank, October 2020), https://databank.worldbank.org/data/download/poverty/987B9C90-CB9F-4D93-AE8C-750588BF00QA/AM2020/Global_POVEQ_NGA.pdf.

p. 81   **to serve unbanked and underbanked clients as well**   Women's World Banking, "BETA Project," internal project preparation materials, 2012–2018; Women's World Banking, *Diamond Bank Storms the Market: A BETA Way to Save* (New York: Women's World Banking, March 5, 2014), https://www.womensworldbanking.org/wp-content/uploads/2014/03/Womens-World-Banking-A-BETA-Way-To-Save.pdf.

p. 82   **bring more people into the formal financial system**   Central Bank of Nigeria, *Circular to All Banks and Other Financial Institutions: Introduction of Three-Tiered Know Your Customer (KYC) Requirements* (Abuja, Nigeria: Central Bank of Nigeria, January 18, 2013), https://www.cbn.gov.ng/out/2013/ccd/3%20tiered%20kyc%20requirements.pdf.

p. 82   **opening a financial account remains out of reach**   Alliance for Financial Inclusion, *KYC Innovations, Financial Inclusion and Integrity in Selected AFI Member Countries* (Kuala Lumpur, Malaysia: AFI, March 2019), https://www.afi-global.org/sites/default/files/publications/2019-03/KYC-Innovations-Financial-Inclusion-Integrity-Selected-AFI-Member-Countries.pdf.

p. 82   **check the personal information she provided against official databases**   Central Bank of Nigeria, *Circular to All Banks and Other Financial Institutions (Know Your Customer)*.

p. 83   **a savings account rather than starting with a lending product**   Women's World Banking, "BETA Project."

p. 83   **everyone bristled at the fees charged by the coordinator**   Women's World Banking, *Diamond Bank Storms the Market*.

p. 83 **conditions that would let Diamond Bank take advantage of them**   Women's World Banking, *Diamond Bank Storms the Market*.

p. 85 **at a higher rate than those with male Friends**   Women's World Banking, "BETA Project"

p. 85 **"The money slips through your fingers"**   Akpe, interview.

p. 85 **saving an impressive 60 percent of their income through informal means**   Women's World Banking, *Diamond Bank Storms the Market*.

p. 86 **cited as one of its most valuable assets**   Access Bank and Diamond Bank, *Access Bank-Diamond Bank Merger Update: Creating Nigeria and Africa's Largest Retail Bank*, January 2019, https://www.accessbankplc.com/AccessBankGroup/media/Investors/Results-2019/Access-Bank-Diamond-Bank-Investor-Presentation.pdf.

p. 86 **only to see its value erode**   Macrotrends, "Nigeria GDP Growth Rate 1961–2021," https://www.macrotrends.net/countries/NGA/nigeria/gdp-growth-rate; Macrotrends, "Nigeria Inflation Rate 1960–2021," https://www.macrotrends.net/countries/NGA/nigeria/inflation-rate-cpi.

p. 86 **making decisions on how to use their business's profits and in making household purchases**   Women's World Banking, "BETA Project Outcomes Research," internal project research.

p. 87 **41 percent of annual wages, compared to 23 percent for men**   PR Newswire, "Men v Women: The Economic and Financial Divide 2013," press release provided by Halifax, UK, Cision, March 28, 2013, https://www.prnewswire.com/news-releases/men-v-women-the-economic-and-financial-divide-2013-200468241.html.

p. 87 **women's savings accounts grow at three times the rate of men's savings accounts in the past decade**   Financial Alliance for Women, "The Opportunity / Untapped Potential," https://financialallianceforwomen.org/the-opportunity/#untappedpotential.

p. 87 **to incentivize opening more women's accounts**   Women's World Banking, "BETA Project."

p. 88 **savings balances outside the formal financial system**   World Bank, *The Little Data Book on Financial Inclusion 2018* (Washington, DC: World Bank, 2018), https://openknowledge.worldbank.org/bitstream/handle/10986/29654/LDB-%20FinInclusion2018.pdf?sequence=1&isAllowed=y.

p. 88 **from these informal financial relationships**   Julie Zollman, *Kenya Financial Diaries: Shilingi Kwa Shilingi—The Financial Lives of the Poor* (Nairobi, Kenya: Financial Sector Deepening Kenya, August 2014), https://www.findevgateway.org/sites/default/files/publications/files/kenya_financial_diaries_shilingi_kwa_shilingi_-_the_financial_lives_of_the_poor.pdf.

p. 89 **they saved the windfall either in cash at home or in a ROSCA**   Jonathan Robinson, "Limited Insurance within the Household: Evidence from a Field Experiment in Kenya," *American Economics Journal: Applied Economics* 4, no. 4 (October 2012): 140–164, https://doi.org/10.1257/app.4.4.140.

p. 90 **reported by both men and women to be the household's primary saver**   Simone Shaner, "The Cost of Convenience? Transaction Costs, Bargaining Power, and Savings

Account Use in Kenya," *Journal of Human Resources* 52, no. 4 (Fall 2017): 919–945, https://doi.org/10.3368/jhr.52.4.0815-7350R1.

p. 90   **distance to a financial service provider as major impediments**   Asli Demirgüç-Kunt, Leora Klapper, Dorothe Singer, et al., *The Global Findex Database 2017: Measuring Financial Inclusion and the Fintech Revolution* (Washington, DC: World Bank, 2018).

p. 90   **more likely to use the bank accounts for various financial activities**   Shawn Cole, Thomas Sampson, and Bilal Zia, "Prices or Knowledge? What Drives Demand for Financial Services in Emerging Markets?," *Journal of Finance* 66, no. 6 (December 2011): 1933–1967, https://doi.org/10.1111/j.1540-6261.2011.01696.x.

p. 91   **a far greater impact on women's ability to save and invest**   Pascaline Dupas and Jonathan Robinson, "Savings Constraints and Microenterprise Development: Evidence from a Field Experiment in Kenya," *American Economic Journal* 5, no. 1 (January 2013): 163–192, https://doi.org/10.1257/app.5.1.163.

p. 91   **lifted one million people out of poverty**   Tavneet Suri and William Jack, "The Long-Run Poverty and Gender Impacts of Mobile Money," *Science* 354, no. 6317 (December 9, 2016): 1288–1292, https://doi.org/10.1126/science.aah5309.

p. 91   **consumption levels by 7 percent in response to these income shocks**   William Jack and Tavneet Suri, "Mobile Money: The Economics of M-PESA," NBER Working Paper No. 16721 (Cambridge, MA: National Bureau of Economic Research, January 2011), https://www.nber.org/system/files/working_papers/w16721/w16721.pdf.

p. 91   **three times more likely to save for health and other emergencies than non-users**   Serge Ky, Clovis Rugemintwari, and Alain Sauviat, "Does Mobile Money Affect Saving Behaviour? Evidence from a Developing Country," *Journal of African Economies* 27, no. 3 (June 2018): 285–320, https://doi.org/10.1093/jafeco/ejx028.

p. 92   **women who received the benefits in cash**   Jenny C. Aker, "Payment Mechanisms and Anti-Poverty Programs: Evidence from a Mobile Money Cash Transfer Experiment in Niger," *Economic Development and Cultural Change* 65, no. 1 (October 2016): 1–37, https://doi.org/10.1086/687578.

p. 92   **not seeing their BETA friend frequently enough**   Women's World Banking, "BETA Project."

p. 93   **a sensitivity to fees**   Tomoko Harigaya, "Effects of Digitization on Financial Behaviors: Experimental Evidence from the Philippines," September 4, 2020, https://tomoko-harigaya.files.wordpress.com/2020/09/harogaya_mfs_sep2020.pdf.

p. 94   **secured the loan using a portion of her BETA savings balance as collateral**   Women's World Banking, "BETA Project."

p. 94   **insufficient to accumulate a lump sum**   Daryl Collins, Jonathan Morduch, Stuart Rutherford, et al., *Portfolios of the Poor: How the World's Poor Live on $2 a Day* (Princeton, NJ: Princeton University Press, 2009), 124–127.

p. 94   **at any retail bank in India**   Sudhinder Chowhan and J. C. Pande, "Pradhan Mantri Jan Dhan Yojana: A Giant Leap towards Financial Inclusion," *International Journal of Research in Management and Business Studies* 1, no. 4 (October–December 2014): 19–22, https://ijrmbs.com/vol1issue4/sudhinder.pdf.

p. 94　a tremendous success in terms of account opening　"Jan Dhan Yojana Makes It to Guinness World Records, 11.5 cr Jan Dhan Accounts Opened," *Economic Times*, last updated January 21, 2015, https://economictimes.indiatimes.com/news/economy /finance/jan-dhan-yojna-makes-it-to-guinness-world-records-11-5-cr-jan-dhan -accounts-opened/articleshow/45955376.cms.

p. 94　that in aggregate hold a total deposit balance of $14 billion　Chowhan and Pande, "Pradhan Mantri Jan Dhan Yojana ."

p. 94　accounts have seen little to no use　Anand Adhikari, "Jan Dhan Yojana Data Shows Rural Area Residents Using Bank Accounts More Often," *Business Today*, November 20, 2019, https://www.businesstoday.in/sectors/banks/zero-balance-dormant-bank-accounts -under-jan-dhan-yojana-on-a-steady-decline/story/390664.html.

p. 94　an overdraft facility up to roughly $130　Chowhan and Pande, "Pradhan Mantri Jan Dhan Yojana ."

p. 95　a credit facility to incentivize even deeper engagement　Women's World Banking, "Pilot Evaluation Findings," PowerPoint presentation to Bank of Baroda Management, December 2, 2020.

p. 95　health insurance policy in addition to their microloan　Women's World Banking, *Gender Performance Indicators 2.0: How Well Are We Serving Women?* (New York: Women's World Banking, 2015), https://www.womensworldbanking.org/wp-content /uploads/2013/06/GenderPerformanceIndicators_2015_WomensWorldBanking.pdf.

p. 96　252 million women paying school fees all in cash　Demirgüç-Kunt et al., *The Global Findex Database 2017.*

p. 96　in thirty countries remittances make up 10 percent or more of GDP　Migration Data Portal, "Remittances," updated February 23, 2021, https://migrationdataportal.org /themes/remittances.

p. 97　training resulted in significant increases in recipients' savings balances　Women's World Banking, "Hatton Remittances," internal project preparation and implementation materials, 2010–2011.

p. 97　"net profit attributable to the future relationship with a customer"　Tanaya Kilara, Barbara Magnoni, and Emily Zimmerman, *The Business Case for Youth Savings: A Framework,* CGAP Focus Note 96 (Washington, DC: Consultative Group to Assist the Poor, 2014), https://www.cgap.org/sites/default/files/Focus-Note-Business-Case-for-Youth-Savings -A-Framework-Jul-2014.pdf.

p. 97　successful and loyal bank employees on graduation　Women's World Banking and Nike Foundation, *Banking on Youth: A Guide to Developing Innovative Youth Savings Programs*, 2012, revised 2014, https://www.womensworldbanking.org/wp-content/uploads /2014/10/Womens-World-Banking-Banking-On-Youth-2014.pdf.

p. 98　compared to the bank's already high average rate of 77 percent　Women's World Banking, *Building a Sustainable Youth Savings Proposition.*

p. 98　served to attract new, younger clients to the bank　Women's World Banking and Nike, *Banking on Youth*; "Diamond Bank Excites Youths with Dreamville, Game-Enabled

Digital Savings Platform," *Daily Post—Nigeria News*, March 16, 2018, https://dailypost
.ng/2018/03/16/diamond-bank-excites-youths-dreamville-game-enabled-digital-savings
-platform; Women's World Banking, "Diamond Youth Savings" internal project preparation and implementation materials, 2012–2018.

CHAPTER 5: MAKING THE BUSINESS CASE FOR ACCESS TO CAPITAL

p. 102 **customer lifetime value of a woman client can be higher than that of a man** Women's
World Banking, "She Counts 2019: Driving Savings—Effective Practices in Product
Bundling" (New York: Women's World Banking, December 20, 2019), https://www
.womensworldbanking.org/insights-and-impact/she-counts-driving-savings-effective
-practices-in-product-bundling.

p. 102 **further growth will only exacerbate existing economic inequality** Thorsten Beck
and Asli Demirgüç-Kunt, "Small and Medium-Sized Enterprises: Access to Finance as
a Growth Constraint," *Journal of Banking & Finance* 30, no. 11 (November 2006):
2931–3256, https://www.sciencedirect.com/journal/journal-of-banking-and-finance/vol
/30/issue/11; World Bank, "Small and Medium Enterprises (SMEs) Finance," https://
www.worldbank.org/en/topic/smefinance.

p. 102 **smaller companies have the highest rate of employment growth, followed by medium-
sized firms** World Bank, "Small and Medium Enterprises (SMEs) Finance."

p. 102 **capacity to expand its number of permanent employees** Meghana Ayyagari, Pedro
Juarros, Maria Soledad Martinez Peria, et al., "Access to Finance and Job Growth: Firm-
Level Evidence across Developing Countries," Policy Research Working Paper 7604
(Washington, DC: World Bank, 2016), http://hdl.handle.net/10986/24146.

p. 102 **even fewer bank loans were made to smaller businesses** Tracey Durner and Liat She-
tret, *Understanding Bank De-risking and Its Effects on Financial Inclusion: An Exploratory
Study* (Oxford: Oxfam, November 2015), https://www-cdn.oxfam.org/s3fs-public/file
_attachments/rr-bank-de-risking-181115-en_0.pdf.

p. 103 **assets valued between $3 million and $15 million** World Bank, SME Finance Forum,
and International Finance Corporation, *Micro, Small and Medium Enterprises: Economic
Indicators (MSME-EI) Analysis Note* (Washington, DC: World Bank, December 2019),
https://www.smefinanceforum.org/data-sites/msme-country-indicators.

p. 103 **makes an accurate calculation of the financing gap extremely difficult, if not impossible** Peer Stein, Oya Pinar Ardic, and Martin Hommes, "Closing the Credit Gap for
Formal and Informal Micro, Small, and Medium Enterprises" (Washington, DC: International Finance Corporation, August 2013), http://hdl.handle.net/10986/21728.

p. 104 **1.3 times the amount of lending currently being done** SME Finance Forum,
"MSME Finance Gap," International Finance Forum, World Bank Group, https://www
.smefinanceforum.org/data-sites/msme-finance-gap.

p. 104 **unable to tap the financing they need to grow** SME Finance Forum, "MSME Finance
Gap."

p. 104 **heavier collateral requirements than men** Alexander Muravyev, Dorothea Schäfer,
and Oleksandr Talavera, "Entrepreneurs' Gender and Financial Constraints: Evidence

from International Data," DIW Discussion Paper 706 (Berlin: Deutsches Institut für Wirtschaftsforschung, 2007), http://hdl.handle.net/10419/27231.

p. 104 **4.5 percent of loans to both men and women are overdue at ninety days** International Finance Corporation, *Women-Owned SMEs: A Business Opportunity for Financial Institutions* (Washington, DC: International Finance Corporation, 2014), https://www.ifc.org /wps/wcm/connect/44b004b2-ed46-48fc-8ade-aa0f485069a1/WomenOwnedSMes +Report-Final.pdf?MOD=AJPERES&CVID=kiiZZDZ.

p. 104 **obstacles to banks' provision of credit to MSMEs** Ratna Sahay, Martin Čihák, Papa N'Diaye, et al., "Financial Inclusion: Can It Meet Multiple Macroeconomic Goals?," IMF Staff Discussion Note SDN/15/17 (Washington, DC: International Monetary Fund, September 2015), https://www.imf.org/external/pubs/ft/sdn/2015/sdn1517.pdf.

p. 105 **assets used as collateral by developing country banks** World Bank, *Secured Transactions, Collateral Registries and Movable Asset-Based Financing* (Washington, DC: World Bank / International Bank for Reconstruction and Development, November 2019), http://documents1.worldbank.org/curated/pt/193261570112901451/pdf/Knowledge -Guide.pdf.

p. 105 **leveraged for badly needed growth capital** Mehnaz Safavian, Heywood Fleisig, and Jevgenijs Steinbuks, "Unlocking Dead Capital: How Reforming Collateral Laws Improves Access to Finance," Viewpoint: Public Policy for the Private Sector, Note 307 (Washington, DC: World Bank, March 2006), http://hdl.handle.net/10986/11190.

p. 105 **who owns or has a security interest in an asset** World Bank, *Secured Transactions, Collateral Registries and Movable Asset-Based Financing.*

p. 105 **the strongest impact of these positive changes was felt by small business** Inessa Love, Maria Soledad Martinez Peria, and Sandeep Singh, "Collateral Registries for Movable Assets: Does Their Introduction Spur Firms' Access to Bank Finance?," Policy Research Working Paper 6477 (Washington, DC: World Bank, Development Research Group, June 2013), http://documents1.worldbank.org/curated/en/731881468314344960/pdf /WPS6477.pdf.

p. 105 **particularly well suited to serving MSMEs** World Bank, *Secured Transactions, Collateral Registries and Movable Asset-Based Financing.*

p. 106 **that lender's rights in a secured transaction** Simeon Djankov, Caralee McLiesh, and Andrei Shleifer, "Private Credit in 129 Countries," *Journal of Financial Economics* 84, no. 2 (May 2007): 299–329, https://doi.org/10.1016/j.jfineco.2006.03.004.

p. 106 **lending to the private sector increased by at least 47.5 percent** Michael Turner and Robin Varghese, *Economic Impacts of Payment Reporting Participation in Latin America* (Durham, NC: Political and Economic Research Council, May 2007), https://www .perc.net/wp-content/uploads/2013/09/Latin_America.pdf.

p. 107 **can be an important stepping-stone to access credit** World Bank, *Women, Business and the Law 2018* (Washington, DC: World Bank, 2018), http://hdl.handle.net /10986/29498.

p. 107 **jumped by 21 percent** World Bank Development Research Group, Better Than Cash Alliance, Bill & Melinda Gates Foundation, and Women's World Banking, *Digital*

Financial Solutions to Advance Women's Economic Participation, prepared for the Turkish G20 Presidency (Washington, DC: World Bank, November 16, 2015), https://www.gpfi .org/publications/digital-financial-solutions-advance-womens-economic-participation.

p. 107 **282 branches throughout the country** KCB Group, *2019 Integrated Report & Financial Statements* (Nairobi, Kenya: KCB Group, 2019), https://kcbgroup.com/wp-content /uploads/2020/11/KCB-Group-Plc-2019-Integrated-Report-and-Financial-Statements -min.pdf.

p. 107 **differentiate itself in an increasingly crowded market** Women's World Banking, "KCB Project," internal project preparation and implementation materials, 2016–2019.

p. 108 **to the country's 300,000 to 400,000 registered MSMEs** Women's World Banking, *Empowering MSMEs: Creating a Better Banking Experience for Women-Led Micro, Small, and Medium Enterprises in Kenya* (New York: Women's World Banking, November 2020), https://www.womensworldbanking.org/wp-content/uploads/2020/11/MSME_Report _2020.pdf.

p. 108 **a lack of external funding was the greatest obstacle to their growth** Government of the Republic of Kenya, *Kenya Vision 2030* (Nairobi, Kenya: Government of the Republic of Kenya, 2007), https://vision2030.go.ke/wp-content/uploads/2018/05/Vision -2030-Popular-Version.pdf.

p. 108 **compared with just 24 percent of men-led firms** International Trade Centre, *Promoting SME Competitiveness in Kenya: Targeted Solutions for Inclusive Growth* (Geneva: International Trade Centre, September 2019), https://www.intracen.org/uploadedFiles /intracenorg/Content/Publications/Kenya_SME_Comp_final_low_res.pdf.

p. 108 **how they differed from the lending needs of retail or corporate customers** Women's World Banking, *Empowering MSMEs*.

p. 108 **build a residential real estate business** Women's World Banking, "KCB Focus Group 4," transcript, April 9, 2016.

p. 109 **youngest children once they finished college** Women's World Banking, "KCB Focus Group 3," transcript, April 8, 2016.

p. 109 **Issues of special importance to entrepreneurial women** Women's World Banking, "KCB Project."

p. 109 **"and I acquired them all through loans"** Women's World Banking, "KCB Focus Group 7," transcript, April 11, 2016.

p. 109 **"with business you have to keep growing your money"** Women's World Banking, "KCB Focus Group 7."

p. 110 **Extended through their husbands rather than directly** Michael Aliber, "The Importance of Informal Finance in Promoting Decent Work among Informal Operators: A Comparative Study of Uganda and India," Social Finance Working Paper 66 (Geneva: International Labour Office, 2015).

p. 110 **maintain any semblance of financial independence** Women's World Banking, "KCB Focus Group 4"; Women's World Banking, "KCB Focus Group 5," transcript, April 9, 2016; Women's World Banking, "KCB Focus Group 7."

p. 110 **"keep it and buy more equipment"** Women's World Banking, "KCB Focus Group 3."

p. 110 **issues of ownership and independence at play for the women** Women's World Banking, "KCB Focus Group 4"; Women's World Banking, "KCB Focus Group 5"; Women's World Banking, "KCB Focus Group 7."

p. 110 **"even if you are bored with him, you have to stay"** Women's World Banking, "KCB Focus Group 4."

p. 111 **use the vehicles as security for business loans** Women's World Banking, "KCB Focus Group 4"; Women's World Banking, "KCB Focus Group 5"; Women's World Banking, "KCB Focus Group 7."

p. 111 **"it helps me to buy things for my children"** Women's World Banking, "KCB Focus Group 4."

p. 111 **"That is my voice, that is my strength"** Women's World Banking, "KCB Focus Group 4."

p. 111 **the membership privilege most valued by men and women alike** Women's World Banking, "KCB Focus Group 3"; Women's World Banking, "KCB Focus Group 4"; Women's World Banking, "KCB Focus Group 5"; Women's World Banking, "KCB Focus Group 7."

p. 111 **"financially it's like zero work"** Women's World Banking, "KCB Focus Group 3."

p. 111 **other event services as a package** Women's World Banking, "KCB Focus Group 4."

p. 112 **"Oh, I saw [her] at the bank today"** Women's World Banking, "KCB Focus Group 4."

p. 112 **"I want to be treated like the boss I am"** Women's World Banking, "KCB Focus Group 7."

p. 112 **the importance of follow-up** Women's World Banking, *Empowering MSMEs: Creating a Better Banking Experience for Women-Led Micro, Small, and Medium Enterprises in Kenya* (New York: Women's World Banking, November 2020), https://www.womens worldbanking.org/wp-content/uploads/2020/11/MSME_Report_2020.pdf.

p. 112 **larger businesses, employing more than ten people** Women's World Banking, *Empowering MSMEs*.

p. 113 **implement new practices and improve their managerial skills** Women's World Banking, *Empowering MSMEs*.

p. 113 **sell it to cover the unpaid loan amount** Women's World Banking, discussions with KCB management, April 2016.

p. 113 **settle an unpaid loan was a lengthy, often arduous process** Vitalis Kimutai, "Rachel Korir's 40-Year Struggle Wins Women Land Rights," Daily Nation, reprinted on The Land Portal, April 15, 2019, https://landportal.org/news/2019/04/rachel-korirs-40-year -struggle-wins-women-land-rights.

p. 114 **before loan applications were submitted to headquarters** Women's World Banking, *Empowering MSMEs*.

p. 114 **accurately measure the success of the program** Women's World Banking, discussions with KCB management.

p. 114 **thanks to the deeper engagement with relationship managers** Women's World Banking, *Empowering MSMEs*.

p. 114 **mandates that they were asked to deliver on** Women's World Banking, discussions with KCB management.

p. 114 **training in the one hundred pilot branches** Women's World Banking, *Empowering MSMEs*.

p. 114 **insufficient evidence to determine what does work and under what conditions** Iris Bohnet, *What Works: Gender Equality by Design* (Cambridge, MA: Belknap Press of Harvard University Press, 2016), 51–53.

p. 115 **increased from 22 percent to over 50 percent of the MSME portfolio** Women's World Banking, *Empowering MSMEs*.

p. 115 **affected KCB's ability to serve women-owned businesses** Women's World Banking, KCB gender sensitization training.

p. 116 **cross-selling, marketing products, and communications training** Women's World Banking, *Empowering MSMEs*.

p. 116 **compared to the average 40 percent increase by nonborrowers** Women's World Banking, *Empowering MSMEs*.

p. 117 **by year three of the project, up from 86 percent at the outset** Women's World Banking, *Empowering MSMEs*.

p. 117 **credit processes, staff training, and product offerings** Women's World Banking, *Empowering MSMEs*.

p. 117 **the secret to winning these customers' business** Women's World Banking, *Global Best Practices in Banking Women-Led SMEs* (New York: Women's World Banking, 2014), http://www.womensworldbanking.org/wp-content/uploads/2014/11/Global-Best -Practices-Banking-Women-Led-SMEs-WomensWorldBanking.pdf.

p. 118 **up to 15 percent higher than loans to male-owned MSMEs** "Untapped Potential," The Opportunity, Financial Alliance for Women, https://financialallianceforwomen.org /the-opportunity/#untappedpotential.

p. 118 **such businesses can be started and run with less capital** Leora F. Klapper and Simon C. Parker, "Gender and the Business Environment for New Firm Creation," *World Bank Research Observer* 26, no. 2 (August 2011): 237–257, https://doi.org/10.1093/wbro /lkp032.

p. 118 **greater obstacles than men to start those businesses in the first place** Reyes Aterido, Thorsten Beck, and Leonardo Iacovone, "Access to Finance in Sub-Saharan Africa: Is There a Gender Gap?," *World Development* 47 (February 2013): 102–120, http://dx.doi .org/10.1016/j.worlddev.2013.02.013.

p. 119 **men are more likely to concentrate their investment in a single high-yielding project** Marco Castillo, Ragan Petrie, and Maximo Torero, "Gender Differences in Risk Preferences of Entrepreneurs," faculty paper, Department of Economics, Texas A&M University, College Station, TX, and Melbourne Institute, University of Melbourne, December 2017), https://www.aeaweb.org/conference/2018/preliminary/paper /BYb6nnGk; Doug Sundheim, "Do Women Take as Many Risks as Men?," *Harvard Business Review*, February 27, 2013, https://hbr.org/2013/02/do-women-take-as-many -risks-as; Jugnu Ansari and Saibal Ghosh, *Are Women Really More Risk-Averse? The Lending Behaviour of Women-owned Cooperatives in India* (Mumbai: Reserve Bank of India), https://www.cafral.org.in/sfControl/content/Speech/621201790348PMAre_Women _Really_More_Risk-Averse.pdf.

p. 119 **men's and women's requested loan sizes and borrowing frequency were roughly equivalent** Humaira Islam, founder of Shakti Foundation, in discussion with the author, October 24, 2015.

p. 119 **not to apply for a loan for fear of rejection** Ciarán Mac an Bhaird, Javier Sanchez Vidal, and Brian Lucey, "Discouraged Borrowers: Evidence for Eurozone SMEs," *Journal of International Financial Markets, Institutions and Money* 44 (September 2016): 46–55, https://doi.org/10.1016/j.intfin.2016.04.009.

p. 120 **the majority of graduates self-selected not to borrow** Noa Meyer, Global Program Director for the 10,000 Women Program at Goldman Sachs, discussion with the author, March 27, 2014.

p. 120 **their own perceived lack of creditworthiness** Hanan Morsy, Amira El-Shal, and Andinet Woldemichael, "Women Self-Selection Out of the Credit Market in Africa," Working Paper 317 (Abidjan, Côte d'Ivoire: African Development Bank Group, July 24, 2019), https://www.afdb.org/en/documents/working-paper-317-women-self-selection -out-credit-market-africa.

p. 120 **even if it is financially disadvantageous to the lender** "Taste-Based Discrimination," Wikipedia, last edited October 10, 2020, https://en.wikipedia.org/wiki /Taste-based_discrimination.

p. 120 **whether they are owned by men or women** Sara Carter et al., "Gender, Entrepreneurship, and Bank Lending: The Criteria and Processes Used by Bank Loan Officers in Assessing Applications," *Entrepreneurship Theory and Practice* 31, no. 3 (May 2007): 427–444, https://doi.org/10.1111/j.1540-6520.2007.00181.x.

p. 120 **with only the gender of the entrepreneur changed** J. Michelle Brock and Ralph De Haas, "Gender Discrimination in Small Business Lending: Evidence from a Lab-in-the-Field Experiment in Turkey," Working Paper 232 (London: European Bank for Reconstruction and Development, October 7, 2019), https://www.ebrd.com/publications /working-papers/gender-discrimination.

p. 121 **inexorably becomes statistical discrimination** Esther Duflo, "Women Empowerment and Economic Development," *Journal of Economic Literature* 50, no. 4 (December 2012): 1051–1079, https://doi.org/10.1257/jel.50.4.1051; Aterido, Beck, and Iacovone, "Access to Finance"; Mala Htun, Francesca Jensenius, and Jami Nelson-Nuñez, "Gender-Discriminatory Laws and Women's Economic Agency," *Social Politics: International Studies in Gender, State & Society* 26, no. 2 (Summer 2019): 193–222, https://doi.org /10.1093/sp/jxy042.

p. 121 **there was far less scope for discriminatory behavior** Muravyev, Schäfer, and Talavera, "Entrepreneurs' Gender and Financial Constraints."

p. 122 **"fades away with gender-specific learning on the job"** Thorsten Beck, Patrick Behr, and Andreas Madestam, "Sex and Credit: Do Gender Interactions Matter for Credit Marker Outcomes?," *Journal of Banking and Finance* 87 (February 2018): 380–396, https://doi.org/10.1016/j.jbankfin.2017.10.018.

p. 123 **Gender discrimination was literally costing the bank money** Brock and De Haas, "Gender Discrimination in Small Business Lending." https://www.ebrd.com /publications/working-papers/gender-discrimination.

p. 123 **did not place stricter requirements on women's loan applications** Brock and De Haas, "Gender Discrimination in Small Business Lending."

p. 123 **no longer showed evidence of discriminatory behavior** Beck, Behr, and Madestam, "Sex and Credit."

p. 124 **male and female loan officers performed similarly** José G. Montalvo and Marta Reynal-Querol, "Gender and Credit Risk: A View from the Loan Officer's Desk," Working Paper 1076 (Barcelona: Barcelona Graduate School of Economics, March 2019), https://www.bde.es/f/webpi/SES/seminars/2019/Fich/sie20190627.pdf.

p. 124 **ensure that low-income households are not put into even greater distress** "Lessons on Digital Consumer Credit from East Africa," CGAP, https://www.cgap.org/topics/collections/digital-credit.

p. 125 **enable women-owned businesses to circumvent the barriers to accessing growth capital** World Bank, *Promoting Digital and Innovative SME Financing* (Washington, DC: World Bank, 2020), https://www.gpfi.org/sites/gpfi/files/saudi_digitalSME.pdf; Rashmi Pillai and Peter Zetterli, "Four Next-Gen Fintech Models Bridging the Small Business Credit Gap," CGAP, June 20, 2019, https://www.cgap.org/blog/4-next-gen-fintech-models-bridging-small-business-credit-gap.

p. 126 **can monitor the status of the loan online** Women's World Banking, due diligence for investment in Amartha, October 2020–February 2021.

p. 126 **is gaining ground throughout the emerging markets** Allied Market Research, "Peer to Peer (P2P) Lending Market to Reach $558.9 Billion by 2027: At 29.7% CAGR," news release, Globe Newswire, May 11, 2020, https://www.globenewswire.com/news-release/2020/05/11/2031233/0/en/Peer-to-Peer-P2P-Lending-Market-to-Reach-558-9-Billion-by-2027-At-29-7-CAGR.html.

p. 126 **greater levels of proven profitability than men and pay higher interest rates** Xiao Chen, Bihong Huang, and Dezhu Ye, "The Gender Gap in Peer-to-Peer Lending: Evidence from The People's Republic of China," ADBI Working Paper 977 (Tokyo: Asian Development Bank Institute, July 2019), https://www.adb.org/publications/gender-gap-peer-peer-lending-evidence-prc.

p. 126 **fintechs can make unsecured digital loans an attractive option for women-owned businesses** Pillai and Zetterli, "Four Next-Gen Fintech Models Bridging the Small Business Credit Gap."

p. 127 **effectively eliminating delinquent loans** Kope Kopo, "Simple Tools for Your Business," https://kopokopo.co.ke.

p. 127 **allowing her to build a credit history** Pillai and Zetterli, "Four Next-Gen Fintech Models Bridging the Small Business Credit Gap"; Tienda Pago, "Tienda Pago Closes Series A to Boost Access to Financing for Small Merchants in Latin America," news release, Accion, April 3, 2018, https://www.accion.org/tienda-pago-closes-series-a-to-boost-access-to-financing-for-small-merchants-in-latin-america.

p. 127 **understanding of the company's cash flows for future lending** Pillai and Zetterli, "Four Next-Gen Fintech Models Bridging the Small Business Credit Gap"; Ruby Hinchliffe, "Nigerian Fintech Lidya Lends $3m to SMEs in Eastern Europe," LendTech, Fintech

Futures, October 8, 2020, https://www.fintechfutures.com/2020/10/nigerian-fintech
-lidya-lends-3m-to-smes-in-eastern-europe; Lidya Homepage, https://www.lidya.info/us
/en/home.

CHAPTER 6: MAKING THE BUSINESS CASE FOR MANAGING RISK

p. 129 **risk management strategies that are estimated to be ten times less effective than
formal protection mechanisms**   Suzy Cheston et al., *Inclusive Insurance: Closing the
Protection Gap for Emerging Customers* (Washington, DC: Center for Financial Inclusion at Accion and Institute of International Finance, January 2018) https://content
.centerforfinancialinclusion.org/wp-content/uploads/sites/2/2018/08/Inclusive-Insurance
-Final-2018.06.13.pdf.

p. 130 **she could not protect her hard-won success**   Nandini, an FWWB India client, as told
to a Women's World Banking researcher, 2013.

p. 130 **recover from a crisis when it does occur**   Craig Churchill and Michal Matul, eds.,
Protecting the Poor: A Microinsurance Compendium, vol. 2 (Geneva: International Labour
Organization, 2012), https://www.munichre-foundation.org/en/Inclusive_insurance
/Protecting_the_poor_A_microinsurance_compendium/Protecting_the_poor_A_micro
insurance_compendium_Volume_II.html.

p. 130 **back down the chute into deeper poverty**   Jayshree Vyas, Managing Director, SEWA
Bank, interview by the author, March 2008.

p. 130 **or reach out to expensive informal money lenders**   Women's World Banking, *Health
Microinsurance: An Inclusive Approach* (New York: Women's World Banking, 2016),
https://www.womensworldbanking.org/wp-content/uploads/2016/11/Health-Micro
insurance-Inclusive-Approach-WWB-2016-Web.compressed.pdf; Anjali Banthia, Susan
Johnson, Michael J. McCord, et al., *Microinsurance That Works for Women: Making
Microinsurance Programs Gender-Sensitive* (Geneva: Microinsurance Innovation Facility
and International Labour Organization, October 2009), https://www.ilo.org/employ
ment/Whatwedo/Publications/WCMS_124368/lang--en/index.htm.

p. 131 **frequently cited reason low-income women's informal businesses fail**   Women's World
Banking, "Caregiver Research," internal project preparation and materials, 2009–2016.

p. 131 **insurers will need to keep costs as low as possible as well**   Cheston et al., *Inclusive
Insurance.*

p. 132 **are all married and also live nearby in Marka**   Hiyam, client, interviews by the author,
August and October 2019.

p. 132 **would have taken her fifteen days before**   Hiyam, interviews.

p. 132 **became the family's sole source of income**   Hiyam, interviews.

p. 133 **limiting her business to pick-up orders at the apartment**   Hiyam, interviews.

p. 133 **painstakingly rebuilt following his earlier illness**   Hiyam, interviews.

p. 133 **more opportunities for contact between insurer and client**   Cheston et al., *Inclusive
Insurance.*

p. 134 **even greater risk of falling deeper into poverty**   Women's World Banking, "Caregiver
Research."

p. 134　**to 146,000 clients, 96 percent of them women**　Early Warning System, "MFW Jordan (IFC-42450)," last modified March 3, 2020, https://ewsdata.rightsindevelopment.org/projects/42450-mfw-jordan.

p. 134　**73 percent of Microfund's staff and management are women**　Women's World Banking, network member financial reporting template, 2006–2010.

p. 136　**with both organizations sharing the premium revenue**　Mazen Ayham Nimri, interview by the author, July 10, 2017; Mazen Ayham Nimri, "How to Turn Your Microinsurance Product into a Success Story," Women's World Banking, February 3, 2016, https://www.womensworldbanking.org/insights-and-impact/how-to-turn-your-micro insurance-product-into-a-success-story; Mazen Ayham Nimri, "Microinsurance: The Jordanian Experience," PowerPoint presentation at the conference Microinsurance: International Experiences and Egyptian Applications, Cairo, Egypt, May 7–8, 2017.

p. 136　**to monitor exclusions can be quite costly**　Nimri, interview.

p. 137　**managed to keep fraudulent claims to less than 2 percent**　Nimri, interview; Nimri, "Microinsurance Product."

p. 137　**premium income represents a valuable source of noninterest earnings**　Nimri, interview.

p. 137　**"the courage to take risks as a smaller insurer that larger companies won't take"**　Nimri, interview.

p. 137　**premium income estimated at $30–$50 billion**　AXA Group, Accenture, and International Finance Corporation (IFC), *She for Shield: Insure Women to Better Protect All* (Washington, DC: IFC and AXA Group, 2015).

p. 137　**a strong preference for enrolling husbands and children in addition to themselves, particularly for health coverage**　Banthia et al., *Microinsurance That Works for Women*.

p. 138　**build trust and familiarity with insurance products**　Cheston et al., *Inclusive Insurance*; Herman Smit, Cat Denoon-Stevens, and Antonia Esser, *InsurTech for Development: A Review of Insurance Technologies and Applications in Africa, Asia, and Latin America* (Cape Town, South Africa: Centre for Financial Regulation and Inclusion, March 2017), https://cenfri.org/wp-content/uploads/2017/11/InsurTech-Research-Study_March -2017.pdf.

p. 138　**exploring expansion to other emerging markets**　Women's World Banking, PULA application to Women's World Banking Fintech Innovation Challenge, October 2019.

p. 139　**limiting distribution to a single decision-maker**　AXA Group et al., *She for Shield*.

p. 139　**would yield $500 billion in new written premiums**　AXA Group et al., *She for Shield*.

p. 139　**may also see improved rates of customer retention**　Global Banking Alliance for Women, *The Women's Market for Insurance: An Emerging Business Opportunity* (Brooklyn, NY: Global Banking Alliance for Women, Brooklyn, 2018), https://financialalliancefor women.org/download/womens-market-insurance-emerging-business-opportunity.

p. 140　**"I plan to keep working, I plan to improve my business. I will open a store."**　Women's World Banking Caregiver Outcomes Research, August 2, 2019.

CHAPTER 7: A CALL TO ACTION

p. 142　**contactless payments were truly in everyone's interest**　Bill & Melinda Gates Foundation, World Bank, Consultative Group to Assist the Poor (CGAP), Women's World

Banking, *Digital Cash Transfers in the Time of COVID 19: Opportunities and Considerations for Women's Inclusion and Empowerment* (Seattle: Bill & Melinda Gates Foundation, World Bank, CGAP, Women's World Banking, 2020), https://www.cgap.org/sites/default /files/publications/2020.Digital-Cash-Transfers-in-Times-of-COVID-19-Opportunities -and-Considerations-for-Womens-Inclusion-and-Empowerment.pdf.

p. 142 **over 95 percent of the Indian population have an Aadhaar number**   G. Shainesh, Shyam Sunder, K. Sudhir, et al., "Aadhaar, Global Network Case 102–18," Yale School of Management, August 6, 2018, https://som.yale.edu/case/2018/aadhaar.

p. 142 **new accounts were opened, primarily by women, to receive these government payments**   Bill & Melinda Gates Foundation et al., *Digital Cash Transfers in the Time of COVID 19.*

p. 142 **176 million poor women who do not yet have a Jan Dhan account**   Rohini Pande et al., *Reaching India's Poorest Women with COVID-19 Relief,* policy brief, Yale Economic Growth Center, Yale University, April 17, 2020), https://egc.yale.edu/reaching -indias-poorest-women-covid-19-relief.

p. 143 **reduce income inequality and foster financial stability**   Martin Čihák and Ratna Sahay, "Finance and Inequality," IMF Staff Discussion Note SDN/20/01 (Washington, DC: International Monetary Fund, 2020).

p. 144 **easy, low-cost entry into the formal financial system**   Nimal Fernando and Robin Newnham, *National Financial Inclusion Strategies: Current State of Practice* (Kuala Lumpur, Malaysia: Alliance for Financial Inclusion, June 2018), https://www.afi-global.org /sites/default/files/publications/2018-06/National%20Financial%20Inclusion%20 Strategies.pdf.

p. 144 **who have opened accounts to facilitate government relief payments**   Bill & Melinda Gates Foundation et al., *Digital Cash Transfers in the Time of COVID 19.*

p. 145 **Banks can use the data to improve their product offerings to women**   Fernando and Newnham, *National Financial Inclusion Strategies*; United Nations Secretary-General's Special Advocate for Inclusive Finance for Development, *Collecting and Using Gender-Disaggregated Data for Financial Policymaking,* September 2020, https://www.unsgsa .org/sites/default/files/resources-files/2020-09/Policy_Note_Gender-Disaggregated _Data_FINAL.pdf.

p. 145 **accountable to national financial inclusion strategies with clearly stated targets**   Fernando and Newnham, *National Financial Inclusion Strategies.*

p. 146 **eliminate the gender gap in financial inclusion by 2024**   Central Bank of Nigeria, *National Financial Inclusion Strategy (Revised)* (Abuja, Nigeria: Central Bank of Nigeria, October 2018), https://www.cbn.gov.ng/out/2019/ccd/national%20financial%20 inclusion%20strategy.pdf.

p. 146 **eliminate financial discrimination if it is enshrined in the legal code**   Asli Demirgüç-Kunt, Leora Klapper, and Dorothe Singer, "Financial Inclusion and Legal Discrimination against Women: Evidence from Developing Countries," Policy Research Working Paper 6416 (Washington, DC: World Bank, 2013), http://hdl.handle.net/10986/15553.

p. 146 **167 countries still have at least one law restricting women's economic opportunity**   "Entrepreneurship: Examining Constraints to Women's Ability to Start and Run a

Business," in World Bank, *Women, Business and the Law 2018* (New York: World Bank, 2018), https://wbl.worldbank.org/en/data/exploretopics/wbl_rb.

p. 146 **to vote and to be counted in a national census**   Alan Gelb and Anna Diofasi Metz, *Identification Revolution: Can Digital ID be Harnessed for Development?* (Washington, DC: Center for Global Development, 2017), https://www.cgdev.org/sites/default/files /identification-revolution-can-digital-id-be-harnessed-development-brief.pdf.

p. 146 **mandatory in over 150 countries**   Lucia Hanmer and Marina Elefante, *Achieving Universal Access to ID: Gender-based Legal Barriers Against Women and Good Practice Reforms* (Washington, DC: World Bank, 2019), http://hdl.handle.net/10986/32474; Bill & Melinda Gates Foundation et al., *Digital Cash Transfers in the Time of COVID-19.*

p. 146 **less likely than men to have the necessary identification documents**   Asli Demirgüç-Kunt, Leora Klapper, Dorothe Singer, et al., *The Global Findex Database 2017: Measuring Financial Inclusion and the Fintech Revolution* (Washington, DC: World Bank, 2018).

p. 147 **encourage greater competition among mobile providers**   Bill & Melinda Gates Foundation et al., *Digital Cash Transfers in the Time of COVID-19*; Women's World Banking, "Reaching Financial Equality for Women: A 10-point Action Plan for Governments and Businesses to Rebuild Stronger after COVID-19 by Prioritizing Women's Digital Financial Inclusion" (New York: Women's World Banking, March 8, 2021), https://www .womensworldbanking.org/wp-content/uploads/2021/03/Reaching_Financial _Equality_2021.pdf.

p. 147 **credit history that banks can rely on to perform due diligence**   World Bank, *Women's Financial Inclusion and the Law 2018.*

p. 147 **20 percent of total loans extended in only eighteen months**   E. MacEachern, email message to author, April 20, 2017.

p. 148 **60 million unbanked women worldwide still receive government social benefits in cash**   Demirgüç-Kunt et al., *Global Findex Database 2017.*

p. 148 **"head of household," more often the man, as the recipient of such payments**   Shelly J. Lundberg, Robert A. Pollak, and Terence J. Wales, "Do Husbands and Wives Pool Their Resources? Evidence from the United Kingdom Child Benefit," *Journal of Human Resources* 32, no. 3 (Summer 1997): 463–480, https://doi.org/10.2307/146179; Jenny C. Aker, "Payment Mechanisms and Anti-Poverty Programs: Evidence from a Mobile Money Cash Transfer Experiment in Niger," *Economic Development and Cultural Change* 65, no. 1 (October 2016): 1–37, https://doi.org/10.1086/687578.

p. 148 **the association of more women on these boards with greater banking sector stability**   Ratna Sahay and Martin Čihák, *Women in Finance: A Case for Closing Gaps* (Washington, DC: International Monetary Fund, September 17, 2018), https://www.imf .org/en/Publications/Staff-Discussion-Notes/Issues/2018/09/17/women-in-finance-a -case-for-closing-gaps-45136.

p. 148 **"decisions that not only impact them directly, but are often made in their name"**   Christopher J. Brummer, "What do the Data Reveal About (the Absence of Black) Financial Regulators?," working paper, (Washington, DC: Georgetown University Law Center, Institute of International Economic Law, July 20, 2020), http://dx.doi.org/10.2139 /ssrn.3656772.

p. 149 **far exceeds the annual revenue of the world's leading financial institutions** Jessica Clempner, *Women in Financial Services 2020: A Panoramic Approach* (New York: Oliver Wyman, 2019), https://www.oliverwyman.com/content/dam/oliver-wyman/v2/publications/2019/November/Women-In-Financial-Services-2020.pdf.

p. 149 **JP Morgan Chase was in the number two position at $114.6 billion** Nathan Reiff, "10 Biggest Banks," Investopedia, January 16, 2021, https://www.investopedia.com/articles/investing/122315/worlds-top-10-banks-jpm-wfc.asp.

p. 149 **it can lead to better products for men as well** Clempner, *Women in Financial Services 2020*.

p. 150 **in choosing to engage with a financial product or service** Kantar, *Winning Over Women: A Commercial Imperative for Financial Service* (London: Financial Alliance for Women, 2017), https://financialallianceforwomen.org/download/winning-women-commercial-imperative-financial-services.

p. 150 **tend to engage more deeply than men with those relationships** Women's World Banking, *Global Best Practices in Banking Women-Led SMEs* (New York: Women's World Banking, 2014), http://www.womensworldbanking.org/wp-content/uploads/2014/11/Global-Best-Practices-Banking-Women-Led-SMEs-WomensWorldBanking.pdf; Financial Alliance for Women, "Untapped Potential/The Opportunity," https://financialallianceforwomen.org/the-opportunity/#untappedpotential.

p. 150 **to track both individual and institutional performance** Women's World Banking, *Global Best Practices in Banking Women-Led SMEs*.

p. 151 **if more women applied for loans, more might receive them** Ciarán Mac an Bhaird, Javier Sanchez Vidal, and Brian Lucey, "Discouraged Borrowers: Evidence for Eurozone SMEs," *Journal of International Financial Markets, Institutions and Money* 44 (September 2016): 46–55, https://doi.org/10.1016/j.intfin.2016.04.009; Ken S. Cavalluzzo, Linda C. Cavalluzzo, and John D. Wolken, "Competition, Small Business Financing, and Discrimination: Evidence from a New Survey," *Journal of Business* 75, no. 4 (October 2002): 641–679, https://doi.org/10.1086/341638; Rose M. Prasad, "Loan Hurdles: Do Banks Discriminate against Women Entrepreneurs?," *Academy of Management Perspectives* 23, no.4 (November 30, 2017): 91–93, https://doi.org/10.5465/amp.23.4.91; Richa Singh, "Gender-Based Financing Preferences of SMEs: Discouraged Borrowers," master's thesis, University of Ottawa, 2014, http://hdl.handle.net/10393/30836.

p. 152 **self-selecting out of this opportunity for business growth** Mac an Bhaird, Sanchez Vidal, and Lucey, "Discouraged Borrowers;" Cavalluzzo, Cavalluzzo, and Wolken, "Competition, Small Business Financing, and Discrimination"; Prasad, "Loan Hurdles"; Singh, "Gender-Based Financing Preferences of SMEs."

p. 152 **to higher profitability and even to greater levels of innovation** Sahay and Čihák, *Women in Finance*; J. Yo-Jud Cheng and Boris Groysberg, "Gender Diversity at the Board Level Can Mean Innovation Success," *MIT Sloan Management Review*, January 22, 2020, https://sloanreview.mit.edu/article/gender-diversity-at-the-board-level-can-mean-innovation-success.

p. 152 **nearly 40 percent of fintechs globally have no women on their boards** Jessica Clempner, Rich Chavez, and Tiphaine Ramenason, "How to Shift Gender Balance in Fintech," Fintech Futures, April 24, 2020, https://www.fintechfutures.com/2020/04/how -to-shift-gender-balance-in-fintech.

p. 152 **tamp down differences in favor of group cohesion** Robin J. Ely and David A. Thomas, "Getting Serious about Diversity: Enough Already with the Business Case," *Harvard Business Review,* November–December 2020, https://hbr.org/2020/11/getting -serious-about-diversity-enough-already-with-the-business-case.

p. 153 **inequality in access to smartphones** Demirgüç-Kunt et al., *Global Findex Database 2017.*

p. 153 **establishing trust with both men and women** Aakanksha Thakur, Samveet Sahoo, Prabir Barooah, et al., "Agency Banking: How Female Agents Make a Difference," MicroSave Consulting, April 5, 2016, http://blog.microsave.net/2016/04/05/agency-banking -how-female-agents-make-a-difference; Women's World Banking, "Pilot Evaluation Findings," PowerPoint presentation to Bank of Baroda management, December 2, 2020.

p. 153 **roughly 90 percent of transactions in the developing world are still completed in cash** Hugh Thomas, "Measuring Progress toward a Cashless Society," Compendium, MasterCard, 2014, https://newsroom.mastercard.com/wp-content/uploads/2014/08 /MasterCardAdvisors-CashlessSociety-July-20146.pdf.

p. 153 **one-third of transactions in the US are settled in cash** Raynil Kumar and Shaun O'Brien, *2019 Findings from the Diary of Consumer Payment Choice* (San Francisco: Federal Reserve Bank of San Francisco, June 2019), https://www.frbsf.org/cash/publications /fed-notes/2019/june/2019-findings-from-the-diary-of-consumer-payment-choice.

p. 153 **with only 12 percent of transactions taking place in cash** Statista, "Share of Cash in Total Payment Transactions in Sweden from 2000–2019," October 2020, https://www .statista.com/statistics/1095529/cash-use-in-sweden.

p. 153 **location of CICO points is an even more significant factor in driving inclusion** William Jack and Tavneet Suri, "Mobile Money: The Economics of M-PESA," NBER Working Paper No. 16721 (Cambridge, MA: National Bureau of Economic Research, January 2011), https://www.nber.org/system/files/working_papers/w16721/w16721.pdf.

p. 153 **doorstep withdrawal based on a customer's biometric ID** Bill & Melinda Gates Foundation et al., *Digital Cash Transfers in the Time of COVID-19.*

p. 155 **if they did not also address her child care responsibilities** Ana Revenga and Meagan Dooley, "What Works for Women Entrepreneurs? A Meta-Analysis of Recent Evaluations to Support Female Entrepreneurship," Global Working Paper 142 (Washington, DC: Brookings Institution, Global Economy and Development program, September 2020), https://www.brookings.edu/wp-content/uploads/2020/09/What-works-for-women -entrepreneurs_final.pdf.

p. 155 **women's financial inclusion might increase both women's agency and opportunity** Lotus McDougal, Jeni Klugman, Nabamallika Dehingiam, et al., "Financial Inclusion and Intimate Partner Violence: What Does the Evidence Suggest?," *PLoS One* 14, no. 10 (October 2019), https://doi.org/10.1371/journal.pone.0223721.

p. 155 **"companies stand to gain the most if they change their approach"** Michael J. Silverstein and Kate Sayre, "The Female Economy," *Harvard Business Review,* September 2009, https://hbr.org/2009/09/the-female-economy.

p. 155 **84 percent of US consumers expecting companies to stand up for women's rights** Cone Communications, "Americans Willing to Buy or Boycott Companies Based on Corporate Values, According to New Research by Cone Communications," May 17, 2017, https://www.conecomm.com/news-blog/2017/5/15/americans-willing-to-buy-or-boycott-companies-based-on-corporate-values-according-to-new-research-by-cone-communications.

p. 156 **inclusive culture, sexual harassment policies, and pro-women brand** Bloomberg, "Gender Equality Index," https://www.bloomberg.com/gei.

p. 156 **reported being misunderstood by their financial advisers** Sylvia Ann Hewlett, Andrea Turner Moffitt, and Melinda Marshall, *Harnessing the Power of the Purse: Female Investors and Global Opportunities for Growth* (New York: Coqual, 2014), https://coqual.org/wp-content/uploads/2020/09/25_harnessingthepowerofthepursefemaleinvestors_keyfindings-1.pdf.

p. 156 **62 percent of women with a net worth of $500,000 or more have built their own wealth** Elizabeth MacBride, "The $11 Trillion Market Sallie Krawcheck Is Betting On," Quarterly Investment Guide, CNBC, last modified May 18, 2016, https://www.cnbc.com/2016/05/11/the-11-trillion-women-investment-market-sallie-krawcheck-is-betting-on.html.

p. 156 **women want their values reflected in their investments** Hewlett, Moffitt, and Marshall, *Harnessing the Power of the Purse.*

p. 156 **over fifty publicly traded gender lens investment funds** Suzanne Biegel and Sandi M. Hunt, *Project Sage 3.0: Tracking Venture Capital, Private Equity and Private Debt with a Gender Lens* (Philadelphia: University of Pennsylvania, Wharton School of Business, 2020), https://socialimpact.wharton.upenn.edu/research-reports/reports-2/project-sage-3.

p. 156 **publicly listed companies that prioritize and advance women's leadership** Fidelity Investments, "Fidelity Women's Leadership Fund," last modified January 2020, https://www.fidelity.com/mutual-funds/investing-ideas/womens-leadership-fund.

p. 157 **as early as kindergarten can have lifelong benefits** Organisation for Economic Co-operation and Development Council, *Recommendations on Principles and Good Practices for Financial Education and Awareness* (Paris: Organisation for Economic Co-operation and Development, July 2005), https://www.oecd.org/daf/fin/financial-education/35108560.pdf.

p. 157 **when it comes to making personal financial decisions** Financial Alliance for Women, "Untapped Potential."

p. 157 **do not always address both facets of the problem** National Network to End Domestic Violence, "About Financial Abuse," https://nnedv.org/content/about-financial-abuse.

p. 158 **this well-educated population would be able to take greater advantage of technological changes** Leora Klapper, Mayada El-Zoghbi, and Jake Hess, "Achieving the Sustainable

Development Goals: The Role of Financial Inclusion," working paper, CGAP and UNSGSA (United Nations Secretary-General's Special Advocate for Inclusive Finance for Development) (Washington, DC: CGAP, April 2016), https://www.cgap.org/sites /default/files/Working-Paper-Achieving-Sustainable-Development-Goals-Apr-2016_0 .pdf.

p. 158 **income grow at a faster pace than the country's average** Klapper, El-Zoghbi, and Hess, "Sustainable Development Goals."

Index